Social Justice and the City

David Harvey

Basil Blackwell

Copyright © David Harvey 1973
Foreword copyright © Ira Katznelson 1988
This edition first published 1988

Basil Blackwell Ltd,
108 Cowley Road, Oxford, OX4 1JF, UK

First published 1973 by
Edward Arnold (Publishers) Ltd

Published in paperback in the United States of America 1975 by
The Johns Hopkins University Press,
Baltimore, Maryland 21218

British Library Cataloguing in Publication Data

Harvey, David, *1935 Oct. 31—*
    Social justice and the city.
1. Urban region.   2. Social planning –
sociological perspective
I. Title.
307.12
ISBN 0–631–16476–6

Printed and bound in Great Britain by T.J. Press (Padstow) Ltd

Contents

Contents

Foreword

by Ira Katznelson

Enough time has elapsed for me to break the usual confidences. In 1972, when *Social Justice and the City* was in production in Britain and Johns Hopkins University Press was considering whether to publish the American edition I was asked to prepare an anonymous review. Apparently, the manuscript had received mixed readings. I was told this was not the usual academic book: it was "hot" and "controversial", but was it any good? I agreed to undertake the task.

What I did not tell the Press' editor was that I was a very inexperienced junior faculty member who had never assessed a manuscript for a university press. More than a decade and a half later, I have reviewed a good number. None has had the verve and significance of *Social Justice and the City*. I remember the details of receiving the heavy parcel in my office at Columbia, lugging it home, and opening it to discover the book's length and my own unfamiliarity with many of its themes, references, and allusions.

I set to work. Just a few pages into the text I put all my apprehensions aside. I gobbled up the manuscript. I read this complex, at times difficult, volume in just two very long sessions. I literally could not put it down, so profound and basic did it seem. It shattered the boundaries, categories, and self-satisfaction of traditional urban scholarship and it provoked many more good questions than it could possibly answer. This is what I said in my report, which ran in length only a fraction of the number of pages of notes I was stimulated to take.

This kind of impact was not unintended. Harvey wanted to redefine and extend the reach of geography and to embed the subject in a theoretical project. He heralded this aim in his first book, *Explanation in Geography*, a massive and influential methodological treatise published in 1969. In the book's concluding comment, he tried to set the agenda for the coming decade by proposing a move away from issues of technique and methodology of the kind he had just been treating toward what he called both a philosophy and a theory of geography. Harvey wrote:[1]

> It should be clear, therefore, that an adequate methodology provides a *necessary* condition for the solution of geographical problems; philosophy provides the *sufficient* condition. Philosophy provides the steering mechanism, methodology provides the power to move us closer to our destination. Without methodology we will lie becalmed, without philosophy we may circle aimlessly without direction. I have mainly been concerned with the nature of the power devices which are available to us. But I would like to close by returning to the interface between methodology and philosophy . . .

> Without theory we cannot hope for controlled, consistent, and rational, explanation of events. Without theory we can scarcely claim to know our own identity. It seems to me, therefore, that theory construction on a broad and imaginative scale must be our first priority in the coming decade. It will take courage and ingenuity to face up to this task. But I feel confident that it is not beyond the wit and intelligence of the current generation of geographers. Perhaps the slogan we should pin up on our study walls for the 1970s ought to read: 'By our theories you shall know us.'

In the ensuing four years, Harvey found such a theory, Marxism, and an object of analysis for this theory within geography, the city.

He signified this discovery and this focus in *Social Justice and the City*. A chronicle of his own intellectual transformations, the book is divided between essays Harvey calls liberal formulations, concerned with such staples of geography as spatial differentiation and distributions of populations and activities in space, and those he calls socialist formulations, rather more concerned with connections between spatial phenomena and modes of production. In making this shift, Harvey sought to reject the narrow morphological character of his discipline, its radical separation of fact and value, its obsession with problems of data and measurement, and its fragmentary qualities. Harvey's book had an immediate and stunning effect on urban studies. With great rigour, it broadened the domain of geography, redefined the

[1] *Explanation in Geography.* London: Edward Arnold; Baltimore: Johns Hopkins University Press, 1979.

objects of urban analysis, and opened up a host of new questions. *Social Justice and the City*, in short, was a foundational text.

Above all, the book, in both its liberal and socialist parts, sought to demonstrate how it was possible to bring social processes and spatial forms together analytically and as a guide to action, and to show their interpenetration. In this volume, spatial forms incorporate social processes; and all social processes are inherently spatial. Joining both sections are four key themes: the nature of theory (in which Harvey seeks to break what he sees as an artificial separation between methodology and philosophy, and in which he tries to make the reader self-conscious about the act and consequences of categorization); the nature of space (in which he replaces the familiar question, what is space?, with the question, "how is it that different human practices create and make use of distinctive conceptualizations of space?"); the nature of social justice (which he moved from "a predisposition to regard social justice as a matter of eternal justice and morality to regard it as something contingent upon the social processes operating in society as a whole"); and the nature of urbanism (seen not as a thing in itself, but as providing a line of sight into society). He turned to Marxism to deal with these issues that span the book's "liberal" and "socialist" moments not on *a priori* grounds, but because it promised to permit these tasks to be accomplished.[2]

Like Manuel Castells in *La question urbaine*, Harvey sought to harness Marxism and the city by engaging a series of important works by Henri Lefebvre published in the late 1960s and early 1970s including *Le droit à la ville*, *La révolution urbaine* and *La pensée marxiste à la ville*.[3] Quite apart from their intrinsic merit, these works were significant because they reinvigorated an urban conversation within Marxism that had been dormant for more than a century. At the moment he was leaving behind the comfortable habitat of mainstream geography Harvey could find no other models or guides within Marxism.

Though inspired by Lefebvre, Harvey rejected completely the independent determinative qualities Lefebvre attributed to spatial relations. For Harvey, space is not an ontological category as such, but is a social dimension that both shapes and is shaped

[2] Below, pp. 10–17.
[3] Henri Lefebvre, *Le droit à la ville*. Paris: Anthropos, 1968; *La révolution urbaine*. Paris: Gallimard, 1971; *La pensée marxiste et la ville*. Paris: Casterman, 1972.

by human agency: "Spatial forms are ... seen not as inanimate objects within which the social process unfolds, but as things which 'contain' social processes in the same manner that social processes *are* spatial."[4]

Approaching two decades since their publication, and taking into account the resurgence of theoretically-informed urban studies they helped to promote, the various essays in *Social Justice and the City* still repay careful reading; in the first part, for their Rawlsian perspective on urban spatial relations with regard to urban planning and income distribution (as in the discussion of "territorial justice," and the balance between centralized and decentralized governance), and, in the second part, for their specification of a Marxist research agenda on the city concerned with reinterpreting the sweep of urban history in terms of the integration of the economy and the circulation of surplus in different modes of production. The wonderful sensibilities about space and meaning systems that Harvey exhibited in the early "liberal" formulations have continued to animate his work since his Marxist turn. These include a concern with the texture of the relationship between individuals, groups and their social space, the connections between different kinds of human activities and their distinctive spaces, architecture and urban landscape as markers of the social order, the work–home linkage, the place of functionalism in urban analysis, and the limits on the capacity of the state in a market society.[5]

To be sure, the second half of *Social Justice and the City* was an early, and in some respects a very preliminary and schematic attempt, lurching at times between the "scientific" and "critical" Marxist camps. This Marxist section includes a paper that demonstrates how ghetto housing for American blacks is underpinned by a "blameless" entrepreneurial set of initiatives; an important paper on the theory of urban land use focusing on the "catalytic moment" of collision between the use and exchange values of land that powerfully utilizes long-neglected discussions in Marx about rent and the micro-economics of land and space that show how rent is a rationing device for land as a permanent and immovable commodity required by all, open to multiple uses and meanings, which changes hands infrequently but decisively;

[4] Below, especially ch. 1.
[5] Below, chs 1–3.

4

and it includes a sweeping macroscopic overview of urban development throughout human history by contrasting different mechanisms of generating and deploying the social surplus. Here, the city is conceptualized historically as "a pivot around which a given mode of production is organized, as a centre of revolution against the established order, and as a centre of power and privilege (to be revolted against)." Cities are formed "through the geographic concentration of social surplus product, which the mode of economic integration must therefore be capable of producing and concentrating." Using Karl Polanyi's categories of economic coordinating mechanisms – reciprocity, redistribution, and market exchange – together with Marx's concept of the mode of production, Harvey presented the city as contained within a field of relations between the social surplus, the dominant mode of economic organization, and the spatial organization of society. Within capitalism, the city is both a locus and stabilizer of accumulation and its contradictions.[6]

These essays remain important for their capacity to repay re-readings in insight and challenges to research, and, too, as markers in the rediscovery of the city for Marxism, and Marxism for the city. In the subsequent fifteen years, Harvey has worked carefully, steadily, and selectively, through the research agenda of *Social Justice and the City* with the aim of expanding and extending Marx's work on capitalist accumulation to give it an explicit spatial dimension.

In this task Harvey has been remarkably successful. His subsequent work in *The Limits to Capital* builds on the suggestive, but sketchy, passages in Marx's *Capital* that deal with rent, and directly introduces spatial elements into the analysis of the circuits of capital accumulation. Harvey's two-volume *Studies in the History and Theory of Capitalist Development* contains a recursive look at, and a mature elaboration of, the main themes in *Social Justice and the City*, as well as attempts to break new ground by inquiring into the questions of disposition, language, meaning, culture, and agency that Harvey had put aside while he had been working out the imbricated relationship of urban space and capitalist accumulation. But Harvey's success in achieving the goals of *Social Justice and the City* is manifest not only in his own

[6] Below, pp. 203, 216.

scholarship. He has the satisfaction of knowing just how much this volume has helped change urban studies and extend the capacity of Marxist social theory.[7]

The book's influence has reached well beyond the bounds of geography to motivate considerations of the city in sociology, political science, economics, history, and anthropology, and it has shaped a robust re-engagement of Marxism with the city. Unlike the situation that prevailed at the time of its publication, there is now a large body of work about the city within the Marxist tradition. In a warm appreciation, Harvey has summarized its key themes and achievements this way:[8]

> Spurred on by events, Marxists turned to a direct analysis of urban issues in the 1960s. They sought to understand the economic and political meaning of urban, community-based social movements and their relation to work-based movements – the traditional focus of attention. The relations between production and social reproduction came under intense scrutiny as the city was variously studied as the locus of production, of realization (effective demand through consumption, sometimes conspicuous), of the reproduction of labour power (in which the family and community institutions, supported by physical and social infrastructures – housing, healthcare, education, cultural life – played a key role, backed by the local state). The city was also studied as a built environment to facilitate production, exchange and consumption, as a form of social organization of space (for production and reproduction), and as a specific manifestation of the division of labour and function under capitalism (finance capital versus production, etc.). The overall conception which emerged was urbanization as the contradictory unity of all these aspects of capitalism.

In assessing this body of work Harvey has pronounced it very good. He is right to do so. If not for the contributions of urbanists who have worked in the Marxist tradition in the 1970s

[7] David Harvey, *The Limits to Capital*. Oxford: Basil Blackwell; Chicago: University of Chicago Press, 1982; *The Urbanization of Capital: Studies in the History and Theory of Capitalist Urbanization*. Oxford: Basil Blackwell; Baltimore: Johns Hopkins University Press, 1985; *Consciousness and the Urban Experience: Studies in the History and Theory of Capitalist Urbanization*. Oxford: Basil Blackwell; Baltimore: Johns Hopkins University Press, 1985.

[8] "Urbanization." In Tom Bottomore, *et al.*, editor, *A Dictionary of Marxist Thought*. Oxford: Basil Blackwell; Cambridge, Mass.: Harvard University Press, 1983, pp. 503–4.

and 1980s studies of the city today would have much less definition and theoretical thrust; and if not for *Social Justice and the City*,
this body of work would rest on much less sturdy foundations.

New School for Social Research
New York
July 1988

Introduction

The biographical details of how this book came to be written are relevant to reading it since they serve to explain features in its construction that might otherwise appear peculiar. After completing a study of methodological problems in geography, which was published under the title *Explanation in Geography*, I began to explore certain philosophical issues which had deliberately been neglected in that book. In particular, I felt it important and appropriate to explore how ideas in social and moral philosophy—ideas that are customarily regarded as distinctive and separate avenues of enquiry from the philosophy of science which had hitherto held my attention—could be related to geographical enquiry and to those fields of intellectual endeavour, such as planning and regional science, with which geography has much in common. It seemed a reasonable starting assumption, for example, that principles of social justice had some relevance for the application of spatial and geographical principles to urban and regional planning. Since I could find scarcely any literature on this topic it seemed important to try to provide something, however inadequate it might turn out to be. In the course of pursuing this general aim it quickly became apparent that it ought not to be pursued in abstraction. I therefore determined to pursue it in a context with which I could become familiar at first hand and yet which was broad enough to provide material examples and a fund of experience upon which to draw whenever necessary. Since I had just moved to Baltimore, it seemed appropriate to use that city, together with other cities with which I was familiar, as a backdrop against which to explore questions that arose from projecting social and moral philosophical considerations into the traditional matrix of geographical enquiry. Hence emerged a preoccupation with urban planning, urban systems and, ultimately, urbanism in general.

The interaction between the exploration of "ideas for ideas sake" and the results of material investigation and experience provoked an evolution in my general conception of urbanism and urban problems as well as in my views on such disparate topics as the nature of space, the nature of theory, and, indeed, the nature of knowledge and scientific enquiry in general. The essays assembled in this volume were written at various points along an evolutionary path and therefore represent the history of an evolving viewpoint. I do not regard this history as idiosyncratic to myself (although there are probably some features in it that may be so interpreted). It is the sort of history that seems inevitable if anyone seeks an adequate and appropriate way to bring together a viewpoint established in social and moral philosophy on the one hand and material questions that the condition of the urban centres in the western world point to on the other.

The evolution which occurs in the essays naturally gives rise to contradictions and inconsistencies between them. The general approach contained in Part 2 is substantially different (and, I believe, substantially more enlightening) than that in Part 1. Yet the later chapters take on more meaning if it is understood how the general viewpoint they espouse was arrived at—hence the importance of recording the search process as it threads its way through the various essays here assembled. It is also important to note that the material content of Part 1 is not rejected but is incorporated and given new meaning by the evolving framework of Part 2.

Reflecting on the evolution of thought which has occurred I can identify an evolution in four fundamental themes which interlock with each other around a central, overwhelming and unchanging concern. Social processes and spatial forms, are, for the most part, distinct in our minds if not in reality and it has been a fundamental concern of mine for several years now to heal the breach in our thought between what appear to be two distinctive and irreconcilable modes of analysis. In the essays contained in this volume there is an evolution in the way this problem is conceived as well as in the solutions to it that are contemplated. In chapter 1, for example, the problem is regarded as linguistic and linguistic solutions are explored. But by chapter 5 the problem has become one of human practice (in which the linguistic problem is itself embedded) and solutions therefore lie in the realm of human practice. The distinction between social processes and spatial form is always regarded as artificial rather than real, but in the later chapters the distinction is regarded as unreal in rather a different sense. Spatial forms are there seen not as inanimate objects within which the social process unfolds, but as things which "contain" social processes in the same manner that social processes *are* spatial. How best to portray the interpenetration between social process and spatial form that arises out of human practice is itself a problem for human practice to overcome rather than a problem which attaches to the properties of reality itself.

The four themes which surround this central concern with social process and spatial form are frequently submerged in the content, but they tend to emerge at crucial points for explicit consideration as signposts are sought to guide the analysis. The themes interact with each other as if they are on a magic roundabout—the figures revolve before one's eyes but they so change their shape and colour that it is difficult to believe that they are the same figures or that they are even distinct from each other. Since the figures may not be readily apparent to the reader as they pirouette around the social-process–spatial-form theme, I shall endeavour in this introduction to set out the salient features of each. The difficulty which this course creates is that the themes relate and reflect upon each other in such a complex fashion that to isolate each for explicit consideration would be to damage the general evolution of thought beyond repair. Since my purpose here is to provide signposts for the reader rather than a carefully assembled replication of the argument, I shall content myself with describing how each theme is viewed at the beginning and how it appears at the end. In this manner I hope to make it easier for the reader to understand how the nature of theory, the nature of space, the nature of social justice and the nature of urbanism each come to be viewed in a substantially different manner as the analysis proceeds.

1 The nature of theory

The initial view of theory stems from an artificial separation of methodology from philosophy. I have never regarded this separation as anything more than a matter of convenience, but it is amazing how far convenience can lure. From this separation flows a tendency to regard facts as separate from values, objects as independent of subjects, "things" as possessing an identity independent of human perception and action, and the "private" process of discovery as separate from the "public" process of communicating the results. All these tendencies are clearly exhibited in *Explanation in Geography* and may be seen in action in the first two chapters in this volume. I now reject these distinctions as injurious to analysis even in their apparently harmless form of a separation of convenience. Initially I also held to the view that the construction of theory requires the manufacture of an adequate and proper language, with fixed definitions and meanings, that could be used to "talk about" phenomena in a logically consistent way. I recognized that definitions could dictate conclusions and that a system of thought erected on fixed definitions and fixed categories and relationships could inhibit rather than enhance our ability to comprehend the world. But these seemed minor problems inherent in the process of scientific enquiry as a whole. I now argue that acts of categorization are quite fundamental: it is vital to understand how categories are established and in particular how they take on meaning and are transformed through and in use. There is a tendency, therefore, to argue in Part 2 for contextually and relationally established meanings— meanings, in other words, which are regarded as moveable, not in some random or arbitrary way, but as a part of the process through which society embraces certain lines of thought in order to rationalize certain lines of action in preference to others.

There is a parallel evolution in the approach to verification. From an initial position in which verification is viewed as a matter of establishing (by some generally accepted means) the empirical relevance and applicability of abstract propositions, I progress to the view that it cannot be separated from social practice in general. There are various types of theory with distinct functions to perform in a social context and each type has particular verification procedures attached to it. The general distinction (set out in the note to chapter 4) between *status quo, revolutionary* and *counter-revolutionary* theory provides some insight into the question of verification. Verification is achieved through practice which means that theory *is* practice in a very important sense. When theory becomes practice through use then and only then is it really verified. Underlying this view, and indeed underlying the whole evolution in the conception of theory contained in these essays, is, of course, a shift away from philosophical idealism towards a materialist interpretation of ideas as they arise in particular historical contexts.

2 *The nature of space*

There are various ways in which we can think about space. It is crucial to formulate a proper conception of it if we are to understand urban phenomena and society in general; yet the nature of space has remained something mysterious to social enquiry. If we regard space as absolute it becomes a "thing in itself" with an existence independent of matter. It then possesses a structure which we can use to pigeon-hole or to individuate phenomena. The view of relative space proposes that it be understood as a relationship *between* objects which exists only because objects exist and relate to each other. There is another sense in which space can be viewed as relative and I choose to call this relational space—space regarded, in the fashion of Leibniz, as being contained *in* objects in the sense that an object can be said to exist only insofar as it contains and represents within itself relationships to other objects. In the first of the essays contained in this volume the case for a relative view of space is put forward. But this case is also argued in a particular way. The argument is ontological, seeking to resolve the question "what is space?" Furthermore, this philosophical question is thought to have a philosophical or linguistic solution independent of everything else. The approach taken is that once we have discovered what space is and have discovered ways of representing it, then we can proceed with our analysis of urban phenomena by fitting our understanding of human behaviour into some general conception of space. This approach fades into insignificance in the later essays (particularly in chapter 5) and space becomes whatever we make of it during the process of analysis rather than prior to it. Further, space is neither absolute, relative or relational *in itself*, but it can become one or all simultaneously depending on the circumstances. The problem of the proper conceptualization of space is resolved through human practice with respect to it. In other words, there are no philosophical answers to philosophical questions that arise over the nature of space—the answers lie in human practice. The question "what is space?" is therefore replaced by the question "how is it that different human practices create and make use of distinctive conceptualizations of space?" The property relationship, for example, creates absolute spaces within which monopoly control can operate. The movement of people, goods, services and information takes place in a relative space because it takes money, time, energy, and the like, to overcome the friction of distance. Parcels of land also capture benefits because they contain relationships with other parcels; the forces of demographic, market and retail potential are real enough within an urban system and in the form of rent relational space comes into its own as an important aspect of human social practice. An understanding of urbanism and of the social-process–spatial-form theme requires that we understand how human activity creates the need for specific spatial concepts and how daily social practice solves with consummate ease seemingly deep philosophical mysteries concerning the nature of space and the relationships between social processes and spatial forms.

3 The nature of social justice

Questions of social justice are initially approached as if social and moral philosophy is a distinct field of enquiry through which absolute ethical principles can be laid down with the full force of moral law. These principles, once established, can then be used, it is supposed, to evaluate events and activities in the urban context. Implicit in this approach is a distinction between observation on the one hand and the values on the basis of which we place the stamp of moral approval or disapproval on the other. This distinction between fact and value (which is consistent with the distinction between methodology and philosophy) is one of the innumerable dualisms which, as many philosophers have remarked, pervade post-Renaissance western philosophy. These dualisms can either be accepted as a fact of life or they can be reconciled in some fashion. Kant, for example, constructed an elaborate system of thought designed to link the dualisms into a coherent philosophy, but in the process was forced to resort to the doctrine of the *a priori*. Marx, however collapses the distinctions and thereby proclaims the end to all philosophy (since there is not much left to philosophize about in the usual sense of the term). Philosophy has proceeded unabated subsequent to Marx's analysis, but I am now inclined to accept Marx's view of the matter. This is not to say that ethics are redundant, for there is a Marxian ethics of sorts. But it deals with how concepts of social justice and morality relate to and stem from human practice rather than with arguments about the eternal truths to be attached to these concepts. For Marx, the act of observing *is* the act of evaluation and to separate them is to force a distinction on human practice that does not in reality exist.

A further aspect to this problem is worth elaborating on for it demonstrates nicely the evolution of ideas in these essays. In chapter 2 the forces governing the redistribution of real income in an urban system are examined in detail. Throughout this chapter the question of distribution is examined as if it is entirely independent of the question of production. This is an approach typical of liberalism (hence the title for Part 1 as "Liberal Formulations"). A contemporary representative of this approach is John Rawls whose voluminous work on *A Theory of Justice* (1971) contains an explicit statement on the nature of distributive justice without mentioning production: this, it is assumed, will be taken care of, presumably through the workings of the market mechanism. Rawls's views are the subject of explicit discussion in chapter 3, but this essay is transitional in the sense that it is there recognized that production and distribution are related to each other and that efficiency in the one is related to equity in the other. But not until chapter 6 is it accepted that production *is* distribution and that efficiency *is* equity in distribution. Here too it is finally recognized that the definition of income (which is what distributive justice is concerned with) is itself defined by production. The forcing of consumption through need-creation and the like is then viewed as part of the process whereby an effective demand for products is ensured.

The collapse of the distinction between production and distribution, between efficiency and social justice, is a part of that general collapse of all dualisms of this sort accomplished through accepting Marx's approach and technique of analysis. The evolution that occurs in these essays is from a liberal to a socialist (Marxist) conception of the problem. I move from a predisposition to regard social justice as a matter of eternal justice and morality to regard it as something contingent upon the social processes operating in society as a whole. This is not to say that social justice is to be regarded as a merely pragmatic concept which can be shifted at will to meet the requirements of any situation. The sense of justice is a deeply held belief in the minds of many (including mine). But Marx posed the question, "why these beliefs?" And this is a disturbing but perfectly valid question. The answer to it cannot be fashioned out of abstractions. As with the question of space, there can be no philosophical answer to a philosophical question—only an answer fashioned out of the study of human practice.

4 The nature of urbanism

A reading of chapters 1 and 6 indicates that the concept of urbanism undergoes considerable change throughout these essays. Initially urbanism is regarded as a "thing in itself" which can be understood as such (provided we can overcome the barriers posed by disciplinary fragmentation and academic imperialism with respect to its analysis). In chapter 6 urbanism appears as a vantage point from which to capture some salient features in the social processes operating in society as a whole—it becomes, as it were, a mirror in which other aspects of society can be reflected. This transformation occurs partly because urbanism comes to be defined relationally. The urban centre, for example, is regarded as "containing" a periphery, for there can be no centre without a periphery and each helps to define the other. The collapse of the distinction between production and distribution likewise has an impact upon the way in which urbanism is viewed. An initial concern with urbanism as a "thing in itself" thus fades into a concern with all facets of man, society, nature, thought, ideology, production, and so on, built around the concept of a relationally defined urbanism. Urbanism then provides a thread of an argument which serves to pin important but seemingly disparate topics together. The complexity of urbanism is not to be attributed to the inherent complexity of the phenomena in itself but reflects merely our ability to weave an intricate woof of argument around the urbanism concept. It follows from this that we cannot promote an understanding of urbanism through interdisciplinary research, but that we can promote an understanding of disciplinary contributions through a study of urbanism. Urbanism and the social and spatial transformations embedded in its evolution form the hard testing ground for socio-geographic theory. And, as chapter 5 demonstrates, many of our theories do not perform too well in such a fierce environment. An analysis of urbanism has, therefore, to be paralleled by an analysis of urban theory.

It bears repeating that the four themes outlined here do not evolve independently of each other. There are similarities and interactions between the evolutions described. The changes in the conception of space and of social justice are consistent with the change in the approach to theory. Space, social justice and urbanism are all initially viewed as topics "in themselves" which can be explored in abstraction—once it has been established what space is, once it has been established what social justice is, then, it is presumed, we can proceed to the analysis of urbanism. The recognition that these topics cannot be understood in isolation from each other and that the pervasive dualisms implicit in western thought cannot be bridged, only collapsed, leads to a simultaneous evolution of thought on all fronts. And it is, of course, the power of Marx's analysis that it promotes such a reconciliation among disparate topics and the collapse of dualisms without losing control over the analysis. The emergence of Marx's analysis as a guide to enquiry (by which token I suppose I am likely to be categorized as a "Marxist" of sorts) requires some further comment. I do not turn to it out of some *a priori* sense of its inherent superiority (although I find myself naturally in tune with its general presupposition of and commitment to change), but because I can find no other way of accomplishing what I set out to do or of understanding what has to be understood. Chapters 1 and 2, for example, are still adequate statements in certain respects, but in both chapters seemingly insoluble problems arise. The approach to the question of space in chapter 1 poses an irreconcilable dilemma that degenerates into a helpless, formless relativism. The approach to urban society in chapter 2 provides a useful framework for understanding certain important mechanisms which operate within "the urban process", but the distinction between fact and value as it affects the concept of income as "command over resources" again allows important questions to be swamped in a helpless formless relativism to which no solution, apart from opinionated moral exhortation, appears possible. Chapter 3 contains a struggle to bring the question of social justice and space into focus, but insofar as solutions emerge they rest upon an arbitrary characterization of the nature of social justice. Chapter 4 marks a liberation from the old approach and in a crude but exuberant way begins the process of reformulating problems as solutions and solutions as problems. Chapters 5 and 6 seek to consolidate the evolving framework making explicit use of Marx's analysis wherever it seems appropriate. It is in these last three chapters that some fundamental lines of thought and ways of thinking are opened up.

I leave it to the reader to judge whether Part 1 or Part 2 contains the more productive analyses. Before making this judgement there are two points I would like to present. First, I recognize that the analysis of Part 2 is a beginning point which opens up new lines of thought. The analysis is rather unfamiliar (of necessity) but its freshness to me may have made it appear at times rather rough and at other times unnecessarily complicated. I beg a certain amount of indulgence on this score. Second, Marx gives a specific meaning to ideology—he regards it as an *unaware* expression of the underlying ideas and beliefs which attach to a particular social situation, in contrast to the *aware* and critical exposition of ideas in their social context which is frequently called ideology in the west. The essays in Part 2 are ideological in the western sense whereas the essays in Part 1 are ideological in the Marxist sense.

The first four chapters in this volume are substantially reproduced from papers already published. Chapter 1 was first published as "Social processes and spatial form: an analysis of the conceptual problems of urban planning", in *Papers of the Regional Science Association* volume 25, and I am indebted to the editor for permission to publish it here. Chapter 2, initially included in chapter 1 but cut out because of length, was expanded to appear in volume 22 of the Colston Papers on *Regional Forecasting* (edited by M. Chisholm and published by Butterworth Scientific Publications, London); I am indebted to the Members of the Colston Society for permission to reproduce this material. Chapter 3 was a paper delivered at the special session on *Geographical Perspectives on American Poverty* at the 67th Annual Meeting of the Association of American Geographers and it was subsequently published in *Antipode Monographs in Social Geography* 1, under the editorship of Richard Peet, who has kindly given permission to republish this material. Chapter 4 appeared in *Perspectives on Geography* volume 2, and I would like to thank the general editor, Harold McConnell, and the Northern Illinois University Press for permission to reproduce this article. Chapters 5 and 6 are contributions original to this volume.

I would also like to thank a number of people who, wittingly or unwittingly, have contributed to the writing of this book. Marcia Merry continuously provoked me to it, Lata Chatterjee provided a fund of experiential data on the dynamics of the housing market, Gene Mumy, Dick Walker and Jörn Barnbrock proved to be interesting fellows, and Barbara, John and Claudia through their warmth and vitality saved me at times when cynicism appeared imminent. Titus, Jerry Cornelius, John Coltrane and the Beatles also played their part. Finally, I would like to dedicate this book to all good committed journalists everywhere.

Hampden, Baltimore   *January, 1973*

Part one

Liberal Formulations

Chapter 1

Social Processes and Spatial Form:

1 The Conceptual Problems of Urban Planning

The city is manifestly a complicated thing. Part of the difficulty we experience in dealing with it can be attributed to this inherent complexity. But our problems can also be attributed to our failure to conceptualize the situation correctly. If our concepts are inadequate or inconsistent, we cannot hope to identify problems and formulate appropriate policy solutions. In this essay, therefore, I want to address myself to the conceptual problems only. I shall ignore the complexity of the city itself and seek instead to expose some of the problems which we ourselves generate by our characteristic ways of looking at the city. One set of conceptual problems arises from academic and professional specialization on certain aspects of city processes. Clearly, the city cannot be conceptualized in terms of our present disciplinary structures. Yet there is very little sign of an emerging interdisciplinary framework for thinking, let alone theorizing, about the city. Sociologists, economists, geographers, architects, city planners, and so on, all appear to plough lonely furrows and to live in their own confined conceptual worlds. Leven (1968, 108) has remarked that much recent research deals "with problems in the city rather than of the city". Each discipline uses the city as a laboratory in which to test propositions and theories, yet no discipline has propositions and theories about the city itself. This is the primary problem to be overcome if we are ever to understand (let alone control) the complexity that is the city. If we are to do this, however, we must overcome some extraordinarily difficult methodological, and conceptual problems.

THE GEOGRAPHICAL VERSUS THE SOCIOLOGICAL IMAGINATION

Any general theory of the city must somehow relate the social processes in the city to the spatial form which the city assumes. In disciplinary terms, this amounts to integrating two important research and educational traditions—I shall call it building a bridge between those possessed of the sociological imagination and those imbued with a spatial consciousness or a geographical imagination.

Mills (1959, 5) defines the "sociological imagination" as something which "enables its possessor to understand the larger historical scene in terms of its meaning for the inner life and the external career of a variety of individuals. . . . The first fruit of this imagination . . . is the idea that the individual can understand his own experience and gauge his own fate only by locating himself within his period, that he can know his own chances in life only by becoming aware of those of all individuals in his circumstances. . . . The sociological imagination enables us to grasp history and biography and the relations between the two in society. . . . Back of its use there is always the urge to know the social and historical meaning of the individual in society and in the period in which he has his quality and his being."

As Mills goes on to point out, this sociological imagination is not the sole possession of sociology: it is the common bond of all disciplines in the social sciences (including economics, psychology, and anthropology) and is the central concern of history and social philosophy as well. The sociological imagination has very powerful tradition behind it. From Plato through Rousseau to Marcuse, there has been a never-ending debate upon the relationship of the individual to society and the role of the individual in history. In the last half century or so, the methodology associated with the social sciences has also become more rigorous and more scientific (some would say pseudo-scientific). The sociological imagination can now feed upon an enormous speculative literature, a plethora of survey research results, and a few well-articulated theories regarding certain aspects of the social process.

It is useful to contrast with this "sociological imagination" the rather more diffuse quality which I have called "spatial

23

consciousness" or the "geographical imagination". This imagination enables the individual to recognize the role of space and place in his own biography, to relate to the spaces he sees around him, and to recognize how transactions between individuals and between organizations are affected by the space that separates them. It allows him to recognize the relationship which exists between him and his neighbourhood, his territory, or, to use the language of the street gangs, his "turf". It allows him to judge the relevance of events in other places (on other peoples' "turf")—to judge whether the march of communism in Vietnam, Thailand, and Laos is or is not relevant to him wherever he is now. It allows him also to fashion and use space creatively and to appreciate the meaning of the spatial forms created by others. This "spatial consciousness" or "geographical imagination" is manifest in many disciplines. Architects, artists, designers, city planners, geographers, anthropologists, historians, and so on have all possessed it. But it has a far weaker analytic tradition behind it, and its methodology still relies heavily upon pure intuition. The main seat of the spatial consciousness in western culture today still lies in the plastic arts.

This distinction between the geographical and the sociological imaginations is artificial when we seek to relate to the problems of the city, but it is all too real when we examine the ways we think about the city. There are plenty of those possessed with a powerful sociological imagination (C. Wright Mills among them) who nevertheless seem to live and work in a spaceless world. There are also those, possessed of a powerful geographical imagination or spatial consciousness, who fail to recognize that the way space is fashioned can have a profound effect upon social processes—hence the numerous examples of beautiful but unlivable designs in modern living.

Into this interface between the sociological and the spatial approach to problems, a number of individuals and groups of individuals and even whole disciplines have crept. Many of those possessed of the sociological imagination have come to recognize the significance of the spatial dimension in social process. Hallowell (1955) and Hall (1966) in anthropology (the latter proposing the new science of proxemics), Tinbergen (1953) and Lorenz (1966) in ethology, Sommer's (1969) studies of the role of personal "psychological" space in influencing

24

human reaction to environmental design, Piaget and Inhelder's (1956) studies of the growth of the spatial consciousness in children, philosophers such as Cassirer (1944; 1955) and Langer (1953) with their clear recognition of the effect of the spatial consciousness upon man's view of his relationship to the world around him, these are but a few examples. We should also find regional economists and regional scientists in this group. Others have moved into this interface from the other direction. Trained in a tradition of spatial consciousness, they have realized how the fashioning of spatial form can influence social process—architects such as Lynch (1960) and Doxiadis (1968) (with his proposed new science of ekistics), city planners such as Howard and Abercrombie. Straddling the interface, we also find the regional geographer who, in spite of his taboo-laden methodology and weak analytic tools, can still on occasion manage to convey some deep insights into the way in which regional consciousness, regional identity, and natural and man-made environment merge into one another over time to create a distinctive spatial structure in human organization. Recently, human geographers have been more active in exploring the relationships between social processes and spatial form (Harvey, 1969; Buttimer, 1969).

There is an enormous but widely scattered literature which relates to the interface. But it is difficult to pull it all together, to distill its message. Perhaps one of our first tasks in seeking to fashion a new conceptual framework for our understanding of the city will be to survey and synthesize this vast diffuse literature. Such a synthesis will probably reveal how difficult it is to work in this area without major conceptual adjustments. It is interesting to consider, for example, how long it has taken for the city planner and the regional scientist to adjust to each other in their attempt to understand city processes. The intricacies of spatial-form problems seem to have escaped early workers in regional science. Space either generated a regional structure (by a process which was assumed rather than understood) to which could then be applied accounting frameworks devised for the national level (from which we have regional accounting and interregional input-output), or else space merely generated transport costs which could be substituted against other costs involved in the production process (from which we have most of location theory and the interregional equilibrium models).

Space was simply one variable in a conceptual framework devised primarily for spaceless economic analysis. Regional scientists and regional economists still exhibit a prediliction for understanding economics and misunderstanding space. However, urban planning, dominated as it traditionally has been by a primary resort to drawing board design and, in particular, by the process of designing from the map (a notorious instrument for self-deception if ever there was one), was completely immersed in the details of human spatial organization as expressed in land use. In making a planning decision about a particular parcel of land, the city planner had little or no use for the aggregated and not very well-substantiated generalizations of the regional scientist, the economist, or the sociologist. He coloured the parcel red or green on his planning map according to his own intuitive evaluation of the design of the spatial form and his rough assessment of economic and social factors as he conceived them (provided, of course, that his decision was not solely determined by the balance of political pressures). Webber (1963, 54), who has been one of the strongest advocates on the spatial design side for pushing the planner into a greater awareness of the social process, considers it vital for the planner to disabuse himself "of some deep-seated doctrine that seeks order in simple mappable patterns, when it is really hiding in extremely complex social organization, instead."

There are, therefore, signs of some pressure for bringing the sociological and geographical imaginations together in the context of the city. But it has been a struggle. More often than not geographical and sociological approaches have been regarded as unrelated or, at best, as viable alternatives to the analysis of city problems. Some have sought, for example, to modify the spatial form of a city and thereby to mould the social process (this has typically been the approach of physical planners from Howard on). Others have sought to place institutional constraints on social processes in the hope that this alone will be enough to achieve necessary social goals. These strategies are not alternatives. They should be regarded as complementary. The trouble is that the use of one sometimes conflicts with the use of the other. Any successful strategy must appreciate that spatial form and social process are different ways of thinking about the same thing. We must therefore harmonize our thinking about them or else continue to create contradictory strategies for dealing with city problems. Webber complains of the "ideological campaign to reconstruct the preconceived city forms that matched the social structures of past eras", and argues for the "emergence of a pragmatic problem-solving approach in which the spatial aspects of the metropolis are viewed as continuous with and defined by the processes of urban society." Leven (1968, 108) has similarly pleaded for "some kind of theoretical framework within which we identify factors which are determinants of city form and which, in turn, produce some spatial form in an analytically predictable way." Then we could "search for some method of evaluating the resultant spatial performance which, in turn, probably would feed back upon the determinants of spatial form themselves."

The general point should be clear: the only adequate conceptual framework for understanding the city is one which encompasses and builds upon both the sociological and the geographical imaginations. We must relate social behaviour to the way in which the city assumes a certain geography, a certain spatial form. We must recognize that once a particular spatial form is created it tends to institutionalize and, in some respects, to determine the future development of social process. We need, above all, to formulate concepts which will allow us to harmonize and integrate strategies to deal with the intricacies of social process and the elements of spatial form. And it is to this task that I now want to turn.

TOWARDS A PHILOSOPHY OF SOCIAL SPACE

It may seem strange to begin the quest to bridge the gap between sociological and geographical imagination by giving detailed consideration to the situation on the geographical side of the fence. But it is useful to begin at this point because those imbued with a keen sense of space have, by and large, failed to articulate a view of space which can be analysed and readily understood by the analysts of social process. If we attempt to understand more thoroughly what we mean by space, then some of the problems which appear to lie in the way of our bridge-building effort will, I hope, disappear.

There is, of course, a very substantial literature dealing with the philosophy of space. Unfortunately most of it is concerned with interpreting the meaning of space as it is conceptualized in modern physics. This is helpful in certain respects, but it is rather a special view of space, and I am not sure that it has any general validity for the examination of social activity. Other views need to be considered. In order to make this point clear, I shall need to develop some simple ideas regarding modes of spatial experience, and the ways in which we can analyse that experience. Cassirer (1944) provides a useful starting point for he is one of the few philosophers who has taken a very general view of space. He differentiates between three basic categories of spatial experience. The first, *organic space*, refers to the kind of spatial experience which appears to be genetically transmitted and, hence, biologically determined. Much of the behaviour examined by ethologists (instinctive spatial orientation and migration, instinctive territoriality, and so on) fits into this category. The second, *perceptual space*, is more complex. It involves the neurological synthesis of all kinds of sense experience—optical, tactual, acoustic and kinesthetic. This synthesis amounts to a spatial experience in which the evidence of various senses is reconciled. An instantaneous schema or impression may be formed and memory may lead to the retention of that schema over time. When memory and learning are involved, the schema may be subject to addition or subtraction by culturally learned modes of thought. Perceptual space is primarily experienced through the senses, but we do not yet know how far the performance of our senses is affected by cultural conditioning. The third kind of spatial experience is abstract; Cassirer calls this *symbolic space*. Here, we are experiencing space vicariously through the interpretation of symbolic representations which have no spatial dimension. I can conjure up an impression of a triangle without seeing one simply by looking at the word "triangle". I can gain experience of spatial form by learning mathematics and in particular, of course, geometry. Geometry provides a convenient symbolic language for discussing and learning about spatial form, but it is not the spatial form itself.

These three levels of spatial experience are not independent of each other. The abstract geometries which we construct require some interpretation at the perceptual level if they are to make intuitive rather than logical sense—hence all the diagrams which a typical textbook in geometry provides. Our perceptual experience may be affected by organic experience. But, if we are to build an analytically tractable theory of spatial form, we must eventually resort for formal geometry. We need, therefore, to find some way of representing events as they occur on the perceptual or organic level by some abstract symbolic system which forms a geometry. Conversely, we may regard it as finding some interpretation at the organic or perceptual level for ideas developed at the abstract level.

I have discussed elsewhere some of the problems that arise in this process of transferring experience gained at one level to a mode of experience operating at another level (Harvey, 1969, chapter 14). The main thrust of the argument was that we need to demonstrate some structural isomorphism between the geometry used and the particular perceptual experience or set of experiences under analysis. Where such an isomorphism exists, we can "map" the information derived from the perceptual plane into a geometry for analytic treatment. A successful mapping is one that allows us to transfer conclusions from the analytic geometry back into the realm of perceptual experience in such a way that we gain control or predictive power over the perceptual situation. On a flat plane surface, for example, I can predict physical distances between many objects from just a few key measurements, and I can do it by the use of Euclidean geometry and its derivative trigonometry. This example is an important one. Long experience of such mapping has taught us that Euclidean geometry is the relevant geometry for discussing the organization of objects in physical space—at least as far as earth-bound phenomena are concerned. Euclidean geometry is also the geometry in which engineering and physical construction processes find automatic expression, since it is the "natural" geometry for working with physical laws as they operate on the earth's surface.

It might appear from this that all we require for an analytic treatment of spatial form is some development out of Euclidean geometry. We do not yet have such a development; we have not yet devised adequate methods for generalizing about shape, pattern, and form on such Euclidean surfaces, for example. But, even given this development, our problems would be far from over simply because social space is not isomorphic with physical space. Here, the history of physics has something very important to teach us. We cannot expect that the kind of geometry appropriate for discussing one kind of process will be adequate to deal with another process. The selection of an appropriate geometry is essentially an empirical problem, and we must demonstrate (either by successful application or by the study of structural isomorphisms) how particular kinds of perceptual experience can validly be mapped into a particular geometry. In general, the philosophers of space tell us, we cannot select an appropriate geometry independent of some process, for it is the process which defines the nature of the coordinate system we must use for its analysis (Reichenbach, 1958, 6). This conclusion can, I believe, be transferred intact to the social sphere. Each form of social activity defines its space; there is no evidence that such spaces are Euclidean or even that they are remotely similar to each other. From this we have the geographer's concept of socio-economic space, the psychologist's and anthropologist's concept of "personal space," and so on. A primary need, if we are to understand the spatial form of the city, therefore, is the articulation of an adequate philosophy of social space. Insofar as we can only understand social space by reference to some social activity, we are forced to attempt an integration of sociological and geographical imagination.

The construction of a philosophy of social space will be difficult, for we need far more knowledge about the processes which go on in the perceptual realm of spatial experience. We know very little, for example, about the exact manner in which the artist or architect fashions space to transmit an aesthetic experience. We know that he often succeeds (or fails), but we scarcely know how. We know that the principles upon which an architect fashions space are very different from the principles employed by the engineer. Good architecture presumably incorporates two sets of principles of spatial organization—one set designed to prevent the structure created from violating physical constraints, and the other set designed to facilitate the transference of some aesthetic experience. The physical principles pose no problem—they are Euclidean and analytically tractable. The aesthetic principles are extremely difficult to deal with. Langer (1953, 72) provides, an interesting starting point for a theory of space in art. She hypothesizes that "the space in which we live and act is not what is treated in art at all", for the space in which we have our physical being is a system of relationships whereas the space of art is a created space built out of forms, colours, and so on. Thus the visual space defined by a painting is essentially an illusion . . . "like the space 'behind' the surface of a mirror, it is what the physicists call 'virtual space'—an intangible image. This virtual space is the primary illusion of all plastic art." In a later section, Langer (p. 93) goes on to extend this concept to architecture. Architecture clearly has actual function, and it also defines and arranges spatial units in terms of actual spatial relationships which have meaning for us in terms of the space in which we live and move. But nevertheless, "architecture is a plastic art, and its first achievement is always, unconsciously and inevitably, an illusion: something purely imaginary or conceptual translated into visual impression."

What is this something which we translate into a visual impression? Architecture, suggests Langer, is an *ethnic domain*— "a physically present human environment that expresses the characteristic rhythmic functional patterns which constitute a culture." In other words, the shaping of space which goes on in architecture and, therefore, in the city is symbolic of our culture, symbolic of the existing social order, symbolic of our aspirations, our needs, and our fears. If, therefore, we are to evaluate the spatial form of the city, we must, somehow or other, understand its creative meaning as well as its mere physical dimensions.

It has been an important principle in art and architecture that spatial form can be manipulated in various ways to yield various symbolic meanings. Until recently we have failed to study this process scientifically. There is a growing literature on the psychological aspects of art and a growing realization that we need some understanding of how the man-made environment takes on meaning for its inhabitants. The interiors of buildings, for example, often signify much about the nature of the social order and the nature of the social processes which are supposed to go on inside it. The design of a medieval church has much to say about the nature of the social hierarchy simply through the spatial relationship which some individual has to the central focal point. It is no accident that those in the choir somehow seemed closer to God (and hence more privileged) than those in the nave. Sommer (1969) has extended this principle and sought to show how different kinds of spatial design in a wide variety of contexts can affect human behaviour and activity systems. This work is young, but it may not be too long before it yields some useful principles for understanding the role that spatial symbolism plays in affecting human behaviour. The same principles are perhaps applicable at a more general scale. Lévi-Strauss (1963) has shown how the spatial layout of a whole village in a primitive culture may reflect in detail the mythology of the people and the social relationships which exist among various groups in the population. The layout of a typical eighteenth-century village in England implies a great deal about the social order as it then existed with its dual sources of power in the church and the nobility. Lowenthal and Prince (1964) have similarly noted how each age fashions its environment to reflect existing social norms. The city as a whole, even the modern amorphous version of it, still possesses this symbolic quality. It is no accident that church and chapel spires dream over Oxford (a town created in the age of church power), whereas, in the age of monopoly capitalism, it is the Chrysler building and the Chase-Manhattan Bank building which brood over Manhattan Island. These are all crude examples, and the interactions between spatial form, symbolic meaning and spatial behaviour are probably very complex. It is important that we understand these interactions if we are not (to quote Webber again) "to reconstruct the preconceived city forms that matched the social structures of past eras". The basic point I am trying to make is that, if we are to understand spatial form, we must first enquire into the symbolic qualities of that form. How can this be done?

I doubt very much whether we will ever truly understand the intuitions which lead a creative artist to mould space to convey a message. But, I think we can go a long way to understanding the impact which that message has upon the people who receive it. In terms of the activity pattern of the total population, it is this reaction which we must learn to gauge. If the city contains all manner of signals and symbols, then we can try to understand the meaning which people give to them. We must seek to understand the message which people receive from their constructed environment. To do this we need a very general methodology for the measurement of spatial and environment symbolism. Here, the techniques of psycholinguistics and psychology have much to recommend them. These techniques allow us to assess the significance of an object or event by examining the behavioural disposition to act with respect to it. We can tap this behavioural disposition in a number of ways. We can sample the mental state of the individual or of a group of individuals and discover their attitudes towards and their perceptions of the space which surrounds them. We can use a variety of techniques to do this from personal construct theory, semantic differential, through to more direct questionnaire techniques. The aim here is to try to evaluate the cognitive state of the individual with respect to his spatial environment. An alternative, favoured by behaviourists and operant psychologists, is simply to observe peoples' behaviour and thus gauge their reaction to objects and events. In this case, it is overt behaviour in space which provides us with the necessary clues to understand spatial significance. Practical considerations make it almost impossible to use anything other than overt behaviour when large aggregates of population are involved as, for example, in the study of journey-to-work and journey-to-shop phenomena as they occur at the total city scale of analysis.

A number of difficulties arise from using these techniques to measure the impact of the spatial symbolism that exists in the city. At the aggregative level, we have to rely upon the information provided by a generalized description of spatial activity in the city and this activity pattern may be a function of all kinds of things which have nothing to do with spatial form and spatial meaning. There is undoubtedly a substantial portion of social process which operates independently of spatial form, and we need to know what portion of the activity is influenced by spatial form and which portion remains relatively independent. Even at the microlevel, we still face the problem that experimental controls over unwanted variables are difficult to institute. We can learn a lot from laboratory experiments on the reaction to various forms of spatially organized stimuli—reactions to complexity, depth perception, associations in meaning, pattern preferences, and so on but it is extremely difficult to relate these findings to complex activity patterns as they unfold in the city. Nevertheless, there is a growing (and very stimulating) literature on the behavioural responses to certain aspects of environmental design and on the way in which individuals react to and schematize various aspects of the spatial form that is the city (Proshansky and Ittelson, 1970). I do not want to review these

33

studies here, but I do want to try to identify the general philosophical framework which they point to.

This framework is one in which space only takes on meaning in terms of "significant relationships", and a significant relationship cannot be determined independent of the cognitive state of some individual and the context in which that individual finds himself. Social space, therefore, is made up of a complex of individual feelings and images about and reactions towards the spatial symbolism which surrounds that individual. Each person, it seems, lives in his own personally constructed web of spatial relationships, contained, as it were, in his own geometric system. All this would make for a depressing picture from the analytic point of view, if it were not for the fact that groups of people appear to identify substantially similar images with respect to the space that surrounds them and also appear to develop similar ways of judging significance and behaving in space. The evidence is far from being secure, but, at this stage, it seems reasonable to adopt as a working hypothesis the view that individuals possess some proportion (as yet undetermined) of "common image" derived from some group norms (and probably certain norms in acting with respect to that image), and a proportion of "unique image" which is highly idiosyncratic and unpredictable. It is the common part of the spatial image with which we must first concern ourselves, if we are to squeeze out some details of the real nature of social space.

I have already suggested that the material so far gathered on spatial images is very sparse. But it is very suggestive. Lynch (1960), for example, indicates that individuals construct spatial schemas which hang together topologically—the typical Bostonian appears to move from one focal point (or node) to another along well-defined paths. This leaves vast areas of the physical space which are not touched and are indeed unknown as far as the individual is concerned. The implication of this particular study is that we should think of city organization with the analytic tools of topology rather than with Euclidean geometry. Lynch also suggests that certain features in the physical environment create "edges" beyond which the individual does not typically penetrate. Both Lee (1968) and Steinitz (1968) confirm his finding that boundaries can be identified for some areas in a city, and these areas seem to form distinctive neighbourhoods. In some cases these boundaries may be easily traversed, but in other cases they may act as barriers to movement in the city—ghetto avoidance behaviour on the part of middle-class whites and the strong prescriptive territoriality which can be found among certain ethnic and religious groups (as in Protest-ant–Catholic areas of Northern Ireland) are good examples. So we can expect strong discontinuities in socially measured spatial structures. At a more aggregated level (say the total journey-to-work pattern in a city), many of the individual differences in mental images may counteract each other and amount to some kind of random noise in a system which is capable of being tackled descriptively. But even at this level the evidence suggests that there is a good deal of inhomogeneity in spatial behaviour even when data has been aggregated into very large groups for the purpose of developing gross interaction models of the city. There are distinctive group behaviours, some but not all of which may be explicable in terms of the sociological characteristics of the group (age, occupation, income, etc.), and there are distinctive activity styles which suggest that rather different parts of the city have rather differ-ent attractive power. In these cases, we may be justified in generalizing to a more continuous geometry; but even here the work of geographers suggests that the space is far from being a simple Euclidean one (Tobler, 1963). At this point we become involved in the question of the exact nature of the socio-econom-ic surface we are dealing with and the problem of finding ade-quate transformations to permit the analysis of events on that surface. In general, we have to conclude that social space is complex, non-homogeneous, perhaps discontinuous, and almost certainly different from the physical space in which the engineer and the planner typically work.

We then have to consider how these notions of personal space arise, how they are moulded by experience, and how stable they are in the face of a changing spatial form. Again, the evidence available to us is sparse. Much of the work of Piaget and Inhelder (1956) has to do with the way in which spatial con-sciousness develops in the young. There seem to be distinctive evolutionary stages going from topology through projective relationships to Euclidean formulation of concepts of physical space. It appears, however, that children do not necessarily learn the same spatial ability in all cultures, particularly as far as schematizing spatial information is concerned (Dart and

Pradhan, 1967). The evidence suggests that cultural conditioning, group learning, and individual learning are involved in the formation of an individual's spatial schema. It is quite probable that different culture groups develop totally different styles of representing spatial relationships, and these styles may, in themselves, be directly related to social processes and norms. Different groups within a population may therefore have rather different spatial schematic abilities, and education undoubtedly plays an important role in determining spatial ability (Smith, 1964). There is a good deal of variance in any population as regards the ability to read maps, to maintain a sense of direction, and so on. There is also considerable variation in the way in which individuals or groups construct mental schemas. Perhaps the simplest is to remember relationships by rote learning (this appears to be characteristic of many primitive and poorly educated peoples). Others may have simple coordinate referencing systems developed to pigeon-hole experiences, and others may have far more complex (and perhaps even inconsistent) ways of schematizing spatial relationships. But much of the information which is built up on a spatial schema must be the result of individual experience, and the schema is likely to undergo continual change with experience. The nature of that experience may be crucial to determining the symbolism—the area of a city you hate to go near because of unhappy memories; the area you always associate with good times. Experience continues to accrue, and that experience may modify or extend the nature of the mental map or the spatial form as recorded in the image. Memory itself may fade and parts of the spatial image which are not reinforced may very quickly disappear. Social space is not only variable from individual to individual and from group to group; *it is also variable over time*.

I have attempted to demonstrate in this section that space is not as simple as the physicists or the philosophers of science would have us believe. If we are to understand space, we must consider its symbolic meaning and its complex impact upon behaviour as it is mediated by the cognitive processes. One of the benefits of developing this view of space is that it seems capable of integrating the geographical and the sociological imaginations, for, without an adequate understanding of social processes in all their complexity, we cannot hope to understand social space in all its complexity.

SOME METHODOLOGICAL PROBLEMS AT THE INTERFACE

In the preceding section, I sought to show that an understanding of space in all its complexity depends upon an appreciation of social processes. It would, I think, be possible to advance a similar argument with respect to social processes: that an understanding of the social process in all its complexity depends upon an appreciation of spatial form. Rather than attempt such an argument, however, I prefer to consider the methodological problems which lie at the interface between sociological and geographical work. This will demonstrate how difficult work at the interface is likely to be, and it will also provide some evidence for the importance of spatial form to study of the social process as it manifests itself in the city.

The bridge between the sociological and geographical imaginations can be built only if we possess adequate tools. These tools amount to a set of concepts and techniques which can be used to weld the two sides together. If the resultant construct is to be capable of analytic elaboration and susceptible to empirical testing, then mathematical and statistical methods will be needed, and we must, therefore, identify them. It seems likely that these methods will not be identifiable except in a given context. If, for example, we are interested in the interaction between spatial symbolism of the city, the mental maps of individuals, their states of stress, and their patterns of social and spatial behaviour, then we will require one set of tools. If we are interested in the gross aggregate changing form of the city and the gross social dynamics which are associated with that changing form, we will require a different set. In the first case, we need a language which is capable of embracing the complexities of varying individual geometries and social activity systems. In the second case, we can afford to ignore the details of individual behaviour and content ourselves with examining the relationship between the spatial form of the city and overt aggregative behaviour in it. We cannot, therefore, set up any general methodological framework for working at the interface. We can, however, demonstrate the kinds of problem we face by examining the tools we possess for bridge-building in a certain context, namely, that of analysing the gross spatial form of a city and aggregate overt behaviour patterns within it. In this context, I want to concentrate upon the problem of inference and predictive control. I choose this particular focus because as Harris (1968) points out, planners are interested in making "conditional predictions regarding function and development", and this does not differ from the interest of the social scientist who uses conditional prediction as a means for validating a theory. Therefore, both prediction and theory formation as regards the city will depend upon the existence of a valid framework for setting up tests and making inferences. As I shall seek to show, such a framework does not exist at the present time. I shall consider only selected aspects of this problem, and I choose to examine the problems of individuation, confounding and statistical inference.

1 Individuation

It is generally agreed that an initial step in setting up a framework for inference is to define a set of individuals which make up a population. The process of defining an individual is termed "individuation", and it is clearly very important. Logicians such as Wilson (1955) and Carnap (1958) have examined some general problems arising from it. One important distinction they draw is that between individuation in *substance languages* and individuation in *space-time languages*. In the first kind of language, an individual may be defined by specifying a set of properties $(p_1, p_2, p_3, \ldots p_n)$ which the individual possesses—we may individuate a "town" by stating the minimum size of the agglomeration, the nature of the employment structure, and so on. In the space-time language, however, the individuation depends upon specifying the location of an object within a coordinate structure which represents space and time (conventionally written as x, y, z, t). These two language systems have rather different properties, and it is therefore dangerous and difficult to mix them in the individuation process. The researcher on social processes characteristically uses a substance language whereas the purely geographical approach makes use of the space-time language. Bridging the gap between the two involves making use of the two languages simultaneously or, preferably, writing some metalanguage which embraces the relevant characteristics of both languages. Such a metalanguage does not at present exist and some of the initial investigations into its properties indicate that its development will not (Dacey, 1965) be easy. For our immediate purposes, therefore, we must remain content with using the two languages in the same context. The dangers in this procedure can best be demonstrated by examining methods of regionalization.

Consider the notion of "equality" in the two languages. It is feasible in the substance language for two individuals to occupy the same position (two towns may have exactly the same population size, etc.) but such a condition is not possible in the space-time language (two towns cannot occupy exactly the same location). But individuals, once identified, can have many properties at a space-time location. One relevant property might be relative location (distances relative to other places). So space can be used to individuate objects, or it may be treated as a property of individuals defined in either a space-time or in a substance language. Thus the two languages have different characteristics and space itself can enter into either language but in different ways (Bergmann, 1964, 272–301). It is scarcely surprising that this situation has generated much philosophical and methodological confusion and that the regionalization problem is a controversial one. The controversy usually results from a failure to identify how and when the different languages are being used. Taylor (1969) has indicated that confusion arises because "of a failure to appreciate that location occurs twice in the problem". We may use location as a discriminant variable (in which case we are treating spatial location as a property of individuals), or we may accept a given division of the space into locational units and use these space-time individuals (such as administrative areas) to collect information in a substance language. Regionalization may then be based on proximity in the substance language. We can also adopt various combinations or strategies, such as introducing contiguity constraints (i.e., using space as a property) in the grouping procedure, or searching for space-time individuals which are homogeneous with respect to certain property characteristics (this yields us uniform regions). Typically the urban planner accepts a set of locational units (usually census tracts), measures variables in each tract, and may then group tracts according to similarity of properties while observing a contiguity constraint. I do not, however, want to discuss these strategies in detail for I have made my main point: the process of individuation at the interface between the sociological and geographical imagination requires a thorough understanding of two rather different languages and an adequate methodology to govern their combination. This may seem an obscure point in some respects, yet it is the basic methodological issue which lies behind the confusion of the planner when trying to combine ideas about physical neighbourhood (usually thought of in the space-time language) and social functioning (usually thought of in the substance language). The policy conclusions which a planner reaches may thus depend upon which language he regards as dominant and upon exactly how he combines the two languages into some framework for analysis.

2 Confounding

One of the trickiest problems to resolve at the interface is to control unwanted variables and to identify the role of each individual variable in complex interacting non-experimental situations. Without an adequate experimental design procedure, it is all too easy to confound one variable with another, to confound causes with effects, to confound functional relationships with causal relationships, and to commit any number of first-order inferential sins. It is easy, of course, to be rather purist and negative about this, but, even if we attempt to be positive and do not insist upon a premature rigour, the problems still impinge upon us at every turn in research design. Consider the following simple example. The sociologist typically looks at the diffusion process as it operates between individuals, groups, social classes, cultures and so on. The relevant variables in predicting the diffusion relate back to the personality characteristics of the individual. The geographer typically looks at the spatial aspect and regards locational proximity as the prime variable in determining the course of a diffusion process. Now it so happens that people of the same class tend to live in proximity to one another. How then are we to distinguish how much the spatial variable contributes, and how much the personality variables contribute? In any situation, we must examine their joint effect, and, unfortunately, the two aspects are not independent of each other. We do not appear to possess adequate nonexperimental research designs to allow us to handle this sort of problem in any but the crudest fashion.

These problems of confounding, however, exist in work on the social process even when it is thought of as being independent of spatial form. It would thus seem as important for the sociologist working in his own sphere to try to eliminate spatial effects from his argument as it is for the geographer to eliminate the social effects from his. If these confounding effects are not eliminated in the research design, then it will be all too easy to get statistically significant but really spurious support for hypotheses. My own suspicion is that much of the work on social processes suffers because it fails to recognize the acute inferential problems which may arise from confounding spatial with sociological effects. Much of the work on the purely spatial side can similarly be criticized. Working at the interface does not, therefore, pose any new problems; it does shed light on the true nature of some of the old, and it also demonstrates that the social analyst and the spatial analyst cannot afford to work in ignorance of each other.

3 Statistical inference

The problems of individuation and confounding lead to those of statistical inference. These are easy enough to explain, but difficult to resolve. Ideally, we need a metalanguage in which we can discuss statistical significance in both a sociological and spatial sense simultaneously. Lacking this, we must resort to tests derived in the two separate languages and somehow combine them into a valid framework for statistical inference. The tests appropriate for validating hypotheses about a spaceless social process are well established. Under a given hypothesis, we can generate certain expectations and then seek to show that there is no significant difference between expectation and observation data. The lack of any significant difference is generally taken to mean that the hypothesis is confirmed, although this is only true under certain assumptions about the way in which the observed results are generated (for example, eliminating all confounding variables), and the way in which the hypothesis is set up, and so on. The tests appropriate for spatial distribution patterns are not so well established. We can generate certain spatial expectations and then compare these expectations with observed spatial distributions. Tests do exist to compare spatial arrangements of cell type data (Cliff and Ord, 1972). The comparison of two surfaces, however, is not so easy, and we have no way of telling when an expected surface is significantly different from an observed surface. Similarly, we have no real understanding of the meaning of significant difference in point pattern arrangement. In general, therefore, there is no accepted definition of statistical significance in spatial inference and consequently there are serious problems inherent in the testing of hypotheses about spatial distributions. It seems that the only way to formulate notions of significance is to make assumptions about the nature of the spatial distribution. Since we are often concerned to identify, rather than to assume, the spatial distribution, this approach is not always helpful. It appears, however, to be the only course open to us at the present time. For this reason, it is very easy to criticize the current methods of dealing with spatial data (Granger, 1969).

The combination of social and spatial procedures into one framework for statistical inference might still seem feasible. Consider the following example in which we seek to predict the spread of some social characteristic over space—say the spread of non-white population over a series of census tracts located in a city. Under a hypothesis, we may generate certain expectations regarding the number of non-whites in each cell. In order to test this hypothesis, we need to show that the hypothesis generates the correct number of people in each cell. We can test this by comparing the distribution of cells in frequency classes as they occur under the hypothesis and as they occur in reality. We may find there is or is not a significant difference at the five per cent level. But, we also need to show that the model predicts the correct spatial arrangement of the cell predictions. We can use a k-colour contiguity test to show that between the spatial pattern generated under hypothesis and the spatial pattern observed in reality. If the two tests are totally independent of each other, we can join these two significance levels by the multiplication rule and say that the joint test operates at the 0·25 per cent level of significance. But, it is clear that the two tests are not independent of each other. In fact, joining the two tests in this manner may (and frequently does) involve us in a conflict in statistical logic. The social process tests rely upon independence in each item of data if their assumptions are not to be violated, yet the spatial statistics are explicitly concerned with measuring the degree of spatial dependence in the data. Automatically, therefore, we inject into the social process test the problem of autocorrelation, and this means that we violate the assumptions of the test unless we can somehow or other take evasive action (by filtering the data, and so on). This problem arises at almost every point in work at the interface. It is certainly unresolved, and often it passes unrecognized. It has always seemed strange to me, for example, that multivariate methods of regionalization rely upon correlation measures which, if they are to be judged significant indicators, require independence in the data observations, when the objective of the whole procedure is to group units into regions which have similar (and hence spatially autocorrelated) characteristics. The method and the objective in this case seem to be logically inconsistent or, at best, to generate a set of regions which cannot be judged significant in any meaningful sense. This seems to me to form an insuperable objection to the use of factor analysis in regionalization schemes. The problem of autocorrelation has, however, been extensively explored in the econometric literature with respect to the time dimension, and we can draw certain encouragement (and certain techniques) from that field. However, as Granger (1969) has observed, there are important differences between the time dimension which conveniently possesses direction and irreversibility and the spatial dimensions which do not possess either of these properties and which may also be characterized by complex non-stationarities and awkward discontinuities. These problems lead Granger to doubt if the techniques evolved in econometrics to deal with time series can be generalized to spatial series except for certain classes of problem. The spatial autocorrelation problem looks like a difficult one to resolve satisfactorily, and a sound framework for statistical inference at the interface depends upon its resolution.

Our tools for dissecting the problems of blending sociological and geographical techniques to deal with urban problems are blunt. Consequently, we must anticipate difficulty in making conditional predictions and in validating theory. This may sound depressing, but we cannot resolve difficulties by pretending they do not exist. Indeed, the proper identification of them

43

is essential if we are to set about sharpening our tools for bridge-building at the interface. Meanwhile, it is important to be aware of the possible sources of error in spatial forecasting and in theory construction. Self-deception regarding these errors is no training for the social scientist, the geographer, or the planner faced with making difficult policy decisions. Each needs a thorough education in the methodological limitations which surround him while working at the interface.

STRATEGY AT THE INTERFACE

We need an adequate analytic framework for coping with the complex problems at the interface between social and spatial analysis. I do not think that an adequate metalanguage will be forthcoming in the near future to integrate the two approaches. We must therefore devise temporary frameworks with which to construct a theory of the city. In making use of these, however, we must be careful, for the framework we select can affect our notions of the proper role of the planner, and our policy priorities. It is unfortunately all too easy for a "logic in use" to become associated with an entrenched philosophical position. This problem can be demonstrated by a look at two rather different modes of approach to city problems.

It is possible to regard the spatial form of a city as a basic determinant of human behaviour. This "spatial environmental determinism" is a working hypothesis of those physical planners who seek to promote a new social order by manipulating the spatial environment of the city. It is also a convenient way to break into some of the complexities of the interaction between spatial form and social process for it sets up a simple causal framework in which spatial form affects social process. In some cases, this point of view appears to have become an entrenched philosophy, and, as such, it has come under attack of late. The democratic notion that what people want is important, together with some evidence (by no means conclusive) that altering the spatial environment may have little effect upon behaviour patterns, has led Gans (1969), Jacobs (1961) and Webber (1963) to attack spatial environmental determinism and to draw attention to an alternative working hypothesis in which a social process is viewed as possessing its own dynamic that often—in spite of the planner—will achieve its own appropriate spatial form. Webber argues that a new spatial order is emerging as a response to changing technology and changing social norms. The planner cannot prevent this order. He can only delay its achievement or impair its efficiency. This working hypothesis, which reverses the cause relationship proposed in the first, seems also to have become an entrenched philosophical position with some writers. The planner, according to this view, should be seen as a servant of the social process and not its master.

The differences between these two seemingly alternative approaches are a good deal more complicated than the argument of the preceding paragraph indicates. Undoubtedly, many of the early physical planners possessed a very naïve kind of spatial environmental determinism in which a few rehousing projects, a few parks, and the like, were regarded as adequate cures for complex social ills. This approach is demonstrably untrue. But the modern environmental designers are very much more aware of the subtleties that exist in the relationship between an environment and a person's behaviour (Sommer, 1969). They recognize that there is little hard evidence upon which to base ideas about good city design which they are concerned to provide. Modern proponents of both approaches are also likely to acknowledge the role of feedback. The spatial environmentalist will know that if he alters the spatial structure of the transport network then the social process will probably generate quite substantial land-use changes. The social determinist will also recognize that if the social process is moving towards some dominant norm (say communication by automobile then the creation of a spatial form suited for that norm can only reinforce it—most modern American cities are not built for walking in and, therefore, reinforce the need for car ownership and use. The differences between the two approaches are more subtle at the present time, but they are still important. Consider the following two quotations:

"There is considerable evidence that the physical environment does not play as significant a role in people's lives as the planner believes. Although people reside, work and play in buildings, their behaviour is not determined by the buildings, but by the economic, cultural, and social relationships within them. Bad design can interfere with what goes on inside a building, of course, and good design can aid it, but design *per se* does not significantly shape human behaviour." (Gans, 1969, 37–8.)

"Good design becomes meaningless tautology if we consider that man will be reshaped to fit whatever environment he creates. The long-range question is not so much what sort of environment we want, but what sort of man we want." (Sommer, 1969, 172.)

The pros and cons of these approaches are not relevant: the evidence is too slender, and the hypotheses are too ambiguous. It is perhaps more reasonable to regard the city as a complex dynamic system in which spatial form and social process are in continuous interaction with each other. If we are to understand the trajectory of the urban system, we must understand the functional relationships which exist within it, and the independent features in the social processes and spatial form which can change the line of that trajectory. It is unnecessarily naïve to think in terms of simple causal relationships between spatial form and social process (whichever way we choose to point the causal arrow). The system is much more complex than that. The two sides are inextricably interrelated. The two approaches should therefore be regarded as complementary rather than as mutually exclusive alternatives. Yet, it is often necessary to break into some complex interacting system, at some point, if any information is to be generated. Whether we choose to do so at the point of spatial form (and regard the social process as an output), at the point of the social process (and regard the spatial form as an output), or to devise some more complicated approach (with feedbacks and so on) should be a decision governed by convenience rather than by philosophy.

But all these approaches are naïve in the sense that they presuppose the existence of an adequate language to discuss spatial form and social process simultaneously. Such a language does not exist. We usually abstract from the complex system that is the city by making use of languages to handle either the social process or the spatial form. Given this mode of abstraction, we cannot meaningfully talk about spatial form *causing* a social process (or vice versa) nor is it really correct to regard spatial form and social process as if they are variables which are somehow in continuous interaction with each other. What we are really attempting is to translate results generated in one language (say a social process language) into another language

46

(the spatial form language). These translations allow us to say something about the implications of one style of analysis for another style of analysis. It is rather like translating from a geometric result to an algebraic result (and vice versa) in that both languages amount to different ways of saying the same thing. The problem with the spatial-form–social-process translation, however, is that there are no well-established rules for it. Under certain conditions, we can build frameworks to handle both dimensions simultaneously. Consider a simple programming problem in which we seek to optimize levels of activity at certain points in a network by minimizing transport costs. The solution is fairly simple all the time the network remains fixed. However, if we allow the network to alter, the number of activity points to change, as well as activity levels to vary, then we have a very complicated problem on our hands: the number of combinations quickly becomes astronomical. Nevertheless, very small problems of this type can be handled by combinatorial analysis, and I suspect that certain simple problems which occur in city planning or in environmental design can be treated in both dimensions simultaneously. But we are, for the most part, forced to keep either spatial form constant (in which case we can solve quite complicated social process problems) or to keep social process constant (in which case we can solve quite complicated spatial form problems). In each case, we can only find a solution on one side by making fairly strict assumptions about the conditions which exist on the other. This suggests that one appropriate strategy for working at the interface is an iterative one in which we move from spatial form manipulation (with social process held constant) to the social process implications (with the new spatial form held constant). We can move in either direction, and there is no reason why we should not manipulate both spatial form and social process at different steps in an iterative sequence. This seems to be the style that is developing in urban modelling. Several alternative spatial designs are generated, and they are then evaluated in terms of some social process (usually economic efficiency or cost-benefit), and evaluations compared to determine the best design. In other cases, one part of the spatial design is altered, and the impact upon other facets of the spatial design is then examined by way of a spatial allocation model which makes strict assumptions about the nature of the social

47

process. This iterative approach is clearly very useful when taken in combination with simulation techniques. But it does, of course, have some important drawbacks, the most important of which is that it involves a translation from one language to another when the rules of translation are assumed rather than known. These assumed rules can have an important impact upon the results. This can be demonstrated by the problems that arise from the usual strategy adopted in location theory.

The starting point of location theory is that space can be translated into an economic commodity by way of transport costs and that transport cost can then be substituted into a social process model designed to find equilibrium production conditions for each industry or firm. Once these equilibrium conditions have been specified, the results are then translated back into spatial form results by making certain assumptions about the nature of the conditions which exist on some surface (equal transport facilities, flat plane surfaces, and so on). It is generally held, however, that these assumptions are mere conveniences and that they do not in any way interfere with the equilibrium conditions defined in the process model. This supposition can be criticized on a number of grounds. In the first place, the problem of feedback has to be overcome. In the Löschian case, for example, the population change which must result from an achievement of equilibrium must disturb the nature of the spatial form conditions which allow that equilibrium to be spatially specified (Isard, 1956, 271–2). The urban system presumably develops some trajectory, and there is no guarantee that any real equilibrium can be reached in the social process because the spatial form is constantly changing. The system may, therefore, be an explosive one which does not stabilize. In the spatial sense the main trend is towards agglomeration, and therefore it might be more appropriate to call the system an implosive one. A second major criticism, however, is that the geometric assumptions themselves have an impact upon the specification of equilibrium. If we assume a beach of finite length, the social activity of three ice-cream sellers becomes theoretically indeterminate: it is no accident that most location theory assumes infinite plane surfaces, for, without this assumption, the social process equilibrium point often cannot be determined. In general, the spatial form assumptions injected into location theory are more than mere conveniences—they are fundamental to the results. Let me make clear that I am not attacking the location theorist or the urban analyst for making assumptions about spatial form. In practice, I believe we have little choice but to use assumptions of that sort. But it is important to recognize that these are frail bridges with which to cross a huge gulf of a problem. We cannot possibly use them to discuss the kinds of complexity indicated earlier in which space itself is seen as multidimensional, non-homogeneous, perhaps discontinuous, highly personalized, and meaningful in different ways in different social activity contexts. The location approach is operational, but we buy this operationalism at a cost. We ought therefore to be aware of how much we are paying in terms of realism when we adopt certain strategies, and in what ways the assumptions involved in a particular strategy are fundamental to the results of any analysis. We cannot avoid such questions in seeking to construct a genuine theory of the city. Ultimately, we may be able to transcend the problems inherent in our way of conceptualizing social processes and spatial form. Until that time, however, all we can do is to attempt some kind of evaluation of their implications and adapt our research strategies and our policy making accordingly. It is, after all, a major tenet of scientific thought that errors can only be estimated and combated if we have an understanding of the sources from which they arise.

Chapter 2

Social Processes and Spatial Form:

2 The Redistribution of Real Income in an Urban System

Any overall strategy for dealing with urban systems must contain and reconcile policies designed to change the spatial form of the city (by which is meant the location of objects such as houses, plant, transport links, and the like) with policies concerned to affect the social processes which go on in the city (i.e., the social structures and activities which link people with people, organizations with people, employment opportunities with employees, welfare recipients with services, and so on). Ideally, we should be able to harmonize these policies to achieve some coherent social objective. We are far from such a capability at the present time. In chapter 1 I tried to examine some of the difficulties in achieving it. These arise partly from the inherent complexity of the city system itself, partly from our traditional and rather myopic disciplinary approach to a system which cries out for interdisciplinary treatment, and also from serious methodological and philosophical problems which stand in the way of a full integration of spatial form and social process in the context of urban systems analysis. When it comes to formulating strategies and policies, however, there is another dimension to the problem—that of making explicit what we mean by the phrase "a coherent social objective".

By and large, the social planner and forecaster tends to dodge this last issue because it involves a set of social, political and ethical judgements upon which it will be very difficult to obtain general agreement. The trouble with merely dodging the issue is that judgements are inevitably *implied* by a decision,

50

whether we like it or not. If, for example, we predict, on the basis of current knowledge and trends, the future population distribution, consumption patterns, travel demands (by mode) and so on, and allocate current investment accordingly, we thereby imply that these future conditions are acceptable to us. Insofar as investment decisions bear fruit, we must also bear some responsibility for bringing about the very conditions predicted. The phenomenal growth of automobile ownership and use in the United States can partly be accounted for by investment policies favourable to highways rather than to other modes of transport. The planner is therefore intricately bound up with the social processes generating change since much publicized plans are almost certain to influence the course of events (though not always in the direction anticipated) if they are not actually self-fulfilling. For this reason, it is impossible for us to set up an "objective" yardstick for measuring the success or failure of planning policies, for that yardstick requires that we invoke a set of ethical standards and social preferences. Is it "right" for example to concentrate so much on the private automobile? Who in the population suffers and who benefits, and is it right that they should do so? These are the kinds of questions which we must eventually face up to. What this demonstrates, of course, is the crying need for a generally accepted and comprehensive social welfare function against which policy decisions and results can be judged. We are not likely in the near or distant future to be able to formulate a generally acceptable social welfare function for an urban system. This difficulty (which most of us tend to ignore in the hope that it will go away) should not be allowed, however, to divert our attention from the mechanisms which connect allocational decisions (whether public or private) on such things as transport networks, industrial zoning, location of public facilities, location of households, and so on, with their inevitable distributional effects upon the real income of different groups in the population. These distributional effects are exceedingly important. Yet they are very poorly understood and the mechanisms relating allocation and distribution remain obscure. There is, of course, good reason for shying away from a study of these mechanisms. If it becomes explicit as to who will lose and who will benefit, and by how much, from a given allocation decision, then we must anticipate far greater difficulty in implementing the decision. But a working philosophy based on the notion that "what the eye doesn't see the heart doesn't pine for" can scarcely be acceptable to any planner of integrity. The rest of this essay therefore concentrates attention upon the mechanisms which tend to redistribute income in an urban population. This question has, of course, been raised by several writers in the recent past (the most thorough works being those of Thompson, 1965, and Netzer, 1968). I shall seek to evaluate the effects of certain "hidden mechanisms" of redistribution which tend to be obscured by our inability to analyse a system which exhibits interdependence between social and spatial variation.

THE DISTRIBUTION OF INCOME AND THE SOCIAL OBJECTIVES FOR A CITY SYSTEM

Most social policies are directly framed as attempts to maintain a given distribution of income within a social system or to redistribute income among the various social groups that make up a society. It has generally been accepted that some redistribution must take place since there are always those elements in a population who by ill-luck, bad judgement, age or frailty, cannot attain an adequate standard of living through the usual means. Exactly how much redistribution of income should occur is, of course, an ethical question which different societies have answered in different ways at different times—this is the central ethical judgement which has to be made in the formulation of any social policy with respect to a city system. If we are to achieve a chosen income distribution, we must have a very clear idea of the mechanisms which generate income inequalities in the first place, for it is presumably by controlling and manipulating these mechanisms that we will achieve our given objective. It is not necessary to state any preference for a given income distribution to investigate these mechanisms, but it will probably become clear in what follows that I am generally in favour of a far more egalitarian social structure than currently exists in either American or British urban systems. It appears that the "hidden mechanisms" of income redistribution in a complex city system usually increase inequalities rather than reduce them. This has immediate implications for social policy in that it indicates the necessity for a policy of "over-kill" in direct redistribution if the general direction of hidden redistribution is to be counteracted. Another possibility is, of course, to seek to control or make use of the hidden mechanisms for redistribution, and I shall give some indications as to how this might be done. These "asides" regarding my own social policy preferences need not interfere, however, with the direct analysis of the mechanisms controlling income redistribution.

It is rather important to begin by seeking out some adequate definition of income. The simplest, and perhaps the most misleading, definition is that income is the amount "received in spendable form in a given year which is actually spent on current consumption in the same year," but Titmuss (1962, 34) provides us with a more comprehensive definition:

"No concept of income can be really equitable that stops short of the comprehensive definition which embraces all receipts which increase an individual's command over the use of a society's scarce resources—in other words his net accretion of economic power between two points of time. . . . Hence income is the algebraic sum of (1) the market value of rights exercised in consumption, and (2) the change in the value of the store of property rights between the beginning and the end of the period in question."

This definition has some interesting implications, one of which is that income includes the change in value of an individual's property rights "irrespective of whether the change has been brought about by the current addition to property which is saving in the narrow sense, or whether it has been caused by accretions to the value of the property. From the point of view of the individual's command over resources, it is the change in the real value of his property which alone matters, and not the process by which that change was brought about."

It should also be clear that the command over society's scarce resources cannot be determined independently of accessibility to and the price of those resources. Resources can be exhausted, modified, or created, according to the nature of the resource and its management. So there are likely to be several ways in which an individual's income can change. The individual can earn more (less), he can receive positive (negative) benefits from a change in the value of his property, he can simply have more (less) resources made available to him at a lower (higher) price, or he can have any combination of these gains

53

and losses over a particular period. In what follows, I shall use the term "income change" to cover all of these different possibilities. The question then arises as to how changes in the spatial form of a city and changes in the social processes operating within the city bring about changes in an individual's income.

It will require detailed theoretical and empirical evidence to answer this question with any certitude. At the present time I can only present suspicions as hypotheses and bits and pieces of information as supporting empirical evidence. I shall argue, for example, that the social process of wage determination is partly modified by changes in the location of employment opportunities (by categories) compared with changes in residential opportunities (by type). The failure of employment and residential opportunities to keep in balance with each other has imposed greater accessibility costs on some groups in the population relative to other groups. I shall also try to show how changes in the value of property rights and in the availability and price of resources can occur through the spatial dynamics of city growth. I shall argue that these changes together have a very substantial effect upon income distribution and that their effects become disproportionately important as the size of an urban system increases. What this really amounts to, of course, is the notion that "fringe benefits" are generated by changes in the urban system and that these fringe benefits are distributed unequally across the urban population. The modern treatment of income distribution is taking more and more account of the fringe benefit problem. The main thrust of Titmuss's argument, for example, is that changes in the structure of fringe benefits in the British social system have more than offset the redistribution of income by progressive taxation in England during the period 1939–1956. In this essay, I am really trying to extend this sort of argument into the urban context. To do so, I shall need to determine how fringe benefits operate in the context of earnings, property values, and resource availability. In the last case we will also be concerned with the differential distribution of certain unpriced or "free" resources among different segments of a population—at the present time this appears to be one of the more important of the differential "fringe benefits" generated in an urban system. In taking this approach, I believe we can partly explain away one of the central paradoxes of modern society—that an increasingly affluent society with a rapidly changing technology is generating awkward structural problems and deepening tensions in the process of urbanization.

SOME FEATURES GOVERNING THE REDISTRIBUTION OF INCOME

It is perhaps invidious to isolate out any particular features which account for the redistribution of income. Nothing less than complete understanding of how an urban system works is really required. But there are a number of recurrent themes in what follows and it is useful to isolate these before proceeding, since by so doing we can avoid repetitious discussion.

1 The speed of change and the rate of adjustment in an urban system

Much of our analytic understanding of the urban system comes from equilibrium analysis. Most of these equilibrium analyses seek to define an optimal allocation of resources (for instance, land resources) under conditions where the *distribution of income is given*. Most of the analyses of the urban housing market, for example, indicate the structure and form of equilibrium assuming a given distribution of income. Only under this assumption is it possible to determine what is usually termed a "Pareto optimum" (a situation in which nobody can become better off from moving without making somebody else worse off). These models provide us with important insights into the allocation mechanisms which underlie the formation of an urban structure, but they tell us little about how a given distribution of income comes about. Even if we accept the assumption of a given distribution of income, however, we still have to consider the speed with which equilibrium is achieved.

It has been an underlying assumption of much of the work on urban modelling that some kind of natural equilibrium can be identified in an urban system. This is true of both the deterministic models of urban structure developed by writers such as Alonso (1964) and Mills (1969) and the statistical models of equilibrium assumed in gravity type and entropy maximizing models (Wilson, 1970). These equilibrium analyses have undoubtedly provided us with some important insights into the urban system, but I believe such equilibrium models can be misleading if they are applied without considerable qualification.

The main question here, of course, is the speed with which different parts of an urban system can adjust to the changes occurring within it. The changes have been rapid in recent decades but there is considerable evidence that the adjustment process takes a relatively long time to work itself out. Furthermore, different parts of the urban system have different capacities for adjustment. Some aspects of urban organization respond immediately whereas others respond very sluggishly. It is therefore misleading to think of adjustment in the urban system as a homogeneous process proceeding at a uniform rate. This varying speed of adjustment means that there are substantial differentials in the disequilibrium in the urban system at any one point in time. To give a simple example: it is clear that there has not been an equal response in the urban population to the potential of mobility associated with the automobile. The time lag is anything from 20 to 40 years between different groups in the population. It would be very surprising indeed if the better educated and more affluent groups had not taken advantage of this time lag to further their own interests and enhance their own income. The allocation of resources then takes place as an adjustment to this new income distribution and a cumulative process of increasing inequality of income distribution gets under way. This is a crude example, but I think it is very general. Certain groups, particularly those with financial resources and education, are able to adapt far more rapidly to a change in the urban system, and these differential abilities to respond to change are a major source in generating inequalities. Any urban system is in a permanent state of differential disequilibrium (by which I mean that different parts of it are approaching equilibrium at different rates). The speed of change and the relative capacities of elements in the urban system to adapt are essential features in the analysis which follows. This implies that we cannot analyse our problem via some general equilibrium framework, although it doesn't prevent us in any way from making use of the theoretical and empirical insights generated from equilibrium analyses.

2 The price of accessibility and the cost of proximity

It is generally agreed that accessiblity and proximity are important features of any urban system. I shall briefly examine both from the point of view of households acting as consumers. Accessibility to employment opportunities, resources and welfare services can be obtained only at a price, and this price is generally equated with the cost of overcoming distance, of using time, and the like. But it is by no means easy to measure the price which people pay. Consider, for example, the difficulty of putting some value upon time in transport studies. And there are other even more complicated problems involved here, for the social price people are forced to pay for access to certain facilities is something which can vary from the simple direct cost involved in transport to the emotional and psychological price imposed upon an individual who has an intense resistance to doing something (the kind of price which may be extorted, for example, from someone who has to take a means test to qualify for welfare). These social and psychological barriers are important. Any discussion of accessibility, therefore, requires that we answer a fundamental question regarding the meaning of "distance" and "space" in an urban system—a problem which I have examined in chapter 1 (see also the excellent review by Buttimer, 1969). In this essay I am going to use the term "proximity" to refer to a rather different phenomenon than accessibility. By proximity, I mean the effects of being close to something people do not make any direct use of. A household may thus find itself proximate to a source of pollution, to a source of noise, or to a run-down environment. This proximity tends to impose certain costs upon the household (for example, cleaning and laundry bills, sound-proofing, etc.).

It should be self-evident that as we change the spatial form of city (by relocating housing, transport routes, employment opportunities, sources of pollution, etc.) so we change the price of accessibility and the cost of proximity for any one household. We will likewise find that these prices and costs are a function of the social attitudes of the population at large insofar as psychological factors play a part. The balance of these changes clearly has the potential for bringing about quite substantial redistributions of income.

3 Externality effects

The activity of any one element in an urban system may generate certain unpriced and perhaps non-monetary effects upon

57

other elements in the system. These effects are usually termed "externalities", "spill-over effects", or "third-party effects". Mishan states:

"External effects may be said to arise when relevant effects on production and welfare go wholly or partially unpriced. Being outside the price system such external effects are sometimes looked upon as the by-products, wanted or unwanted, of other people's activities that immediately or indirectly affect the welfare of individuals." (1969, 164.)

Such external effects can arise from both private and public activity. Some of the simplest examples can be found in the pollution field, for waste discharge into water and into the air are classic examples of by-product effects which, until recently, have gone unpriced and uncontrolled. Externalities can be viewed as either costs or benefits according to whether the producer or the consumer is affected and according to the nature of the effect. A hydroelectric power operation, for example, may create positive benefits in the way of flood control and recreational opportunities. Waste discharge may create external losses through environmental degradation. Casual observation of urban problems indicates that there is a whole host of externality effects which have to be taken account of—a fact which is implicitly recognized in Lowry's (1965, 158) comment that "in the city everything affects everything else". Many of these relationships are transmitted as third-party effects. Until recently, however, the role of externalities in an urban system was largely ignored. But recent statements have drawn attention to the fact that "external economies and diseconomies are a pervasive and important feature in the urban scene" (Hoch, 1969, 91; see also Gaffney, 1961; Margolis, 1965; 1968; Mishan, 1967, 74–99; Rothenberg, 1967). I think it is a reasonable working hypothesis that "as societies grow in material wealth the incidence of these effects grows rapidly" (Mishan, 1969, 184). In urban systems it seems reasonable to suppose that the larger and more complex they are the greater is the significance of externality effects. In what follows I shall tend to the view that much of what goes on in a city (particularly in the political arena) can be interpreted as an attempt to organize the distribution of externality effects to gain income advantages. Insofar as these attempts are successful, they are a source of income inequality. Even if this interpretation is not accepted, however, there are still some vast unanswered questions concerning the redistributive effects of decisions made in the public sector of an urban system (Thompson, 1965, 118; Margolis, 1965).

The significance of externality effects for an economic analysis of urban structure cannot be underrated. The larger they are "in range and magnitude the smaller is the faith that can be reposed in the allocative virtues of the market mechanism even when working under ideal conditions" (Mishan, 1969, 181). The inability of the market mechanism to allocate resources efficiently when externalities are present has posed a major problem for economic theory. From a policy viewpoint, it has provided a rationale for public interference with the market mechanism and it has also led into the thorny question of who should be responsible (and how) for the production of public goods. The externality problem has therefore received considerable attention from economists in the past decade (see the review by Mishan, 1969, chapter 7; and the work of Buchanan, 1968). Almost all this extensive literature has focused on allocation problems and very little attention has been paid to distributional effects, mainly because any theory of the distribution of external costs and benefits involves those ethical and political judgements about the "best" distribution of income which most of us prefer to avoid. The economic theory of external effects does not tell us all we want to know when it comes to distribution. But it does provide us with some insights into the problem of how externalities arise and how arguments over their allocation can be resolved by resorting to a game-theoretic framework for decision making (Davis and Whinston, 1962).

It is useful to begin by dividing goods into purely private goods (which can be produced and consumed without any third-party effects being present) and purely public goods (which, once produced, are freely available to everyone). As Buchanan (1968, 56–7) points out, however, most of the interesting cases lie between these two extremes—i.e., goods which are partly private and partly public. It is of interest to note that one example of an "impure" public good used by Buchanan concerns location. The very fact of location of a public facility such as a fire station (or for that matter any public service) means that the population does not enjoy exactly homogeneous quality and quantity of fire protection as far as consumption is concerned, even though they have the same quantity and quality of fire protection available to them in terms of production. From the point of view of distribution and consumption, therefore, location is an absolutely vital factor in understanding the impact of externality effects in a city system. From the point of view of the production of public goods, on the other hand, location may be irrelevant. The recent shift towards decentralization of city services may thus be seen as a shift from a policy based on the production of public goods to a policy based on the consumption of public goods. To understand the distributional impact it is necessary to combine the notions of accessibility and proximity developed earlier with the notion of an impure public good. All localized public goods are "impure" and the externality exists as a "spatial field" of effects. We might generalize these spatial fields by distance-decay functions of by diffusion equations (such as those which describe the general field of external costs imposed by a source of atmospheric pollution). These spatial fields of externality effects will vary in intensity and extent, from the influence of a derelict property on the values of the adjacent properties to the extensive field of influence of airport noise. Externality fields can be positive or negative or, sometimes as in the case of an airport, both (since an airport is a nuisance from the point of view of pollution and noise close by but has important benefits for employment and movement). We know very little about the shape and form of these externality fields in an urban environment. But there can be no doubt that their location has a very powerful effect upon the real income of the individual. Changes in them can be a factor in the redistribution of income and, hence, a potential source of income inequality. The political process has a profound influence over the location of external benefits and costs. Indeed, a case can be made for regarding local political activity as the basic mechanism for allocating the spatial externality fields in such a way as to reap indirect income advantages.

THE REDISTRIBUTIVE EFFECTS OF THE CHANGING LOCATION OF JOBS AND HOUSING

Cities have grown very rapidly in the past twenty years or so and this growth has resulted in some significant changes in the spatial form of the city. There has thus been (and always presumably will be) a significant reorganization in the location and distribution of various activities in the city system. It is very easy to regard these changes as somehow "natural" and "right" and simply a manifestation of adjustment in the urban system to changing technology, changing demand patterns, and the like. From the policy point of view, however, it should be clear that these adjustments in the spatial form of the city are likely to bring about a redistribution of income in a variety of ways. It will not be possible in this essay to discuss all the ways in which this might occur. I shall, therefore, proceed largely by way of examples.

The changing location of economic activity in a city means a changing location of job opportunities. The changing location of residential activity means a changing location of housing opportunities. Both these changes are likely to be associated with changing expenditures on transport. Changes in transport availability certainly affect the cost of obtaining access to job opportunities from housing locations. These changes are fairly well understood (indeed they are invariably built into any model of urban growth) but their implications for the redistribution of income are not always so clearly perceived. Consider, for example, the situation in many American cities in which there has been a very rapid suburbanization in both the location of residences and the location of employment opportunities (Kain, 1968; Kerner Commission Report, 1968). If we look at the way in which the location of jobs (by category) and housing (by type) has changed, together with the typical adjustments in transport facilities, it will be clear that a redistribution of wealth has occurred. There is considerable evidence that the supply of low income housing is less than elastic (Muth, 1968, 128) and that it is locationally fixed partly by the characteristic pattern of the housing stock available in any city and partly by the existence of a strong social contiguity constraint. For these reasons, we can expect that the main source of supply of low income housing will be in central city areas. The urban system seems to have reacted very sluggishly indeed to the demand for low-income housing in suburban areas. The difficulty of expanding the supply in the inner city (partly due to institutional constraints such as zoning regulations) means that poor quality, low income housing is relatively high priced and frequently more profitable for property owners than we would expect under true equilibrium conditions (Muth, 1968, 126). Low income families therefore have little option but to locate in the relatively high priced inner city. In most American cities, of course, this condition has been exacerbated by the lack of an open housing market for the black population which, of course, just happens to constitute a large segment of the poor. Meanwhile most of the growth in new employment has been in the suburban ring and hence the low income groups have gradually been cut off from new sources of employment. They have had to resort to the local employment opportunities in the fairly stagnant industrial areas of the inner city or in the central business district (CBD), which in any case only offers a small proportion of its employment in the unskilled low-income category. By contrast, residents in the suburban communities have a far wider range of options open to them. They can make use of rapid transit facilities into the CBD, they can seek employment locally in growing suburban employment centres, or they can make use of the pattern of ring-roads and beltways to move around the suburban ring.

The process of relocation within the urban system has thus served to improve the options for the affluent suburbanite and cut down the possibilities for the low-income family in the inner city. This situation could be partly counteracted by transport policy, but by and large that policy has facilitated the existing trend rather than counteracted it. Meyer thus comments on the implications of developing different kinds of urban transport systems:

"It should be quite clear that since the groups served by these . . . different basic urban transportation systems are rather different, the incidence of benefits derived from improvements in these systems will vary considerably. For example, improvement in the long distance, high performance suburb to downtown system will tend primarily to benefit higher income groups. To the extent that development of these systems is subsidized from public funds, the implicit income transfer probably would be regressive. By contrast, expenditures aimed at improving conventional short-haul central city transit will almost certainly benefit mostly low- to middle-income groups." (1968, 68.)

Meyer goes on to comment that the one kind of system which has been very weakly developed (and in most cases totally neglected) is the *inside-out system* for conveying people from central city areas to job opportunities in the suburbs:

"The Negro female domestic working in a suburban home and living in a centrally located ghetto is the archetype: today, however, she is increasingly joined by male Negroes because employment opportunities in manufacturing, inter-city transportation, and even wholesaling and retailing are increasingly found at suburban locations whereas housing opportunities remain restricted to the central ghetto."

In general, the adjustments to transport systems have favoured suburban areas and neglected the needs of inner areas as far as access to employment is concerned. But even if transport policy reversed this trend, there is something paradoxical about expecting low-income households, whose rationale for locating in the inner city in the first place (we are told) depended upon minimizing their outlays on transport cost, to lay out the expenditure necessary to reach suburban employment centres simply because the housing market cannot adjust (in terms of quantity or location) to the changing location of employment. This seems a classic case of the inflexibility of a city's spatial form generating almost permanent disequilibrium in the city social system. From the policy point of view, it indicates the need for public interference in the housing market (by, for example, constructing low income housing close to suburban employment opportunities). Otherwise, there seems little hope of achieving the so-called "natural equilibrium solution" in any reasonable time period, even if we concede that this natural equilibrium is one which is socially acceptable.

The general picture which emerges from this brief survey of the mechanisms governing redistribution of income by way of locational shifts can be summarized as follows:

1   The predominantly low-income inner city area has a decreased opportunity to tap new sources of employment since these are mainly located in suburban areas. As a result there is a trend towards a high and growing incidence of unemployment in inner city areas.

2   Because of inelasticity and locational inflexibility in the supply of low-income housing, the low-income household has little opportunity to migrate into suburban areas, and faces rising housing prices in the inner city area.

3   If the low-income household of the inner city does obtain employment in the suburbs, it is faced with greater outlays

63

on transport costs than it should theoretically be able to withstand (a situation which has not been helped by the lack of attention paid to *inside-out* transit systems.

Differential disequilibrium in the spatial form of the city can thus redistribute income. In general, the rich and relatively resourceful can reap great benefits while the poor and necessarily immobile have only restricted opportunities. This can mean a quite substantial regressive redistribution of income in a rapidly changing urban system.

REDISTRIBUTION AND THE CHANGING VALUE OF PROPERTY RIGHTS

I do not want to examine all aspects of the changing value of property rights, so for illustrative purposes I shall consider that particular property right which remains embedded in the spatial form of the city—land parcels and the buildings thereon. The value of such property rights can change differentially in a city quite markedly over fairly short periods of time. These changes are often thought of as the result of demographic movements, changes in local facilities, swings in fashion, changing investment policies, and so on. It is also evident that the value of any one property right is very much affected by the values of neighbouring property rights (Mishan, 1967, 60–63; Muth, 1969, 118–19). The actions of individuals and organizations other than the owner can therefore affect property values. These external effects on the value of a property holder's rights are not under the property holder's control nor are they adequately catered for in the pricing system operating in a supposedly free market. In reality, of course, there is never a free and open housing market nor do all operators in it have perfect information. Also, as we have already seen, there are different elasticities of supply for different types of housing (low-income housing being in general far less responsive to changes in demand than middle- or high-income housing). But even if we assume away these complications, we still have to deal with the theoretically thorny problem of externalities in the housing market. These externalities can arise from many different sources—they are, so to speak, constantly hovering over the

land and property market. Insofar as the property market is
sensitive to them, we can expect them to influence land values—
for instance, a new source of pollution will lead to a decline in
land values, a new park facility may lead to a rise in land values.
I shall examine these kinds of externality from rather a different
point of view in the next section. In this section, I shall concentrate upon their impact upon the land market itself. Davis
and Whinston put the theoretical problem in these terms:

"If dependence is present, then individual action is sufficient
for the market mechanism to produce prices with sufficient information content to lead the system to Pareto optimality. On
the other hand if independence is not present, then purely individual action alone cannot be expected to achieve Pareto
optimality via the unrestricted pricing mechanism." (1964, 443.)
The meaning given here to independence is that the "utility
payoffs to any person are not affected by the choice of sites
made by any other person." This condition is clearly violated in
the housing market since the utility payoffs of one person are
very sensitive indeed to the choice of sites made by other people
and to the investment decisions of other land and property owners. The problem then arises of how a Pareto-optimum can be
achieved. Government intervention could suffice, provided the
central government possessed enough information regarding
the varying utility which individuals attach to different sites.
Such a situation seems very unlikely (which is not a sufficient
reason for dismissing ultimate government intervention in the
housing market). But one way of attaining a Pareto optimum
is by group action in the housing market. Thus "if group action
is allowed and if properly defined boundary constraints result
in group independence, then prices have sufficient information
content to lead to a two-step or multi-step solution" (Davis and
Whinston, 1964, 433). These groups must be organized into a
spatial structure of zones and conditions in each zone must have
a negligible effect upon conditions in other zones. This zonal
independence is, of course, unlikely to hold in practice; but the
Davis and Whinston model is interesting in that it illustrates how
group action in a housing market can serve to counter the difficult problems posed by the existence of externalities and thereby enhance the value of property rights. Different kinds of
coalition can form:

"First, consumers who mutually impose interaction costs

65

upon each other might coordinate their strategies by selecting sites which are separated by some specific distance, thus reducing interaction costs and raising their security levels. This kind of coalition is called a non-homogeneous group. Second, consumers may coordinate their strategies by selecting sites which are adjoining and thus excluding from the specified sub-area uses which impose interaction costs upon them. This latter type of coalition is called a homogeneous group."

The logical outcome of this is a territorial organization of the city in which each territory contains a group with relatively homogeneous values and utility functions and behaviours (insofar as these relate to property). This amounts to a spatial organization designed in such a way as to share out externalities (and create externalities for others). At this juncture, it is interesting to employ that shadowy form of inference (beloved of economists) called by Buchanan (1968a, 3) "inferential prediction" to derive some kind of institutional order which would facilitate sharing externalities in the housing market. Zoning obviously fulfils this role and Davis and Whinston use their model primarily as a justification for zoning operations. Even without this institution, however, it would be tempting to hypothesize that the social organization of a city gains much of its efficiency and stability through a spatial organization designed to protect external benefits and eliminate external costs as they arise within each community or neighbourhood. Some externalities can effectively be dealt with in this way (for instance, those associated with the tone of a neighbourhood). There appears, therefore, to be some theoretical justification for the existence of territorial social organization in a city. If we accept this proposition for the moment, it is interesting to go on and ask how the city can be partitioned in some rational manner. Should the communities be large and face the costs and difficulties of devising a cooperative strategy for a large number of people or should they be small (and be unable to control the externalities imposed by other small groups)? Implicit, therefore, in this whole approach to a rational sharing of external costs and benefits in the housing market is the awkward question of defining an appropriate regional or territorial organization. An infinite number of regionalizations could be devised, but presumably we need to identify that particular regionalization which maximizes the sum of individual utilities (Davis and

Whinston, 1964, 442). But problems of this sort have no easy or obvious answer.

A number of criticisms and qualifications may be made of the preceding analysis. First, the rationality of the coalition procedure assumes an equal ability and willingness on the part of individuals to negotiate. The history of zoning indicates, however, that such a condition is unlikely to hold, particularly in situations where there is considerable imbalance in the distribution of economic and political power (Makielski, 1966). Second, we are forced to assume no externality effects between zones and this condition is usually violated. It is possible to devise strategems for "between-community" conflict resolution and it should, theoretically, be possible to resolve such conflicts provided an adequate negotiating machinery exists. This raises some awkward problems about inter-community bargaining processes, however, and I shall therefore leave this issue for detailed examination in a later section. It is sufficient to note here that interdependencies of this sort destroy the conditions for a Pareto optimum. Third, we have to consider the problem posed by the assumed simultaneity of site selection. Site selection proceeds sequentially and this implies that late arrivals in the market "have the advantage of additional information since they can observe what had taken place" (Davis and Whinston, 1964, 433). The pattern of externalities in the housing market is, therefore, changing sequentially as the occupation of new sites will invariably impose new costs and benefits on sites already developed. If there were no costs or resistance to moving, no problems would arise; but since there are, we cannot expect the market to operate in an optimal fashion. Early-comers to the market will presumably either try to bribe or coerce the late-comers in order to maintain the pattern of externalities to their own benefit. Since the ability to do either of these things depends entirely upon the economic and political power of the groups concerned, we are likely to find a spatial evolution in the housing market and a pricing system which will tend to yield external benefits to the rich and impose external costs upon the poor and politically weak.

What this analysis of the housing market shows us is that a free market cannot give rise to prices conducive to a Pareto optimum and that the housing market, for reasons of its own spatial internal logic, must contain group action if it is to function coherently. This explains, in turn, why the housing market is so peculiarly susceptible to economic and political pressures, since it is only by organizing and applying these pressures that individuals can defend or enhance the value of their property rights relative to those of other individuals. In this, as in most things, it is the economically and politically weak who probably suffer most, unless institutional controls exist to rectify a naturally arising but ethically unacceptable situation.

THE AVAILABILITY AND PRICE OF RESOURCES

The real income of an individual can be changed by changing the resources available to him (Thompson, 1965, 90). This change can be brought about in a number of ways. The quantity of a free unpriced resource (such as fresh air and quiet) may be altered, the price of a resource may be changed, or the cost of access to a resource may be changed. There is, of course, a connection between the value of land and housing and the price of resources, since changes in the latter are supposedly capitalized by changes in the former. Given the inadequacies in the housing market, we have grounds for thinking that this capitalization is not necessarily rational. In any case, the capitalization only reflects and does not match actual differentials in those operating costs affected by the availability and price of resources. We are, therefore, forced to consider the direct impact upon income distribution of the changing availability and price of resources as an urban system grows and develops.

It is perhaps useful to begin by setting up a working definition for the term "resource" in an urban system. The concept of a resource as a commodity which enters into production is no longer adequate and probably would have been abandoned long ago, were it not for the fact that this concept is basic to conventional forms of economic analysis. Recently, the concept has been extended to things like amenities and open space, but there is still an unfortunate tendency to think of resources as "natural". I think it far more satisfactory to regard the city as a gigantic resource system, most of which is man-made. It is also an areally localized resource system in the sense that most of the resources we make use of in the city system are not ubiquitous

68

and their availability, therefore, depends upon accessibility and proximity. The urban system thus contains a geographical distribution of created resources of great economic, social, psychological and symbolic significance. Unfortunately, when we get away from the simple production-based definition of resources to a definition linked to consumption, we increase the appropriateness of the concept for examining income inequalities and distribution effects, but decrease our ability to define quantitative measures for resource availability. The reason for this is easy to state. We •nust first of all take account of the externality effects inherent in the exploitation of any resource. Secondly, we have to face up to the fact that resources are also technological and cultural appraisals—in other words, their quantity is dependent upon the individual preferences existing in the population and the cognitive skills which people possess to help them exploit the resource system.

Natural and man-made resources are usually localized in their distribution. Location decisions, in turn, lead to the further evolution of the spatial availability of man-made resources. A general tenet of location theory and spatial interaction theory is that the local price of a resource or proximity is a function of its accessibility and proximity to the user. If accessibility or proximity changes (as it must do every time there is a locational shift) then the local price changes and, by extension, there is an implied change in the real income of the individual. Command over resources, which is our general definition of real income, is thus a function of locational accessibility and proximity. Therefore, the changing spatial form of the city and the continuous process of run-down, renewal and creation of resources within it, will affect the distribution of incomes and may form a major mechanism for the redistribution of real income. Consider, as an example, the resource of open space.

Let us assume that each person throughout a city system has an identical need for open space. The price of that open space is low if it is accessible and high if it is not. Assume also a complete inelasticity in the demand for open space and we can then treat the variation in access price within the city as a direct effect on income. The allocation of open space in and around the city will thus affect the distribution of income. Clawson writes:

"Any use of rural open space, relatively close to the city, as a substitute for or supplement to open space within the city has unfortunate effects in terms of income class participation. Truly poor people have no chance to live in the country and commute to work, nor to play golf in the country. These uses of rural open space are limited to middle and upper income levels. Moreover, if the more articulate and politically most active parts of the total population see such use of rural open space as one major solution to the open space problem, they may neglect or oppose costly programs which would provide at least some open space in the city centres where it is most lacking and most urgently needed." (1969, 170.)

Obviously, we could write much the same thing about the provision of any facility in an urban system—health and educational services, sanitation services, police and fire services, shopping opportunities, entertainment and other recreational facilities, transport facilities, to say nothing of the intangible features usually subsumed under the catch-all phrase "quality of urban environment". Many of these resources are located by public action and it is, therefore, important to recognize that "the redistributive aspect of general governmental functions is far from trivial and increases with city size" (Thompson, 1965, 117). But others result from the decision of private entrepreneurs. No matter who the decision-maker, however, the very act of locational choice has distributional significance. In other words, public goods are involved. From the consumer's point of view, these are really impure public goods since they do not allow him a homogeneous quantity and quality of the good in question. At this point, therefore, we have to remind ourselves that a maximum-profit or maximum-efficiency solution for producers is not necessarily the same as a maximum social-benefit solution for consumers. Thus, in location theory we know that the forces governing location from the producer's point of view are not necessarily beneficial when analysed from the consumer's point of view—as Hotelling's classic example of the case of two ice-cream sellers on a beach demonstrates. Hence we also know that in any situation of monopoly, duopoly or oligopoly, the market process is unlikely to produce a location pattern which is the most beneficial for the consumer. Similarly, we know too that the very fact of externalities in the decision process can wreck our confidence in the market mechanism.

There are plenty of theoretical reasons, therefore, for expecting considerable imbalance in the availability and accessibility of resources in an urban system. There are also good theoretical reasons (which will be examined later) for anticipating that this imbalance will usually operate to the advantage of the rich and to the detriment of the poor. The fact that this occurs is not hard to document from most American cities, as a casual reading of the Kerner Commission report (1968) will show. Some of the local costs imposed upon a community by the differential availability and accessibility of resources are quantifiable (such as the real extent of overcharging for consumer goods), but there are many other costs (such as a high infant mortality rate, mental disturbance and nervous tension) which are real enough but extraordinarily difficult to measure.

This style of analysis can be used to deal with differential costs imposed by proximity to those features in the urban environment which generate external costs. I am thinking here of such things as air and water pollution, noise, congestion, criminal activity and the like. The cost to the individual in each case will be a function of his location with respect to the generating source. The intensity of air pollution, for example, will vary according to the diffusion and dispersal rates from the source and the cost to the individual will depend on his location with respect to a spatial field of effects. The costs imposed in the air pollution case are difficult to total up. We can get reasonable estimates of the cleaning and maintenance costs (Yocum and McCaldin, 1968, 646–9; Ridker, 1967), but the indirect costs to mental and physical health are extraordinarily difficult to estimate. We can likewise get some estimate of the impact of criminal activity in terms of the value of goods lost or damage inflicted, but the indirect costs of being cut off from normal physical and social activity on account of fear are incalculable (it may mean that an elderly person is cut off from an amenity resource such as a park, for example). The pattern of these costs clearly varies quite substantially throughout the urban system, so that some groups go fairly cost free while others suffer very considerable cost burdens.

We have briefly examined some of the ways in which the real income of an individual may be affected by the accessibility, availability and price of resources and by the costs imposed by the external effects of various activities contained in the city

71

system. If we could measure these and somehow or other add them all up, what would the total effect be? This may appear an unanswerable question (since so few of the costs can be quantified), but it is nevertheless useful to ask it for doing so directs our attention to an important set of mechanisms generating inequalities in income. It is quite possible, of course, for diverse effects upon real income to cancel each other out—a cost of air pollution here may be balanced by a cost of criminal activity there, etc. Obtaining such a balance over all impure public goods and services over all time periods is essential if there is to be any logic to the provision and financing of such goods (Buchanan, 1968, 162). It is difficult to resist the conclusion, however, that in general the rich and privileged obtain more benefits and incur lower costs than do the poor and politically weak. In part, this conclusion is an intuitive assessment. But it becomes more acceptable since it can be given some theoretical justification and this I now hope to do, albeit in a very sketchy fashion.

We are essentially concerned in this discussion with the distributive effects of activities arranged in a given spatial form and the redistributive effects of changes in that spatial form. Locational changes bring about redistribution mainly through the externalities associated with them. Locational decisions may be made by individual households, entrepreneurs, organizations, public agencies, and so on. Most of these decision makers (except, in theory at least, the last) locate for their own benefit and do not take account (unless legally obliged to) of the third-party effects of their decision. The real income of any one individual in an urban system is thus susceptible to change through the decisions of others. Since these decisions rarely take his welfare into account, there is little or nothing he can do about them except (1) by changing his own location (which will cost him something) to maintain or improve his real income, or (2) by joining together with others and exercising group or collective pressure to seek to prevent locational decisions which diminish his real income and to encourage locational decisions which enhance his real income. The way in which the spatial form of an urban system changes, therefore, will partly be a function of the way in which groups form, bargain with each other and take collective action over the positioning of the various externality fields which will affect their real income. It is in this sense that the political processes in the urban system may be viewed as a way of sharing out external benefits and allocating external costs. In this manner one powerful group may be able to obtain real income advantages over another. The realities of political power being what they are, the rich groups will probably thereby grow richer and the poor groups will thereby be deprived. It seems that the current real income distribution in a city system must be viewed as "the predictable outcome of the political process" (Buchanan, 1968b 185). Any attempt to understand the mechanisms generating inequalities in income must, therefore, involve an understanding of the political processes which operate in a city. This is such an important issue that I shall devote a separate section to it.

POLITICAL PROCESSES AND THE REDISTRIBUTION OF REAL INCOME

It is very difficult to devise an adequate framework for grappling with the complexities of the political process as they are manifest in an urban system. All I shall try to demonstrate in this section is the rather obvious relationship which exists between the redistribution of real income and political decisions. I shall, however, seek to interpret much of the political activity of the city as a matter of jostling for and bargaining over the use and control of the "hidden mechanisms" for redistribution (Wood, 1968). I shall also draw attention to certain aspects of this bargaining process and thereby provide some kind of theoretical basis for the assertion that redistribution of real income via these hidden mechanisms naturally tends to benefit the rich and disadvantage the poor.

Consider a simple case in which there are two communities (each forming a homogeneous group) located close enough to each other so that the actions of one community impose external benefits or costs on the other community. Such interdependence between communities poses considerable theoretical problems —it will, for example, destroy one of the conditions necessary to achieve a Pareto optimum in the housing market. How can these two communities resolve a conflict generated from such a situation? If community A invests heavily in a facility which also benefits community B, should community B be allowed in as a "free rider" or should community B contribute to the

73

investment, and if so, by how much? Similarly, if community A contemplates an action which is detrimental to B, how would B negotiate with A and what should A pay to B in the way of compensation? This problem can be formulated as a two-person non-zero sum game. It is then possible (provided certain conditions are met) to identify rational or "optimal" solutions. Davis and Whinston (1962), for example, use this approach to allocate costs and benefits between two firms whose activities are interdependent through the existence of externalities. The definition of an optimal solution depends upon the way in which the game is structured and the behavioural characteristics of the participants. The outcome will thus depend upon the amount of information available to the participants, their willingness to co-operate, their pessimism or optimism, and so on. Isard *et al.* (1969, chapters 6 and 7) have reviewed these variations on the two-person non-zero sum game in depth. They also indicate how the problem of external effects between communities can be resolved through the extension of game theory to what are called *location games*. These games vary from the joint development and exploitation of a resource by two or three participants, through the allocation of funds across a system of regions, to the location and financing of a public facility (such as an airport or a high school). In all these cases, it is possible to identify optimal solutions and thus provide a rational basis for resolving a conflict between communities over external benefits and costs. In general, of course, something as complicated as a city system requires a more extensive analytic framework—such as that provided by *n*-person, non-zero sum games in which side-payments are allowed (the latter condition is essential for the analysis of coalition formation; in the city political system, coalitions are extremely important). But these games are difficult to analyse and apply (Isard *et al.*, 1969). Nevertheless, we may conclude that it is theoretically possible to harness, by political activity and bargaining, the "hidden mechanisms" of income redistribution so as to achieve a balanced allocation of all impure goods and services over a spatially distributed population. But we can also conclude that this will only happen if the political process is so organized that it facilitates "equality in bargaining" between different but internally homogeneous interest groups. This condition is unlikely to exist and an analysis of the reasons why will provide a justification for the expectation that the rich will generally benefit to the detriment of the poor.

In game theory, we usually assume that the participants are equal in their command over resources. In coalition analysis, however, we can drop this assumption and consider a "weighted decision game" (Isard *et al.*, 1969, 400–402). In this type of game, each person brings to a coalition a certain "resource" which can then be used in the bargaining process. This resource may be a vote, it may be money (for instance, for side-payments, both legal and illegal), it may be influence (for instance, contacts with members of another group), or it may be information (for instance, about competitors or about appropriate strategies). It is interesting to note that a vote is probably the least important of these resources to most aspects of political activity and this is the only resource which is divided equally among all members of the coalition. In a weighted decision game, the outcome depends on the emergence of a coalition which has enough resources to "win". The payoffs are usually positive for the winning coalition and zero to the losers. This sort of situation is quite common in urban politics and explains our expectation that the more powerful community (in financial, educational or influence terms) may be able to dominate locational decisions to its own advantage. Inequality of resources available for the political bargaining process thus creates a condition for the further disposition of resources so as to reinforce that inequality.

I have assumed so far that there is such a thing as an homogeneous "community" or "group" which can function effectively within the bargaining process. This condition is rarely approximated. Therefore, we need some understanding of how and why groups form and how, once formed, they operate as a force in the political arena. This is a complicated question. I am primarily concerned, however, with the likelihood that a group will form, that it will act coherently, that it will exercise power in the political bargaining process, and that it will succeed in providing itself with collective goods. Here it seems that a major distinction is to be made between "small groups" and "large groups". This distinction is brought out most clearly in the analysis of group choice provided by Olson (1965). The analysis proceeds on the assumption of self-interested behaviour on the part of individuals and then goes on to show that "the larger the group, the farther it will fall short of providing an optimal amount of the collective good". The proof of this conclusion need not detain us. The important point is that small groups may well be effective in providing themselves with collective goods particularly when one person in the group has an overwhelming interest in the production of the good. But larger more balanced groups are likely to fall short in this respect. This conclusion is similar to that developed by several analysts of group choice and collective behaviour (Buchanan, 1968). It is not difficult to extend it to the political bargaining process and predict that

"The smaller groups—the privileged and intermediate groups —can often defeat the large groups—the latent groups—which are normally supposed to prevail in democracy. The privileged and intermediate groups often triumph over the numerically superior forces in the latent or large groups because the former are generally organized and active while the latter are normally unorganized and inactive." (Olson, 1965, 128.)

That this condition can be predicted from an assumption of self-interest on the part of all individuals may seem surprising, even though bitter experience teaches us that small, resourceful, well-organized groups can usually defeat the wishes of a widespread mass of unorganized people. Olson points out that large masses of people motivated by self-interest can be organized for their own collective good only through inducements (such as retirement and insurance benefits) or through coercion (such as that imposed by a trade union closed shop policy).

These general conclusions have important implications for our understanding of the political system as it operates in the urban context. We can directly predict from it, for example, that

"neighbouring local governments in metropolitan areas that provide collective goods (like commuter roads and education) that benefit individuals in two or more local government jurisdictions would tend to provide inadequate amounts of these services, and that the largest local government (for instance, the one representing the central city) would bear disproportionate shares of the burdens of providing them." (Olson, 1965, 36.)

Any activity which generates strong external benefits throughout the political system will naturally tend to be underprovided and it is tempting to hypothesize that any activity that generates strong external costs will be undercontrolled or undercompensated for. Since small groups are likely to be more influential in the political decision making process, we can also infer that most of the decisions (both allocational and locational) will disproportionately reflect the desires of small pressure groups as opposed to the mass of the population. Since these groups rarely act from altruism, we can expect these decisions to provide direct and indirect benefits to the members of the group rather than to members of other groups. There are two other predictable consequences of Olson's analysis. First, it is unlikely that a member of a large group will give up voluntarily a very small quantity of his resources in order to achieve a collective aim even when the achievement of that aim will make each individual in the community better off. It is not hard to find examples of this kind of behaviour (the study by Keene and Strong, 1970, of reactions to the Brandywine plan is a good case in point). Second, it is unlikely that a large group will be able to retain voluntarily coherent policies and objectives since, if it is to do so effectively, it must by consensus or apathy allow a small group to negotiate and implement policy on its behalf. As there is always the possibility that the small group will, in the large group's name, achieve policies most appropriate for the small group, we must anticipate considerable within-group rivalry for executive power which will weaken the group's negotiating position. Again, this is a familiar event in the urban context and its frequency is a very influential force governing the outcome of a "land use planning game" (Keyes, 1968).

We may conclude that it is unlikely for self-interested individuals to come together to form a large group which will then act voluntarily for the collective good of everyone in the group. Large-group action is only likely when external inducements can be provided, when sanctions can be applied, or when institutional arrangements are created which formalize the "rules of the game" for large-group decision making and within- and between-group negotiation. This conclusion is obviously not universally true and exceptions will undoubtedly be found (usually depending on the importance of the issue, the homogeneity of attitudes towards them, the subtlety and altruism of the executive group operating on behalf of the large group, and so on). This conclusion directs our attention to the existing institutional framework for reaching collective decisions and

77

arbitrating between the competing needs and desires of different pressure groups within the population. I do not intend any detailed account of how these institutions operate in bringing about a redistribution of income. But it is worth noting two things about them. In the first place, they partly reflect existing group activities and they are, therefore, far more able to take account of small-group pressures (special lobbies and special interests) than they are able to react to the needs and wishes of large groups—hence the recent rhetoric in many American cities about making city administration more responsive to the needs of the people. In the second place, an institutional structure, once it is created, may well become closed or partially closed. In a recent study of antipoverty policy in Baltimore for example, Bachrach (1969) found that low-income groups experienced great difficulty in actually getting into a negotiating position. In other words, groups can effectively be excluded from the negotiating and bargaining game by institutional barriers or by the manoeuvres of other groups. Only a strong and cohesive group will be able to overcome such barriers and get around the problem of what is called "non-decision making". This explains why the urban planning game often bears more resemblance to solitaire than to an n-person non-zero sum game.

The import of the preceding paragraphs is that we can expect considerable imbalance in the outcome of within- and between-group bargaining over external benefits and costs and collective goods because (1) different groups have different resources with which to bargain, (2) large groups in the population are generally weaker and more incoherent than small groups; and (3) some groups are kept away from negotiation altogether. If income redistribution is a "predictable outcome of the political process" it is not hard to predict the general flow of that redistribution. In the first place, we can expect a "central business district imperialism" in which the well-organized business interests of the central city (with their small-group oligopolistic structure) effectively dominate the looser and weaker coalitions found in the rest of the city. This thesis has recently been powerfully argued by Kotler (1969). In the second place, we can also anticipate a "suburban exploitation of the central city" hypothesis (Netzer, 1968, 438–48; Thompson, 1965, chapter 7). In other words, we can expect a "pecking order" among various groups in the population for the exploitation of the various

resources which the city has to offer. Those at the bottom of this pecking order are the losers:
"The slum is the catch-all for the losers, and in the competitive struggle for the cities' goods the slum areas are also the losers in terms of schools, jobs, garbage collection, street lighting, libraries, social services, and whatever else is communally available but always in short supply. The slum, then, is an area where the population lacks resources to compete successfully and where collectively it lacks control over the channels through which such resources are distributed or maintained. This may suggest some new approaches to metropolitan planning—recognizing the necessity for redistribution of power, broader access to resources, and expansion of individual choice to those who have been consistently denied." (Sherrard, 1968, 10.)

The prospects for equity or for a just redistribution of income in an urban system through a naturally arising political process (particularly one based on a philosophy of individual self-interest) are bleak indeed. The extent to which a social system has recognized this fact and adjusted itself to counteract this natural tendency is, I believe, correlated with the degree to which that social system has succeeded in avoiding the structural problems and deepening social tensions consequent upon the process of massive urbanization.

SOCIAL VALUES AND THE CULTURAL DYNAMICS OF THE URBAN SYSTEM

The notion of "real income" presupposes that values can be attached to individual property rights and to command over resources. The measurement of external costs and benefits also presupposes the existence of some value system against which we can measure (and thereby compare) the impact of an environmental change upon one individual or a social group. Casual observation teaches us that people value different things in different ways. This elementary fact of life has bedevilled economic and political theory ever since the abandonment of the neoclassical cardinal utility principle which assumed the existence of some common, identically calibrated instrument for measuring the "intensity of preference" of individuals. The replacement of cardinal by ordinal utility provided more realism in measurement but posed problems of its own—in particular, it led to the impasse described by Arrow (1965) in which it is impossible to derive a social preference or welfare function from a set of individual ordinal utility functions. There are two ways out of this impasse. The first is to try to get some measure of intensity of preference without necessarily assuming complete cardinality. If an individual's preferences can be weighted to reflect his intensity of feeling, then it is possible to derive some kind of social welfare function (Minas and Ackoff, 1964). A good deal of attention has been paid in psychology and psychophysics to this whole question of measuring subjective values: the work accomplished indicates that information can be gained on preferences and weightings, and techniques exist for manipulating, for example, ordinal data to obtain metric information (Shepard, 1966). This work (summarized by Coombs, 1964 and Nunnaly, 1967) has not been integrated as well as it might into the main body of the theory of consumer choice even though good statements do exist (for instance, Fishburn, 1964). The second way out of the Arrow paradox, and one which is usually taken by theoretical economists, is to assume the problems away by stating a "unanimity rule" which conveniently assumes that everyone in the population has the same ranking of preferences over a set of alternatives (Buchanan, 1968). Only under this assumption is it possible to derive a Pareto optimum. When the unanimity rule applies, the alternatives are said to be "Pareto-comparable" and when it does not they are "Pareto-noncomparable" (Quirk and Saposnik, 1968, 117). The usual economic theories of urban structure (such as the Davis and Whinston model examined above) and theories of location require that alternatives are Pareto-comparable. The question then arises as to what happens when they are not.

The implications for a theory of the allocation of public goods are serious. The existence of interpersonal utility functions "plays havoc" with game theoretic formulations (Luce and Raiffa, 1957, 34). Bargaining between two communities which have completely different utility functions cannot be handled in any rational fashion and voting procedures can lead us to a position which is far from optimal. Likewise, the whole question of compensation between parties takes on a new dimension. A transfer payment may be very significant to a poor man and almost irrelevant to a rich man. By the same argument, the poor can less afford to lose an external benefit or incur an external cost. This leads us to an intriguing paradox in which the poor are willing to incur external losses for a far lower transfer payment than are the rich. In other words, the rich are unlikely to give up an amenity "at any price", whereas the poor who are least able to sustain the loss are likely to sacrifice it for a trifling sum—a prediction for which there is some empirical support. In this case, however, we are dealing with the simple problem which arises when different parties express different orders of preference over a given set of outcomes. There are far more serious difficulties. What happens, for example, when groups do not perceive the same alternative choices or potential outcomes? In this case, each group has its own perceived action space, and conflict may arise because neither can see or understand the action space as perceived by the other. A similar difficulty arises when groups cannot agree on the "rules of the game" and since the establishment of these rules largely predetermines the outcome there is likely to be as much conflict over the rules as there is in negotiation itself. What this means is that heterogeneity in social and cultural values may make it impossible for groups to get into a "valid" negotiating position such as that which is specified in one of Isard's location games. From this it follows that an urban system will be unable to function smoothly (in the sense that conflicts between individuals and groups will not easily be resolved) if there is widespread heterogeneity in the social and cultural values of the population. It seems that the "natural" way for this sort of difficulty to be minimized is to seek out a pattern of territorial organization which minimizes both social contact between individuals holding different social and cultural values and also the probability of quarrels over externalities. Territorial and "neighbourhood" organization on ethnic, class, social status, religious and other lines thus has an important role to play in minimizing conflict in the urban system.

Heterogeneity in social cultural values also plays havoc with any simplistic theory of the redistribution of income in an urban system. This can perhaps best be demonstrated by returning to an issue raised but not discussed in the section on the availability and price of resources, i.e., that resources should be considered as technological and cultural appraisals. Since the definition adopted of real income contains the phrase "command over resources", cultural and technical variations in a population automatically affect the measurement of real income. Two individuals can command exactly the same resource but if they value it differently they have different real incomes. It is useful to ask, therefore, what the impact of this fact is for a theory of income redistribution.

Let me first define some terms. By a technological appraisal, I mean that an individual must possess the various cognitive skills and technological equipment to be able to make use of the resource system that is the city. By a cultural appraisal, I mean that individuals must possess value systems which motivate them to want to make use of these resources. The technology is partly comprised of the relevant "hardware" such as machinery, tools, etc., and partly made up of the cognitive skills necessary for the use of that hardware. People raised in rural areas often lack the necessary cognitive skills to handle the city or the suburbs; the suburbanite might likewise lack those skills necessary for the country and the inner city; while the inner-city person may well not be able to handle the country or the suburbs. Cognitive skills are learned and it is possible to learn how to handle a great diversity of environments. But the skills are unlikely to be equally distributed throughout a population and since learning is affected by successful experience (or reinforcement), individuals will become most practised in the art of dealing with their own environment insofar as it impinges upon them. Environmental learning is not, therefore, independent of environment. The kind of environment created in an urban system affects which cognitive skills become developed. Under conditions of relative isolation, we may expect to find specialized sub-populations with particular cognitive skills relevant to a particular kind of urban environment—the slum dweller indeed possesses quite different skills from the rural dweller. Cognitive skills are not, of course, simply a function of environment. Innate intelligence and education obviously play a part. Consider, for example, the ability to think abstractly about and to schematize spatial relationships—a skill which is closely correlated with other aspects of intelligence (Smith, 1964). Such a schematic skill allows the individual to transcend space and command it as a resource. Those who lack such a skill are likely to be trapped by space. This kind of difference has significance for our understanding of income redistribution since it directly affects mobility and accessibility. Thus Pahl (1965) suggests that the higher income and better educated groups tend to make an active use of space whereas lower income groups tend to be trapped by it. Duhl (1963, 137) similarly remarks that higher income groups "use the physical environment as a resource in contrast with the lower socio-economic groups who incorporate the environment into the self". Webber (1963) also hypothesizes that all but the lowest income groups have now freed themselves from restrictions of "territoriality". Whatever the truth of the contentions, it seems reasonable to assume that cognitive skills are dependent upon education, intelligence, and *experience with respect to environment*, and these cognitive skills in turn affect the value of a resource to a given individual.

In like manner, we may assume that cultural values are affected by (among other things) the opportunities created in the city environment. Cultures evolve in part through "a specialized patterning of the individual stimulus situation, and a special patterning of the response that could be made to it" (Smith *et al.*, 1956, 25; see also Kluckhohn, 1954). So we may anticipate cultural evolution within the city system partly through the reorganization of the physical and social stimuli which exist within it. Environmental designers (for instance, Sommer, 1968) would point to the importance of physical stimuli in determining behaviour patterns—which is not to say that these are the *only* stimuli for culture change, as naïve environmental determinists would suggest. Let us now consider the import of this fact for the cultural dynamics of the urban system. Most of the decisions made on the physical planning of the urban system are likely to be made or strongly influenced by small and powerful oligopolistic groups. These groups are in effect rearranging the physical stimuli (a highway here, a power plant there) for large masses of poorly organized people. A few small influential subcultures within the urban culture are patterning stimuli situations for the other subcultures. Most of the subcultures in the urban system have very little control over the different configurations of stimuli (visual, kinesthetic, social, etc.) in different parts of the urbanized area that are likely to generate quite strong cultural divergence. The sort of thing that can happen is demonstrated by a survey of attitudes to air pollution in St. Louis. In suburban areas there was an acute awareness of air

83

pollution, whereas in the central city area, where the problem was at its worst, attitudes were only weakly formed. There were so many other problems in the inner city (jobs, housing, recreational facilities, etc.) that the negative stimuli from air pollution passed virtually unnoticed. The formation of attitudes is thus dependent upon the particular configuration of stimuli existing in a particular urban context. Once cultural heterogeneity develops and social barriers to movement are imposed, cultural divergence may proceed apace within the city system (Thompson, 1965, 106). The cultural attitudes of the inner city have always been different from those of the suburbs and it does not seem that these differences are decreasing. Therefore, I find it hard to accept either Marcuse's thesis (1964) that there is a growing homogeneity in cultural values (and, therefore, no force for change in society) or the spatial form equivalent of it in which a "one dimensional man" dwells in what Melvin Webber (1964) calls "an urban non-place realm". There are strong forces working towards cultural heterogeneity and territorial differentiation in the urban system.

The implications of this conclusion are of interest. First, any theory of real income distribution must involve cross-cultural comparisons. Second, the decisions made about the location and allocation of goods and services in the urban system are "Pareto non-comparable". Thus, it is very difficult to compare the value of, say, open space from one part of a city system to another. Different groups will exhibit different elasticities with respect to their use of it and some groups may have no use for it at all. Consequently, the provision of large parks for inner city dwellers who may not (perhaps) be technically equipped or culturally motivated to make use of them will do absolutely nothing for them from the point of view of income redistribution —it may in fact be equivalent to giving ice cream mixers to the Boro Indians of Brazil.

If resources mean different things to different people, how can we measure their impact upon the real income of individuals and develop location policies with respect to them that achieve a given redistributional goal? This problem could partly be overcome if we could separate out those resources which everyone agreed upon as important from those which only part of the population valued. At least the first kind could be treated as if the unanimity rule held good. Whether or not we could identify such groupings is an empirical question to which there is no easy answer. It is reasonable to assume, for example, that housing opportunities and health services are in the former category. Yet even in these categories there are subtle but important differences in cultural values. Low-income groups, for example, often identify very closely with their housing environment and the psychological cost of moving is to them far greater than it is to the mobile upper middle class. Well-meaning but culturally insensitive middle-class planners can consequently (through rehousing projects and the like) inflict heavy costs upon lower socio-economic groups (Duhl, 1963, 139). The story of the provision of mental health services to the poor similarly shows how inappropriate services can result from a failure of the predominantly middle-class group providing the service to appreciate the specialized subculture of a different socio-economic group (Riessman, *et al.*, 1964).

Equating real income with command over resources thus leads us into an impasse because cultural heterogeneities in the population make it difficult to measure real income. It is very tempting at this juncture to return to the simplest concept of income as monetary income. This I refuse to do because the problems inherent in the impasse are real enough and extremely relevant to our understanding of the urban system. If we fail to investigate them, we abandon all hope of arriving at a firm basis for making socially meaningful decisions. But there are even deeper long-range questions to which this style of analysis directs our attention. By the constant rearrangement of stimuli in the urban system we are provoking a gradual process of cultural evolution. Evolution towards what? One way of making sure that a subculture places no value upon open space is to deny it all experience of it. The evolution of the urban system, whether we like it or not, can lead to large scale sensory deprivation with respect to certain phenomena (such as clean air, wilderness, etc.) and overexposure to others (such as suburban vistas, air pollution, etc.). In the long run, therefore, we must evaluate decisions about the growth of the city against a set of overriding cultural values which we wish to preserve or augment. If we do not do this, we may see the emergence of new sets of cultural values and, if present trends are anything to go by, these may lead to violent conflict and, perhaps, to an ultimate social self-destruction. The sensibilities of mankind cannot remain permanently immune from the environmental changes man is bringing about through his own actions. It is, therefore, salutary to remind ourselves occasionally that "the long-range question is not so much what sort of environment we want, but what sort of man we want." (Sommer, 1969, 173.)

SPATIAL ORGANIZATION AND POLITICAL, SOCIAL AND ECONOMIC PROCESSES

The redistribution of income can be brought about by changes in

1 the location of jobs and housing
2 the value of property rights
3 the price of resources to the consumer.

These changes are themselves affected by the allocations of external costs and benefits to different regions in the urban system and by changes in accessibility and proximity. Populations seek to control these hidden mechanisms governing redistribution through exercising political power. It is in the box marked "social and cultural values" that the whole process feeds back into itself, for these values are both a cause and an effect—any theory of income distribution must be based upon them and yet they are themselves susceptible to change through the allocation of opportunities throughout the urban system. But also inherent in these social processes lies the question of spatial organization. Externality effects are localized, so are job and housing opportunities, resource benefits, communication links, etc. Political power is partly areally based. Many of the hidden mechanisms for redistributing income come to fruition in the act of location. This leads us to the last fundamental question I wish to pose in this chapter. Is there some spatial structure or set of structures which will maximize equity and efficiency in the urban system or, at least, maximize our ability to control the powerful hidden mechanisms which bring about redistribution? This is both a normative and a positive question for it suggests that we can explain current distributional effects by looking at existing spatial structures and also devise spatial structures to achieve a given distributional goal. I will not try

86

to separate these aspects of the problem in the analysis that follows.

The physical spatial form of a city system is a construction in three dimensional Euclidean geometry. The phenomena within it can be conceptualized as points (retail stores, schools, hospitals), lines (transport links), areas (constituencies, territories) and volumes (buildings). This form should presumably facilitate the coherent functioning of social processes. The spatial form is not, however, infinitely adaptable nor are the social demands on it easily reconciled with each other. The actual physical form is necessarily a compromise between a whole set of conflicting demands. When we make decisions about spatial form we are presumably trying to reach an efficient compromise. This is not easy to do. It is the kind of problem which gives rise to lengthy Royal Commission deliberations (such as the Redcliffe–Maud Commission) in Britain and interminable arguments over the relative merits of community control or metropolitan government in the United States. I cannot consider all of these problems here and so I shall proceed by example.

1 The provision and control of impure public goods in an urban system

Impure public goods, once produced, are freely but not equally available (in terms of quantity or quality) to all individuals in the city system. Many goods are of this sort. In particular, all goods and facilities freely available but provided through some locational mechanism fall into this category—hence the interest in spatial form policies in an urban setting. Indeed, it is not unreasonable to treat much of location theory as a specific form of the theory governing the provision of impure public goods (Tiebout, 1961, 80–81).

It is useful to distinguish between three different policy situations. The first concerns goods which confer benefits upon all individuals. Here the policy issue is to ensure that the good is provided (by private or public action) in sufficient quantity and quality at the right locations to achieve a particular distributive objective. The second case is that of impure public goods (such as air pollutants) which impose costs through "involuntary" consumption. Here the policy problem is to regulate location patterns so as to minimize the incidence of these costs and control their distributional effects. The third case (and this is probably the commonest) concerns a mixed situation in which a good provides both benefits and losses.

The provision of beneficial impure public goods can be accomplished through private or public action. In the former case, we rely upon some natural market mechanism to achieve a "reasonable" location pattern (for instance, in retail opportunities and entertainment facilities) and, hence, to minimize (as far as production technology will allow) the differential income effect. Prices thus act to resolve the conflict between the technological necessity for a few productive points and the physical necessity for a large number of spatially distributed consumption points. Lösch's (1954) analysis provides us with some of the necessary equipment for discussing the general form of spatial equilibrium which will result. He indicates that an hierarchical solution is inevitable since production functions, consumption functions, and sets of elasticities (with respect to prices, incomes and the like) vary considerably from one good to another. It would be unrealistic to expect the spatial pattern of private provision of impure public goods to conform to Löschian expectation for a whole host of reasons (concerning the conditions for entry for the firm, stochastic fluctuations in demand and supply conditions, product differentiation, bounded areas, interpenetration of market areas, and so on). There are, therefore, good theoretical reasons for expecting that the market mechanism will be no more efficient in guiding the location of privately supplied impure public goods to Pareto equilibrium than it is in the housing market. The empirical evidence also points in this direction. Consider, for example, the location of supermarket facilities. The supermarket is itself an impure public good (although it is selling wholly private goods) and its location is presumably a function of balancing the need for economies of scale in operation against the effects of rising transport costs to the consumer as the market area is extended. Yet the Kerner Commission (1968, 277) comments on the general lack of these facilities in ghetto areas. It is difficult to tell, of course, whether this is due to genuine market failure, time-lag in achieving equilibrium, or social and economic conditions in ghetto areas which make supermarket operations uneconomic. But even in those areas of the private economy providing impure public goods (such as opportunities for shopping, recreation, and the like) there is no guarantee that, because a set of demand and supply curves can be determined, a locational pattern will automatically result which is anywhere near Pareto optimality. There are sufficient imperfections (through product differentiation and so on) and interdependencies to call into question any assumption of "natural" competitive efficiency even given an ethically acceptable income distribution in the first place. It is not unreasonable, for example, to expect entrepreneurs to locate initially in those areas where excess profits are maximized—hence the "natural" tendency for the affluent areas to be serviced well before the low-income areas and this, as usual, generates an implicit redistribution of real income. Even in the private sector, therefore, there is some ground for public interference if only to encourage the speedier achievement of equilibrium. There is an even stronger justification for interference if the objective is to attain some progressive redistribution in kind.

Many impure public goods cannot be provided through the normal market mechanism because it is difficult to determine a set of market prices. These goods (educational services, fire and police protection, and so on) are provided by public action. It is strange that there are so few criteria developed for determining the location of public activities. Public finance concepts have "up to now been largely spaceless", (Thompson, 1965, 257), while location theorists, as Teitz (1968) points out, have by and large neglected the problem of public facility location. Given that no adequate location criteria have been developed, we can hardly be surprised if locational decisions on public activities are almost entirely the result of those unbalanced political pressures reviewed in a previous section (pp. 73–79). Since "local public services bid fair to become the chief means of income redistribution in our economy" (Thompson, 1965, 118), we ought to pay far more attention to the policies which govern their location if we are to control the process of redistribution. It will not be easy to formulate a theory for the location of public activity. In principle, of course, the problem is exactly the same as it is in the private sector—to find a location pattern which is most efficient subject to a set of distributional constraints. Thus the Löschian framework has some utility (Berry, 1967; Teitz, 1968). But the problem of finding a solution is theoretically obscured by the quasi-monopolistic structure of public organization and the inability to find any realistic pricing mechanisms.

89

Liberal Formulations

In effect, public facility location requires the simultaneous solution of problems of (1) finance (2) production technology (3) quantity and quality of supply (4) location (5) demand estimation and (6) welfare impact. Clearly, it is not easy to define an optimal solution. As in the private sector, we can anticipate some kind of hierarchical arrangement in the location of, for example, medical facilities, yet it is very difficult to determine the best form of this arrangement or to evaluate alternative forms of spatial organization (Schneider, 1967; 1968; Schultz, 1969). More generally, the state of the art in the theory of public facility location has not progressed very much beyond the point of relatively simple model articulation (Teitz, 1968).

Much the same conclusion can be reached with respect to the regulation of those impure public goods which generate costs. There has been very little investigation of the form and nature of the spatial field of influence of particular externalities. We know, however, that they vary greatly in scale, a fact which indicates the necessity for some kind of hierarchical regulation (small-scale effects being controlled at the community level while large-scale effects must be controlled at the metropolitan level). The investigation of externality field effects is a problem in pure spatial analysis. It requires that we be able to specify or generalize the extent and varying intensity of the spatial surface. The regulation problem is then partly a matter of shifting the locations of the sources of these external costs to achieve a desired spatial surface, or locating activity with respect to an existing surface in such a way that certain social objectives (such as freedom from certain levels of air pollution) are achieved. We possess scarcely a vestige of a theory to guide policy decisions of this sort at the present time.

Variations in cultural values and, hence, variations in demands and needs in the population, complicate policy decisions very substantially. We find the same general dilemma we encountered in the housing market case—if a central agency is to make a decision, it must presumably possess information concerning the utility scales of each individual in the population. Since the government obviously cannot possess this information, how should it proceed? One answer is to bend to voting pressure but we have seen how this was likely to lead to inequity. Tiebout suggests instead a fragmented community structure in which

"The consumer voter may be viewed as picking that community which best satisfies preference patterns for public goods. . . . The greater the number of communities and the greater the variance among them, the closer the consumer will come to fully realizing his preference position."

In some respects, this is not an unattractive proposition, since theoretically it maximizes the consumer's range of choice through some community control system whereby communities of individuals with relatively homogeneous values and utility functions express their desires in group choice. Again, we find there is a certain logic to territorial organization in the city and there can be no doubt that consumers do shift from one community to another to satisfy their preference for public goods. There are many specific reasons for doubting the efficacy of Tiebout's proposal (for instance, assumptions of perfect mobility and information) but there are also some very general questions concerning territorial organization in an urban system and it is perhaps appropriate to close by examining these general arguments.

2 Regional and territorial organization in an urban system

There are various natural forces making for territorial organization in an urban system: kinship and ethnic groupings, communities with shared value systems, individuals with similar ideas about quality of urban environment, are good examples. These forces do not remain static. Ethnic and kinship groupings are breaking down (Webber, 1963) and traditional notions of "community" and "neighbourhood" are being replaced by something rather different—a neighbourhood concept which is implicit rather than explicit with respect to social organization (Keller, 1969). There are also good logical reasons for arguing in favour of territorial organization. An "appropriate" organization can do much to minimize conflict and maximize group coherence and efficiency. Whether or not we can achieve such an organization of space and thereby facilitate the achievement of social objectives depends very much upon whether we can find out what is meant by "appropriate".

Territorial organization has many functions to perform within the city system. The classical problem of regionalization is to find a hierarchy of regions which will perform all of these functions reasonably well (see for instance, Boudeville, 1968). Some functions must be performed at the metropolitan level (for instance, the planning of transport systems, parkland facilities) while others can best be operated at the local level (for instance, play areas, child care centres). The first problem, therefore, is to find a form of organization capable of dealing with the obvious fact that different facilities have to be provided at different spatial scales. The second problem is to identify a form of organization which is flexible enough to deal with growth (social and economic), spatial overspill effects, changing spatial relationships, and so on. If the organization is not flexible, it will act as an automatic constraint upon what Friedmann (1969) calls a general process of polarized development (Darwent, 1969). In other words, any territorial organization must be designed so as to be reactive to the dynamics of the urban system. This is perhaps the most difficult problem of all to resolve, and I shall therefore confine my attention to the static aspects of it.

Consider first the political, social and economic benefits to be had from a territorial organization based purely on local neighbourhood groups. According to Olson's (1965) analysis, the smaller the group the more willing it is likely to be to provide itself voluntarily with collective goods. The smaller the group, the more it is likely to achieve some collective aim. This has important economic implications, for it indicates the possibility of higher motivation in small community settings than in large —a quality which Liebenstein (1967) calls "x-efficiency" as opposed to the usual economic measures of efficiency. Certainly, at election time, small communities usually show a higher percentage turn-out (other things being equal) than large communities. In part, this may be a function of the greater potential for individual participation in small communities—a quantity which Isard *et al.* (1969, Chapter 3) have sought to measure as "participation potential". It may also be the result of what Thompson (1965, 263) calls the "personalized styling and control which comes with small scale." It has also been argued on more doctrinaire grounds that the only way to achieve a genuine democracy is through community control based on local neighbourhood units—only then, it is argued, will it be possible to ensure that everyone has a voice in decisions, when presumably that voice will be used to help control the mechanisms generating income inequalities. Thus Kotler (1969, 71) argues that "the poor need neighbourhood government to secure the liberty to achieve prosperity". Before accepting this argument (and it is worth noting that Davis and Whinston's arguments on zoning and Tiebout's on the provision of public services point in this general direction), we must consider some of the disadvantages.

There is no doubt that some goods and services can be supplied and some operations effectively carried out at the local level. But what about those goods which must be supplied on a far broader scale? In these cases there are bound to be significant externalities involved. It has generally been shown by Olson (1965), Weisbrod (1965) and others that there is a tendency for public services to be underprovided when externalities exist (although Williams, 1966, dissents from this view and suggests that the problem is one of non-optimal provision rather than underprovision). One way to rectify this situation is to negotiate with neighbouring communities, but the problems of non-centralized information gathering and negotiation costs (including those to be imputed to a delay in decision making) are likely to make this an inefficient way of rationalizing the provision of these services. An alternative solution is to internalize the externalities by forming a higher level territorial system which will be better able to provide the service in question. We have to be careful that we do not lose more in "x-efficiency" than we gain in economic efficiency. It will not be possible to internalize the externalities completely, of course, and so the determination of an optimal regional organization will depend upon reducing externalities to an acceptable level rather than eliminating them entirely. It therefore becomes feasible to think of an upper level organization which will provide services such as transport, sewage disposal, large recreational facilities, and the like. There is also the problem of financing to be considered. One of the more serious problems in American cities in the recent past has been the loss of a tax-base in many central areas (Netzer, 1968). Locally financed local government is a disastrous proposition—it will simply result in the poor controlling their own poverty while the rich grow more affluent from the fruits of their riches. The redistributional implications are clearly regressive. Indeed, the existing territorial structure of local finance and public service provision in American cities must be regarded as one of the prime culprits in bringing about

93

an inequitable allocation of fringe benefits to different parts of the urban system. Hence arises a very powerful argument for metropolitan-wide government. This argument is further reinforced by the existence of many regulatory problems which can only be solved on an urban or regional basis (for example, regulating the general spatial form of the city and pollution levels).

There are powerful arguments for decentralization and neighbourhood government but there are just as powerful arguments for metropolitan-wide government. Doubtless we could make out arguments for intermediate-size units or even broader "megalopolis-wide" government. These arguments are not irreconcilable, since it should be possible to devise a territorial organization which is hierarchical in nature and which allows maximum local participation while at the same time ensuring a closer to optimal provision of general urban services. In fact, this kind of hierarchical organization already exists in both Britain and the United States. The problem is to determine whether the existing organization is appropriate or whether it is in fact a hindrance—a question which the Redcliffe-Maud Report set out to solve. Unfortunately, there is no easy answer to this kind of question even though it has such important implications for the control of the mechanisms governing redistribution of real income. In effect, if we can provide a correct answer we will have solved the general question which this paper started out with posing—is it possible to harmonize the policies governing spatial form and social processes so as to ensure the achievement of some overall social objective?

A CONCLUDING COMMENT

Forecasting the future of an urban system requires a thorough understanding of the processes generating change and a realistic evaluation of the direction in which the social system as a whole is being moved by those processes. I have concentrated my attention upon the mechanisms governing the redistribution of income and I have suggested that these seem to be moving us towards a state of greater inequality and greater injustice. Unless this present trend can be reversed, I feel that almost certainly we are also headed for a period of intense conflict (which may be violent) within the urban system. In the United States, there is enough evidence to indicate that open conflict is beginning. In Britain, the same processes are at work. I therefore conclude that it will be disastrous for the future of the social system to plan ahead to facilitate existing trends—this has been the crucial planning mistake of the 1960s. As Hoover (1968, 260) suggests, planning frequently makes an ideal out of the status quo, which is objectionable "if we believe the status is nothing to quo about". I therefore find the notion that we are moving in easy stages into an era of enormous affluence and electronic bliss unacceptable since it is at variance with my own analysis and the evidence of my own eyes. In part, the problem is an ecological one, for we may well be, as Mishan (1967) suggests, rolling out the carpet of opportunities in front of us while rolling it up even faster behind us. But in part it is a problem of exercising a wise control over social and spatial organization within the city system. Here an enormous task confronts us. We really do not have the kind of understanding of the total city system to be able to make wise policy decisions, even when motivated by the highest social objectives. The successful formation of adequate policies and the forecasting of their implications is going to depend on some broad interdisciplinary attack upon the social process and spatial form aspects of the city system.

Chapter 3

Social Justice and Spatial Systems

Normative thinking has an important role to play in geographical analysis. Social justice is a normative concept and it
is surprising, therefore, to find that considerations of social justice
have not been incorporated into geographical methods of
analysis. The reason is not far to seek. The normative tools
characteristically used by geographers to examine location
problems are derived from classical location theory. Such
theories are generally Pareto-optimal since they define an
optimal location pattern as one in which no one individual can
move without the advantages gained from such a move being
offset by some loss to another individual. Location theory has
therefore characteristically relied upon the criterion of *efficiency*
for its specification. Efficiency may be defined in a variety of
ways, of course, but in location theory it usually amounts to
minimizing the aggregate costs of movement (subject to demand
and supply constraints) within a particular spatial system.
Models of this type pay no attention to the consequences of
location decisions for the distribution of income. Geographers
have thus followed economists into a style of thinking in which
questions of distribution are laid aside (mainly because they
involve unwelcome ethical and political judgements), while
efficient "optimal" location patterns are determined with a
particular income distribution assumed. This approach obviously lacks something. In part the reaction away from
normative thinking towards behavioural and empirical formulations may be attributed to the search for a more satisfying
approach to location problems. This reaction has been healthy,
of course, but partly misplaced. It is not normative modelling
which is at fault but the *kind* of norms built into such models.
In this chapter, therefore, I want to diverge from the usual
mode of normative analysis and look at the possibility of con-

96

structing a normative theory of spatial or territorial allocation based on principles of social justice. I do not propose this as an alternative framework to that of efficiency. In the long run it will be most beneficial if efficiency and distribution are explored jointly. The reasons for so doing are evident. If, in the short run, we simply pursue efficiency and ignore the social cost, then those individuals or groups who bear the brunt of that cost are likely to be a source of long-run inefficiency either through decline in what Liebenstein (1966) calls "x-efficiency" (those intangibles that motivate people to cooperate and participate in the social process of production) or through forms of anti-social behaviour (such as crime and drug addiction) which will necessitate the diversion of productive investment towards their correction. The same comment can be made about the single-minded pursuit of social justice. It is counter-productive in the long-run to devise a socially just distribution if the size of the product to be distributed shrinks markedly through the in-efficient use of scarce resources. In the long-long-run, therefore social justice and efficiency are very much the same thing. But since questions of social justice have been neglected (except in political rhetoric) and there is a persistent tendency to lay them aside in short run analysis, I shall do the opposite and lay aside questions of efficiency. This should not be taken to imply, how-ever, that efficiency is irrelevant or unimportant.

The concept of social justice is not an all-inclusive one in which we encapsulate our vision of the good society. It is rather more limited. Justice is essentially to be thought of as a principle (or set of principles) for resolving conflicting claims. These conflicts may arise in many ways. Social justice is a particular application of just principles to conflicts which arise out of the necessity for social cooperation in seeking individual advancement. Through the division of labour it is possible to increase production: the question then arises as to how the fruits of that production shall be distributed among those who co-operate in the process. The principle of social justice therefore applies to the division of benefits and the allocation of burdens arising out of the process of undertaking joint labour. The prin-ciple also relates to the social and institutional arrangements associated with the activity of production and distribution. It may thus be extended to consider conflicts over the locus of power and decision-making authority, the distribution of influence, the bestowal of social status, the institutions set up to regulate and control activity, and so on. The essential characteristic in all such cases, however, is that we are seeking a principle which will allow us to evaluate the distributions arrived at as they apply to individuals, groups, organizations, and territories, as well as to evaluate the mechanisms which are used to accomplish this distribution. We are seeking, in short, a specification of a just distribution justly arrived at.

Unfortunately there is no one generally accepted principle of social justice to which we can appeal. Yet the notion of social justice underpins social philosophical thought from Aristotle's *Ethics* onwards. Its two most important forms are derivative of the social contract (initially formulated by Hume and Rousseau) and utilitarianism (initially formulated by Bentham and Mill). Recently, there has been a resurgence of interest in these principles resulting in modern versions of them which seem much more acceptable for a number of reasons—the work of Rawls (1969; 1971), Rescher (1966) and Runciman (1966), being outstanding in this respect. There are other strands to this thinking of course. The detailed discussion of the concept of equality by writers such as Tawney (1931), and the now voluminous literature on the question of the proper distribution of income in society have added their weight to the argument. I do not wish to review this literature here, however, and I shall confine myself to one possible argument concerning social justice and endeavour to show how it can be formulated in a manner that is geographically relevant and useful.

The principle of social justice which I shall explore starts with the skeleton concept of "a just distribution justly arrived at". The main task of this chapter is to put flesh on this skeleton and to formulate its geographic variant. Two preliminary questions may be asked about it:

What are we distributing? It is easy enough to say that we are distributing the benefits to be had from social cooperation but it is very much more difficult to specify what those benefits are, particularly as they relate to individual preferences and values. For the purpose of this paper I shall leave this question unanswered and merely call whatever it is that we are distributing "income". This indicates a very general definition of income—such as Titmuss's (1962) "command over society's scarce resources" or an even more general one such as that proposed by Miller and Roby (1970). I shall assume here that we can devise a socially just definition of income—for it would indeed be a net injustice to devise a socially just distribution of something defined in an unjust manner!

Among whom or what are we distributing it? There is general agreement that the ultimate unit with which we should be concerned is the human individual. For convenience it will often be necessary to discuss distribution as it occurs among groups, organizations, territories, and so on. Geographers are particularly interested in the territorial or regional organization of society and it will be convenient to work at that level of aggregation. But we know enough about the various forms of ecological fallacy (see Alker, 1969) to know that a just distribution across a set of territories defined at one scale does not necessarily mean a just distribution achieved at another scale or a just distribution among individuals. This scale or aggregation problem poses some thorny methodological difficulties. In principle, we may hold that distribution made at any scale or across any aggregates should be accountable to distribution as it occurs at the individual level of analysis. This is difficult to do, but for present purposes I shall assume that justice achieved at a territorial level of analysis implies justice achieved for the individual, even though I am too aware that this is not necessarily the case.

"A JUST DISTRIBUTION"

Having assumed away two rather important questions, I shall now undertake an analysis of the principle of social justice. This can be split into two parts and here I shall seek an understanding of what is meant by a "just distribution". To do this I must first establish a basis for that distribution. This is, of course, an ethical problem which cannot be resolved without making important moral decisions. These decisions essentially concern what it is that justifies individuals making claims upon the product of the society in which they live, work, and have their being. Several criteria have been suggested (see Rawls, 1969; 1971; Rescher, 1966).

99

1   *Inherent equality*—all individuals have equal claims on benefits irrespective of their contribution.
2   *Valuation of services in terms of supply and demand*—individuals who command scarce and needed resources have a greater claim than do others. It is perhaps important to differentiate here between situations in which scarcity arises naturally (inherent brain and muscle power) and situations in which it is artificially created (through the inheritance of resources or through socially organized restrictions on entry into certain occupations).
3   *Need*—individuals have rights to equal levels of benefit which means that there is an unequal allocation according to need.
4   *Inherited rights*—individuals have claims according to the property or other rights which have been passed on to them from preceding generations.
5   *Merit*—claims may be based on the degree of difficulty to be overcome in contributing to production (those who undertake dangerous or unpleasant tasks—such as mining—and those who undertake long periods of training—such as surgeons—have greater claims than do others).
6   *Contribution to common good*—those individuals whose activities benefit most people have a higher claim than do those whose activities benefit few people.
7   *Actual productive contribution*—individuals who produce more output—measured in some appropriate way—have a greater claim than do those who produce a lesser output.
8   *Efforts and sacrifices*—individuals who make a greater effort or incur a greater sacrifice relative to their innate capacity should be rewarded more than those who make little effort and incur few sacrifices.

These eight criteria are not mutually exclusive and they obviously require much more detailed interpretation and analysis. I shall follow Runciman (1966) and suggest that the essence of social justice can be embodied in a weak ordering of three of these criteria so that *need* is the most important, *contribution to common good* is the second and *merit* is the third. I shall not argue the case for this decision. It necessarily rests, however, on an appeal to certain controversial and ethical arguments. But as will become apparent in what follows, the issues raised in the

detailed examination of these three criteria are sufficiently comprehensive to subsume many of the issues which could legiti-
mately be raised under the other headings. These three criteria
could be examined in detail in a variety of contexts. I choose at
this juncture to introduce the geographic aspect to the argument
and examine how they might be formulated in the context of a
set of territories or regions. For purposes of exposition I shall
mainly consider the problem as one of a central authority
allocating scarce resources over a set of territories in such a way
that social justice is maximized. As I have already stated, I
shall assume that territorial distributive justice automatically
implies individual justice.

TERRITORIAL DISTRIBUTIVE JUSTICE

The first step in formulating a principle of territorial distributive justice lies in determining what each of the three criteria—
need, contribution to common good, and merit—means in the
context of a set of territories or regions. Procedures may then
be devised to evaluate and measure distribution according to
each criterion. The combination of the three measures (presumably weighted in some way) provides a hypothetical figure
for the allocation of resources to regions. This figure can then
be used, as happens in most normative analysis, to evaluate
existing distributions or to devise policies which will improve
existing allocations. A measure of territorial justice can be devised by correlating the actual allocation of resources with the
hypothetical allocations. Such a procedure allows the identification of those territories which depart most from the norms
suggested by standards of social justice: but this is not, of course,
easy. Bleddyn Davies (1968), who first coined the term
"territorial justice" has published a pioneering work on the
subject, which indicates some of the problems involved.

1 Need

Need is a relative concept. Needs are not constant for they are
categories of human consciousness and as society is transformed
so the consciousness of need is transformed. The problem is to
to define exactly what it is that need is relative to and to obtain

an understanding of how needs arise. Needs can be defined with respect to a number of different categories of activity—these remain fairly constant over time and we can list nine of them:

1 food
2 housing
3 medical care
4 education
5 social and environmental service
6 consumer goods
7 recreational opportunities
8 neighbourhood amenities
9 transport facilities.

Within each of these categories we can set about defining those minimum quantities and qualities which we would equate with needs. This minimum will vary according to the social norms at a given time. There will also be a variety of ways of fulfilling such needs. The need for housing can be met in a number of ways but at this time these would presumably not include living in shacks, mud-huts, tents, crumbling houses, and the like. This raises a whole host of issues which I can best examine in the context of a particular category—medical services.

Nobody, presumably, would deny that medical care is a legitimate form of need. Yet that need is not easily defined and measured. If we are to obtain a normative measure of social justice we have first to define and measure need in a socially just way. For example, the category "health services" comprises a multitude of subcategories some of which, such as cosmetic surgery and back massages, can reasonably be regarded (in our present society at least) as non-essential. An initial decision has to be made, therefore, on which subcategories should be regarded as "needs" and which should not. Decisions then have to be made as to what are reasonable standards of need within each subcategory. Let us consider some of the methods for doing this.

(i) Need can be determined through looking at *market demand*. Wherever facilities are working very close to capacity we may take it that there is an unfulfilled need in the population and thereby justify the allocation of more resources to expand medical services. This procedure is only acceptable if we can reasonably assume that nothing is inhibiting demand (such as lack of money or lack of access to facilities). To accept market demand as a socially just measure of need requires that the other conditions prevailing in society (affecting both demand and supply) are themselves socially just. This is usually not the case and this method of determining need is therefore likely to be socially unjust.

(ii) *Latent demand* may be assessed through an investigation of relative deprivation as it exists among individuals in a set of regions. Individuals would be relatively deprived if (1) they do not receive a service (2) they see other people (including themselves at a previous or an expected time) receiving it (3) they want it, and (4) they regard it as feasible that they should receive it (Runciman, 1966, 10). The concept of relative deprivation (basically similar to perceived or felt need) has been associated in the literature with the concept of a reference group (a group against which an individual measures his or her own expectations). The reference group may be socially determined—i.e. all blacks or all blue-collar workers—or spatially determined—i.e. everybody in a neighbourhood or even in a large region. The difference between the expectations of the group for health care and actual services received provides a measure of relative deprivation. This measure can be obtained either by direct survey data, or if we know something about reference groups we can calculate likely relative deprivation by looking at variance in provision within different groups. The advantages of the latter approach are that it incorporates a behavioural element so that legitimate differences in group preferences can be expressed, while also providing a measure of dissatisfaction and therefore an indicator of likely political pressure. Its disadvantage is that it assumes that "real" needs are reflected by felt needs. This is often not the case. Very poorly served groups often have very low standards of felt need. Also, all kinds of social inequities are likely to be incorporated into the measure of need if, as is usually the case in class differentiated and (or) segregated societies, the reference group structure is itself a response to conditions of social injustice.

(iii) *Potential demand* can be evaluated by an analysis of the factors which generate particular kinds of health problem. Population totals and characteristics will have an important impact on territorial needs. Health problems can be related to age, life-cycle, amount of migration, and so on. In addition there are special problems which may relate to occupational characteristics (such as mining), to sociological and cultural circumstances, as well as to income levels. Health problems can also be related to local environmental conditions (density of population, local ecology, air and water quality, and so on). If we knew enough about all of these relationships we should be able to predict the volume and incidence of health care problems across a set of territories. This requires, however, a far more sophisticated understanding of relationships than we currently possess; even so, various attempts have been made to employ this method. Its attraction, of course, is that it does provide a reasonably objective method for measuring potential demand for health care. Unfortunately, we are still left with the problem of converting this demand into a measure of need, which in this case requires that we determine appropriate forms and levels of response to these statistically determined potential demands. The response usually amounts to setting standards, which is usually done with a given quantity of resources in mind.

(iv) We could also seek to determine needs through *consultation* with experts in the field. Experts tend to determine need with one eye on available resources. But those who have lived and worked in a community for a long period of time can often draw upon their experience to provide subjective assessments which are nevertheless good indicators of need. The resolution of opinions provided by judiciously selected experts in the health field (health planners, hospital administrators, physicians, community groups, social workers, welfare rights groups, and so on) may provide a socially just determination of need. The method relies upon the subjective judgements of a selected set of individuals, but it has the considerable benefit of drawing directly upon the experience of those who have been most concerned with the health care problem. The disadvantage, of course, lies in the possibility that the experts are selected on the basis of socially unjust criteria—for example, to place the determination of need in the hands of a committee of the American Medical

Association would at present be disastrous from the point of view of social justice.

We must select among the various methods for determining need in such a way that we maximize on the social justice of the result. In the current circumstances I would discard (i) altogether in the health field and I would only accept (ii) if I felt that legitimate variations in preference were being expressed rather than variations in a felt need arising out of a socially unjust social situation or out of ignorance or false consciousness. Both (iii) and (iv) provide possible methods for establishing needs in the health field, but neither are easy to employ and both contain within them the possibility of a socially unjust determination of need.

If need is a primary criterion for assessing the social justice of a distribution of resources across a set of territories, then we are first obliged to establish a socially just definition and measurement system for it. The various methods (and their attendant difficulties) outlined in the medical care case can be applied to each of the categories—education, recreation, housing, consumer goods, and so on. It is not easy to decide upon a socially just definition of need within each category. The appropriate method may also vary from category to category—it may be best to determine consumer need through conventional supply and demand analysis, recreational needs through relative deprivation analysis, housing needs through statistical analysis, and medical care needs through resolution of expert opinion. These, however, are open questions. Defining social justice in terms of need thrusts onto us the whole uncomfortable question of what is meant by need and how it should be measured. It is imperative that we make socially just decisions on these issues. Otherwise our pursuit of a principle of social justice for evaluating geographic distributions will be worthless.

2 Contribution to common good

The concept of contribution to common good can be translated into existing geographic concepts with relative ease. We are here concerned with how an allocation of resources to one territory affects conditions in another. A technology exists to handle some of these questions in the work on interregional multiplier analysis, growth poles and externalities. The spread effects may be good or bad—pollution being an example of the latter. The notion of contribution to common good (or common "bad" in the case of pollution) suggests that our existing technology should be used to extend our understanding of interregional income transfers, interregional linkages, spatial spread effects and so on, insofar as these have actual or potential consequences for the distribution of income in society. This is not an easy task, as is demonstrated by the problems which have plagued the attempt to evaluate the benefits of urban renewal (Rothenberg, 1967). There are two rather different aspects to this problem. We can seek to improve on existing allocations given the existing pattern of interregional multipliers or we can take a more radical approach and seek to restructure the pattern of interregional multipliers by reorganizing the spatial system itself. If we take the latter approach we seek a form of spatial organization which will make the greatest contribution to fulfilling needs through the multiplier and spread effects generated by a particular pattern of regional investment. Common good may have a second component to it, that of increasing the total aggregate product. In this case contribution to common good comes close to the usual efficiency and growth criteria with externalities and side-effects incorporated into the analysis. In the search for social justice this sense of contributing to the common good should remain subsidiary to the concern for distributive consequences.

3 Merit

I shall translate the concept of "merit" into a geographical concept which relates to the degree of environmental difficulty. Such difficulties may arise out of circumstances in the physical environment. Certain hazards, such as drought, flood, earthquakes and so on, pose extra difficulty to human activity. If there is a need for a facility (say a port in an area subject to hurricane damage) then extra resources should be allocated to counter this hazard. In terms of the weak ordering that I have imposed on the criteria for social justice, this means that if a facility is needed, if it contributes to the common good in some way, *then and only then* would we be justified in allocating extra resources for its support. If people live in flood plains when they have no need to live in flood plains and if they contribute nothing to the common good by living there, then under the principle of social justice they ought not to be compensated for damage incurred by living there. If, however, individuals are forced by circumstances (such as lack of alternative choice) to live there then the primary criterion of need may be used to justify compensation. The same remarks apply to problems which arise in the social environment. Hazards posed by crimes against property, fire and riot damage, and the like, vary according to the social circumstances. Individuals need adequate security if they are to be able to contribute meaningfully to the common good and if they are to be able to allocate their productive capacity to fulfil needs. Under a principle of social justice it can therefore be argued that society at large should underwrite the higher costs of insurance in areas of high social risk. To do so would be socially just. The same argument can be applied to the allocation of extra resources to reach groups who are particularly difficult to service—as Davies (1968, 18) points out "it may be desirable to over-provide needy groups with services since they have not had access to them in the past and have not formed the habit of consuming them." This issue arises particularly with respect to the education and health care facilities extended to very poor groups, recent immigrants, and the like. Merit can therefore be translated in a geographical context as an allocation of extra resources to compensate for the degree of social and natural environmental difficulty.

The principles of social justice as they apply to geographical situations can be summarized as follows:

1 The spatial organization and the pattern of regional investment should be such as to fulfil the needs of the population. This requires that we first establish socially just methods for determining and measuring needs. The difference between needs and actual allocations provides us with an initial evaluation of the degree of territorial injustice in an existing system.
2 A spatial organization and pattern of territorial resource allocation which provides extra benefits in the form of need fulfilment (primarily) and aggregate output (secondarily)

in other territories through spillover effects, multiplier effects, and the like, is a "better" form of spatial organization and allocation.

3 Deviations in the pattern of territorial investment may be tolerated if they are designed to overcome specific environmental difficulties which would otherwise prevent the evolution of a system which would meet need or contribute to the common good.

These principles can be used to evaluate existing spatial distributions. They provide the beginnings of a normative theory of spatial organization based on territorial distributive justice. There will be enormous difficulties in elaborating them in detail and there will be even greater difficulties in translating them into concrete situations. We have some of the technology at hand to do this. It needs to be directed towards an understanding of just distributions in spatial systems.

TO ACHIEVE A DISTRIBUTION JUSTLY

There are those who claim that a necessary and sufficient condition for attaining a just distribution of income lies in devising socially just means for arriving at that distribution. Curiously enough this view prevails at both ends of the political spectrum. Buchanan and Tullock (1965)—conservative libertarians in viewpoint—thus suggest that in a properly organized constitutional democracy the most efficient way to organize redistribution is to do nothing about it. Marx (*A Critique of the Gotha Programme*, 11) attacked those "vulgar socialists" who thought that questions of distribution could be considered and resolved independent of the prevailing mechanisms governing production and distribution. Marx and constitutional democrats have a basic assumption in common—that if socially just mechanisms can be devised then questions of achieving social justice in distribution will look after themselves. In the literature on social justice (and in the arena of practical policy determination) there is a varied emphasis on "means" or "ends" with liberal and some socialist opinion apparently believing that social justice in the latter can be achieved without necessarily tampering with the former. But most writers indicate that it is foolhardy to expect socially just ends to be achieved by socially unjust means. It is instructive to follow Rawls's (1969) argument in this respect:

"the basic structure of the social system affects the life prospects of typical individuals according to their initial places in society. . . . The fundamental problem of distributive justice concerns the differences in life-prospects which come about in this way. We . . . hold that these differences are just if and only if the greater expectations of the more advantaged, when playing a part in the working of the social system, improve the expectations of the least advantaged. The basic structure is just throughout when the advantages of the more fortunate promote the well-being of the least fortunate. . . . *The basic structure is perfectly just when the prospects of the least fortunate are as great as they can be.*" (Emphasis mine.)

The problem then, is to find a social, economic and political organization in which this condition is attained and maintained. Marxists would claim, with considerable justification, that the only hope for achieving Rawls's objective would be to ensure the least fortunate always has the final say. From Rawls's initial position it is not difficult by a fairly simple logical argument to arrive at a "dictatorship of the proletariat" type of solution. Rawls tries to construct a path towards a different solution:

"if law and government act effectively to keep markets competitive, resources fully employed, property and wealth widely distributed over time, and to maintain the appropriate social minimum, then if there is equality of opportunity underwritten by education for all, the resulting distribution will be just."

To achieve this Rawls proposes a fourfold division in government in which an allocation branch acts to keep the market working competitively while correcting for market failure where necessary; a stabilization branch maintains full employment and prevents waste in the use of resources; a transfer branch sees to it that individual needs are met; and a distribution branch looks after the provision of public goods and prevents (by proper taxation) any undue concentration of power or wealth over time. From Rawls's initial position it is possible to arrive, therefore, at a Marx or a Milton Friedman, but in no way can we arrive at the liberal or socialist solutions. That this is a sensible conclusion is attested by the fact that the socialist programmes of post-war Britain appear to have had little or no impact upon the distribution of real income in society, while the liberal anti-poverty programmes in the United States have been conspicuous for their lack of success. The reason should be obvious: programmes which seek to alter distribution without altering the capitalist market structure within which income and wealth are generated and distributed, are doomed to failure.

Most of the evidence we have on group decision-making, bargaining, the control of central government, democracy, bureaucracy, and the like, also indicates that *any* social, economic and political organization which attains any permanence is liable to cooptation and subversion by special interest groups. In a constitutional democracy this is usually accomplished by small well-organized interest groups who have accumulated the necessary resources to influence decision-making. A dictatorship of the proletariat solution is likewise subject to bureaucratic subversion as the Russian experience all too readily demonstrates. An awareness of this problem has led good constitutional democrats, such as Jefferson, to look favourably on an occasional revolution to keep the body politic healthy. One of the practical effects of the sequence of revolutions in China since 1949 (and some have attributed this to Mao's conscious design) has been to prevent what Max Weber (1947) long ago called the "routinization of charisma". The question of the appropriate form of social, economic and political organization and its maintenance for the purpose of achieving social justice is beyond the scope of this essay. Yet the way in which it is resolved effectively determines both the mode and likelihood of achieving territorial justice. I shall therefore confine myself to considering how considerations of the means of achieving distribution take on a specific form in the territorial context.

The geographical problem is to design a form of spatial organization which maximizes the prospects of the least fortunate region. A necessary initial condition, for example, is that we have a socially just way of determining the boundaries of territories and a just way of allocating resources among them. The former problem lies in the traditional field of "regionalizing" in geography, but in this case with the criterion of social justice put foremost. The experience of gerrymandering indicates only too well that territorial aggregates can be determined in a socially unjust way. Boundaries can be placed so that the least advantaged groups are so distributed with respect to the more advantaged groups in a set of territorial aggregates that whatever the formula devised for allocation of resources the latter always benefit more than the former. It should be possible to devise territorial boundaries to favour the least advantaged groups—in which case social justice in allocation becomes the normative criterion for regionalization. In the actual allocation of resources we may take Rawls's objective to mean that the prospects for the least advantaged territory should be as great as they can be. How to determine when this condition exists is itself an intriguing problem, but the prospects for its achievement are presumably contingent upon the way in which a central authority decides on the territorial disposition of the resources under its control. Since poor areas are often politically weak, we are forced to rely on the sense of social justice prevailing in *all* territories (and it takes an assumption of only mild self-interest to counter that hope), upon the existence of a benevolent dictator or a benevolent bureaucracy at the centre (the latter perhaps prevails in Scandinavia), or upon a constitutional mechanism in which the least advantaged territories have the power of veto over all decisions. Exactly what arrangements are made for arbitrating among the demands of political territories (demands which do not necessarily reflect need) and for negotiating between a central authority and its constituent territories are obviously crucial for the prospect of achieving territorial justice. It is arguable, for example, whether a greater centralization of decision-making (which has the potential for ironing out differences between territories) should prevail over a greater decentralization (which has the merit of being able to prevent the exploitation of disadvantaged territories by the richer territories). The answer to this probably depends upon the initial conditions. When they are characterized by exploitation (as they appear to be in the United States), a tactical decentralization may be called for as an initial step; when exploitation is not so important (as in Scandinavia), centralization may be more appropriate. Advocacy of metropolitan control or neighbourhood government should be seen in this light.

Similar kinds of problem arise if we examine the impact of the highly decentralized decisions over capital investment characteristic of a freely working capitalist economy. Leaving aside the problems inherent in the tendency for modern capital to congeal into monopoly forms of control, it is useful to examine how an individualistic capitalist system typically operates with respect to territorial justice. Under such a system it is accepted as rational and good for capital to flow to wherever the rate of return is highest. Some (Borts and Stein, 1964) argue that this process will continue until rates of return are equalized over all territories, while others (Myrdal, 1957) suggest that circular and cumulative causation will lead to growing imbalances. Whatever the long term implications of this process are for growth, capital clearly will flow in a way which bears little relationship to need or to the condition of the least advantaged territory. The result will be the creation of localized pockets of high unfulfilled need, such as those now found in Appalachia or many inner city areas. Most societies accept some responsibility for diverting the natural stream of capital flow to deal with these problems. To do so without basically altering the *whole* capital flow process seems impossible however. Consider, as an example, the problems arising out of the housing situation in inner city areas of British and American cities. It is no longer profitable for private capital to flow into the inner city rental housing market. In London in 1965 a return of nine per cent or more would have been necessary to encourage private investment and conditions were such that there was no hope of obtaining such a return by reasonable or legal means (Milner–Holland Report, 1965). In Baltimore in 1969 a rate of twelve to fifteen per cent would be required but actual rates were probably nearer six to nine per cent (Grigsby *et al.*, 1971). It is hardly surprising that the private inner city rental housing market has collapsed in most cities as capital is withdrawn, buildings have depreciated, and capital has been transferred to other sectors or out to the much more profitable private building market in the suburban ring. Thus arises the paradox of capital withdrawing from areas of greatest need to provide for the demands of relatively affluent suburban communities. Under capitalism this is good and rational behaviour —it is what the market requires for the "optimal" allocation of resources.

Is it possible to reverse this flow using capitalist tools? Government can (and often does) intervene to make up the difference between what is now earned in the inner city and what could be earned elsewhere. It can do this in a number of ways (rent supplements to tenants, negative income taxes, direct grants to financial institutions, etc.). But whatever the means chosen the effect is to bribe financial institutions back into the inner city rental market where the government would otherwise have to take over responsibility for provision (through public housing). The first solution initially appears attractive, but it has certain flaws. If we bribe financial institutions, one effect will be to create a greater relative scarcity of capital funds for (say) suburban development. The more advantaged suburbs will adjust the rate of return they offer upwards to bring back the capital flow. The net effect of this process will be a rise in the overall rates of return which is obviously to the advantage of financial institutions—most of which are owned, operated and managed by people who live in the suburbs anyway! Thus there appears to be a built-in tendency for the capitalist market system to counteract any attempt to divert the flow of funds away from the most profitable territories. More specifically, it is impossible to induce action in one sector or territory without restricting it at the same time in other sectors and territories. Nothing short of comprehensive government control can do this effectively.

What this suggests is that "capitalist means invariably serve their own capitalist, ends" (Huberman and Sweezy, 1969), and that these capitalist ends are not consistent with the objectives of social justice. An argument can be formulated in support of this contention. The market system functions on the basis of exchange values and exchange values can exist only if there is relative scarcity of the goods and services being exchanged. The concept of scarcity is not an easy one to comprehend although we are constantly making reference to it when we talk of the allocation of scarce resources. It is questionable, for example, whether there is any such thing as a naturally arising scarcity. Pearson thus writes:

"the concept of scarcity will be fruitful only if the natural fact of limited means leads to a sequence of choices regarding the use of these means, and this situation is possible only if there is alternativity to the uses of means and there are preferentially graded ends. But these latter conditions are socially determined; they do not depend in any simple way upon the facts of

113

nature. To postulate scarcity as an absolute condition from which all economic institutions derive is therefore to employ an abstraction which serves only to obscure the question of how economic activity is organized." (1957, 320.)

The concept of scarcity, like the concept of a resource, only takes on meaning in a particular social and cultural context. It is erroneous to think that markets simply arise to deal with scarcity. In sophisticated economies scarcity is socially organized in order to permit the market to function. We say that jobs are scarce when there is plenty of work to do, that space is restricted when land lies empty, that food is scarce when farmers are being paid not to produce. Scarcity must be produced and controlled in society because without it price fixing markets could not function. This takes place through a fairly strict control over access to the means of production and a control over the flow of resources into the productive process. The distribution of the output has likewise to be controlled in order for scarcity to be maintained. This is achieved by appropriative arrangements which prevent the elimination of scarcity and preserve the integrity of exchange values in the market place. If it is accepted that the maintenance of scarcity is essential for the functioning of the market system, then it follows that deprivation, appropriation and exploitation are also necessary concomitants of the market system. In a spatial system this implies (the ecological fallacy permitting) that there will be a series of appropriative movements between territories which leads some territories to exploit and some to be exploited. This phenomenon is most clearly present in urban systems, since urbanism, as any historian of the phenomenon will tell us, is founded on the appropriation of surplus product (see chapter 6).

Certain benefits stem from the operation of the market mechanism. The price system can successfully coordinate a vast number of decentralized decisions and it can consequently integrate a vast array of activities into a coherent social and spatial system. The competition for access to scarce resources, on which the capitalistic market system rests, also encourages and facilitates technological innovation. The market system therefore helps to increase, immeasurably, the total product available to society. It is also expert at promoting overall growth, and this has led some to argue that, since the market mechanism successfully promotes growth, it follows as a matter of course that the prospects for the least fortunate territory are naturally as great as they possibly can be. Appropriation obviously takes place but this appropriation, it is held, should not be characterized as exploitation because the appropriated product is put to good use and is the source of benefits which flow back into the territories from which it was initially exacted. Appropriative movements which occur under the price system are therefore justified because of the long-term benefits which they generate. This argument cannot be rejected out of hand. But to concede that appropriation is justifiable under certain conditions is not to concede that the appropriation achieved under the market mechanism is socially just. In any economy appropriation and the creation of a social surplus product is necessary, but the pattern achieved under the market economy is not in many respects a necessary one unless the internal logic of the market economy itself is regarded as a form of justification. In a capitalist market economy an enormous concentration of surplus product (at the present time this is mainly located in large corporations) has to be absorbed in ways which do not threaten the continuance of that scarcity upon which the market economy is itself based. Hence the surplus product is consumed in socially undesirable ways (conspicuous consumption, conspicuous construction in urban areas, militarism, waste): the market system cannot dispose of the socially won surplus product in socially just ways. It therefore seems necessary, from the point of view of social justice, to increase total social product without the use of the price-fixing market mechanism. In this regard the Chinese and Cuban efforts to promote growth with social justice are probably the most significant so far undertaken. The third world is otherwise presumably doomed to repeat the experience of individual or state capitalism in which growth is achieved at huge social and human cost.

In contemporary "advanced" societies the problem is to devise alternatives to the market mechanism which allow the transference of productive power and the distribution of surplus to sectors and territories where the social necessities are so patently obvious. Thus we need to move to a new pattern of organization in which the market is replaced (probably by a decentralized planning process), scarcity and deprivation systematically eliminated wherever possible, and a degrading wage system steadily reduced as an incentive to work, without in any way diminishing the total productive power available to society. To find such a form of organization is a great challenge, but unfortunately the enormous vested interest associated with the patterns of exploitation and privilege built up through the operation of the market mechanism, wields all of its influence to prevent the replacement of the market and even to preclude a reasoned discussion of the possible alternatives to it. Under conditions of social justice, for example, an unequal allocation of resources to territories and appropriative movements would be permissible if (and only if) those territories favoured were able, through their physical and social circumstances and through their connections with other territories, to contribute to the common good of all territories. This pattern of appropriation will obviously be different to that achieved under the market mechanism for the latter is institutionally bound to maintain patterns of appropriation, deprivation, and scarcity, and institutionally incapable of distributing according to need or of contribution to common good. The social organization of scarcity and deprivation associated with price-fixing markets makes the market mechanism automatically antagonistic to any principle of social justice. Whether the market mechanism can be justified on grounds of efficiency and growth depends on how it compares with those alternatives which most are not prepared even to discuss.

A JUST DISTRIBUTION JUSTLY ACHIEVED: TERRITORIAL SOCIAL JUSTICE

From this examination of the principles of social justice we can arrive at the sense of *territorial social justice* as follows:

1   The distribution of income should be such that (a) the needs of the population within each territory are met, (b) resources are so allocated to maximize interterritorial multiplier effects, and (c) extra resources are allocated to help overcome special difficulties stemming from the physical and social environment.

2   The mechanisms (institutional, organizational, political and economic) should be such that the prospects of the

least advantaged territory are as great as they possibly can be.

If these conditions are fulfilled there will be a just distribution justly arrived at.

I recognize that this general characterization of the principles of territorial social justice leaves much to be desired and that it will take a much more detailed examination of these principles before we are in a position to build some kind of theory of location and regional allocation around them. It took many years and an incredible application of intellectual resources to get to even a satisfactory beginning point for specifying a location theory based on efficiency and there is still no general theory of location—indeed we do not even known what it means to say that we are "maximizing the spatial organization of the city" for there is no way to maximize on the multiplicity of objectives contained in potential city forms. In the examination of distribution, therefore, we can anticipate breaking down the objectives into component parts. The component parts are as follows:

1   How do we specify need in a set of territories in accord with socially just principles, and how do we calculate the degree of need fulfilment in an existing system with an existing allocation of resources?

2   How can we identify interregional multipliers and spread effects (a topic which has already some theoretical base)?

3   How do we assess social and physical environment difficulty and when is it socially just to respond to it in some way?

4   How do we regionalize to maximize social justice?

5   What kinds of allocative mechanisms are there to ensure that the prospects of the poorest region are maximized and how do the various existing mechanisms perform in this respect?

6   What kinds of rules should govern the pattern of interterritorial negotiation, the pattern of territorial political power, and so on, so that the prospects of the poorest area are as great as they can be?

These are the sorts of questions which we can begin to work on in some kind of single-minded way. To work on them will undoubtedly involve us in making difficult ethical and moral decisions concerning the rights and wrongs of certain principles for justifying claims upon the scarce product of society. We cannot afford to ignore these questions for to do so amounts to one of those strategic non-decisions, so prevalent in politics, by which we achieve a tacit endorsement of the *status quo*. Not to decide on these issues is to decide. The single-minded exploration of efficiency has at best amounted to a tacit endorsement of the *status quo* in distribution. To criticize those who have pursued efficiency for this reason is not to deny the importance of analysis based on efficiency itself. As I indicated at the beginning of this chapter, we need to explore efficiency and distribution jointly. But to do so we first need a detailed exploration of those questions of distribution which have for so long been left in limbo.

Part two

Socialist Formulations

Chapter 4

Revolutionary and Counter-revolutionary Theory in Geography and the Problem of Ghetto Formation

How and why would we bring about a revolution in geographic thought? In order to gain some insight into this question, it is worth examining how revolutions and counter-revolutions occur in all branches of scientific thought. Kuhn (1962) provides an interesting analysis of this phenomenon as it occurs in the natural sciences. He suggests that most scientific activity is what he calls normal science. This amounts to the investigation of all facets of a particular paradigm (a paradigm being a set of concepts, categories, relationships, and methods which are generally accepted throughout a community at a given point in time). In the practice of normal science, certain anomalies arise—observations or paradoxes which cannot be resolved within an existing paradigm. These anomalies become the focus of increasing attention until science is plunged into a period of crisis in which speculative attempts are made to solve the problems posed by the anomalies. Out of these attempts there eventually arises a new set of concepts, categories, relationships, and methods which successfully both resolves the existing dilemmas and incorporates the worthwhile aspects of the old paradigm. Thus, a new paradigm is born and is followed once more by the onset of normal scientific activity.

Kuhn's schema is open to criticism on a number of grounds. I shall discuss two problems very briefly. First, there is no explanation as to how anomalies arise and how, once they have arisen, they generate crises. This criticism could be met by distinguishing between significant and insignificant anomalies.

For example, it was known for many years that the orbit of Mercury did not fit Newton's calculations, yet this anomaly was insignificant because it had no relevance to the use of the Newtonian system in an everyday context. If, for example, certain anomalies had arisen in bridge construction, then they would obviously have been deemed highly significant. Therefore, the Newtonian paradigm remained satisfactory and unchallenged until something of practical importance and relevance could *not* be accomplished using the Newtonian system. Secondly, there is the question, never satisfactorily answered by Kuhn, concerning the way in which a new paradigm becomes accepted. Kuhn admits that acceptance is not a matter of logic. He suggests rather that it involves a leap of faith. The question is, however, what this leap of faith should be based on. Underlying Kuhn's analysis is a guiding force which is never explicitly examined. This guiding force amounts to a fundamental belief in the virtues of control and manipulation of the natural environment. The leap of faith, apparently, is based on the belief that the new system will allow an extension of manipulation and control over some aspect of nature. Which aspect of nature? Presumably it will once again be an aspect of nature which is important in terms of everyday activity and everyday life at a particular point in history.

The central criticism of Kuhn, which these two cases point out, is his abstraction of scientific knowledge from its materialistic base. Kuhn provides an *idealist's* interpretation of scientific advancement, while it is clear that scientific thought is fundamentally geared to material activities. The materialistic basis for the advancement of scientific knowledge has been explored by Bernal (1971). Material activity involves the manipulation of nature in the interests of man, and scientific understanding cannot be interpreted independently of that general thrust. However, at this juncture, we are forced to add a further perspective because "the interest of man" is subject to a variety of interpretations, depending on which sector of society we are thinking of. Bernal points out that the sciences in the West have until very recently, been the preserve of a middle-class group, and even recently, with the rise of what is often called the "meritocracy", the scientist is often drawn into middle-class ways of life and thought in the course of his or her career. We may thus expect the natural sciences tacitly to reflect a drive for manipulation and control over those aspects of nature which are relevant to the middle class. Far more important, however, is the harnessing of scientific activity by a process of patronage and funded research to the special interests of those who are in control of the means of production. The coalition of industry and government heavily directs scientific activity. Consequently, "manipulation and control" means manipulation and control in the interests of particular groups in society (specifically, the industrial and financial community together with the middle class) rather than in the interests of society as a whole (see Bernal, 1971; Rose and Rose, 1969). With these perspectives we are better able to understand the general thrust of scientific advancement hidden within the recurrent scientific revolutions which Kuhn has so perceptively described.

It has frequently been questioned whether Kuhn's analysis could be extended to the social sciences. Kuhn appears to view the social sciences as "pre-scientific" in the sense that no one social science has really established that corpus of generally accepted concepts, categories, relationships and methods which form a paradigm. This view of the social sciences as pre-scientific is, in fact, quite general among philosophers of science (see Kuhn, 1962, 37; Nagel, 1961). However, a quick survey of the history of thought in the social sciences shows that revolutions do indeed occur and that they are marked by many of the same features which Kuhn identified in the natural sciences. There is no question that Adam Smith provided a paradigmatic formulation for economic thought which was subsequently built upon by Ricardo. In modern times Keynes succeeded in doing something essentially similar to Smith and he provided a paradigmatic formulation which has dominated economic thought in the West until the present day. Johnson (1971) explores such revolutions in thought in economics. His analysis parallels in many respects that of Kuhn's, adding, however, several extra twists. At the heart of the Keynesian revolution, Johnson asserts, was a crisis generated by the failure of preKeynesian economics to deal with the most pressing and significant problem of the 1930s—unemployment. Thus, unemployment provided the significant anomaly. Johnson suggests that:

"By far the most helpful circumstance for the rapid propagation of a new and revolutionary theory is the existence of an established orthodoxy which is clearly inconsistent with the most salient facts of reality, and yet is sufficiently confident of its intellectual power to attempt to explain those facts, and in its efforts to do so exposes its incompetence in a ludicrous fashion." Thus the objective social realities of the time overtook the conventional wisdom and served to expose its failings.

"In this situation of general confusion and obvious irrelevance of orthodox economics to real problems, the way was open for a new theory that offered a convincing explanation of the nature of the problem and a set of policy prescriptions based on that explanation."

So far, the similarity to Kuhn is quite remarkable. But Johnson then adds new considerations, some of which really stem from the sociology of science itself. He asserts that a newly accepted theory had to possess five main characteristics:

"First, it had to attack the central proposition of conservative orthodoxy . . . with a new but academically acceptable analysis that reversed the proposition. . . . Second, the theory had to appear to be new, yet absorb as much as possible of the valid or at least not readily disputable components of existing orthodox theory. In this process, it helps greatly to give old concepts new and confusing names, and to emphasize as crucial analytical steps that have previously been taken as platitudinous. . . . Third, the new theory had to have the appropriate degree of difficulty to understand . . . so that senior academic colleagues would find it neither easy nor worthwhile to study, so that they would waste their efforts on peripheral theoretical issues, and so offer themselves as easy marks for criticism and dismissal by their younger and hungrier colleagues. At the same time the new theory had to appear both difficult enough to challenge the intellectual interest of younger colleagues and students, but actually easy enough for them to master adequately with sufficient investment of intellectual endeavour. . . . Fourth, the new theory had to offer to the more gifted and less opportunistic scholars a new methodology more appealing than those currently available. . . . Finally, [it had to offer] an important empirical relationship . . . to measure."

The history of geographic thought in the last ten years is exactly mirrored in this analysis. The central proposition of the old geography was the qualitative and the unique. This clearly could not resist the drive in the social sciences as a whole towards tools of social manipulation and control which require an understanding of the quantitative and the general. Nor can there be any doubt that during the transition process old concepts were given new and confusing names and that fairly platitudinous assumptions were subject to rigorous analytical investigation. Moreover, it cannot be denied that the so-called quantitative revolution allowed the opportunity to pillory the elder statesmen in the discipline, particularly when they ventured into issues related to the newly emerging orthodoxy. Certainly, the quantitative movement provided a challenge of appropriate difficulty and opened up the prospect for new methodologies—many of which were to be quite rewarding in terms of the analytic insights they generated. Lastly, new things to measure were in abundance; and in the distance-decay function, the threshold, the range of a good, and the measurement of spatial patterns, geographers found four apparently crucial new empirical topics which they could spend an inordinate amount of time investigating. The quantitative movement can thus be interpreted partly in terms of a challenging new set of ideas to be answered, partly as a rather shabby struggle for power and status within a disciplinary framework, and partly as a response to outside pressures to discover the means for manipulation and control in what may broadly be defined as "the planning field". In case anyone misinterprets these remarks as pointing a finger at any one particular group, let me say that all of us were involved in this process and that there was and is no way in which we could or can escape such involvement.

Johnson also introduces the term "counter-revolution" into his analysis. In this respect his thought is not very enlightening, since he clearly has an axe to grind in criticizing the monetarists whom he designates as counter-revolutionaries, even though a significant anomaly (the combination of inflation and unemployment) exists as a pressing challenge to the Keynesian orthodoxy. But there is something very important in this term which requires analysis. It seems intuitively plausible to think of the movement of ideas in the social sciences as a movement based on revolution and counter-revolution, in contrast to the natural sciences to which such a notion does not appear so immediately applicable.

We can analyse the phenomena of counter-revolution by

using our insight into paradigm formation in the natural sciences. This is based on the extension of man's ability to manipulate and control naturally occurring phenomena. Similarly, we can anticipate that the driving force behind paradigm formation in the social sciences is the desire to manipulate and control human activity and social phenomena in the interest of man. Immediately the question arises as to who is going to control whom, in whose interest is the controlling going to be exercised, and if control is exercised in the interest of all, who is going to take it upon himself to define that public interest? We are thus forced to confront directly in the social sciences what arises only indirectly in the natural sciences, namely, the social bases and implications of control and manipulation. We would be extraordinarily foolish to presuppose that these bases are equitably distributed throughout society. Our history shows that usually these bases are highly concentrated within a few key groupings in society. These groups may be benevolent or exploitive with respect to other groups. This, however, is not the issue. The point is that social science formulates concepts, categories, relationships and methods which are not independent of the existing social relationships. As such, the concepts are the product of the very phenomena they are designed to describe. A revolutionary theory upon which a new paradigm is based will gain general acceptance only if the nature of the social relationships embodied in the theory are actualized in the real world. A counter-revolutionary theory is one which is deliberately proposed to deal with a revolutionary theory in such a manner that the threatened social changes which general acceptance of the revolutionary theory would generate are, either by cooptation or subversion, prevented from being realized.

This process of revolution and counter-revolution in social science is explicit in the relationship between the political economic theories of Adam Smith and Ricardo and those of Karl Marx, about which Engels, in his Preface to Volume 2 of *Capital*, provides some quite extraordinary insights (see Althusser and Balibar, 1970). At issue was the charge that Marx had plagiarized the theory of surplus value. Marx, however, clearly acknowledged that both Adam Smith and Ricardo had discussed and partially understood the nature of surplus-value. Engels sets out to explain what was new in

Marx's utterances on surplus value and how it was that Marx's theory of surplus value "struck home like a thunderbolt out of a clear sky". To accomplish this he describes an incident in the history of chemistry (quite coincidentally, this turns out to be one of the inspirations for Kuhn's (1962, 52–6) thesis regarding the structure of revolutions in the natural sciences) concerning the relationship between Lavoisier and Priestley in the discovery of oxygen. Both conducted similar experiments and produced similar results. However, there was an essential difference between them. Priestley insisted for the rest of his life on interpreting his results in terms of the old phlogiston theory and therefore called his discovery "dephlogisticated air". Lavoisier, on the other hand, recognized that his discovery could not be reconciled with the existing phlogiston theory and, as a consequence, was able to re-construct the theoretical framework of chemistry on a completely new basis. Thus Engels, and Kuhn after him, states that Lavoisier was the "real discoverer of oxygen vis-à-vis the others who had only produced it without knowing what they had produced." Engels continues:
"Marx stands in the same relation to his predecessors in the theory of surplus value as Lavoisier stood to Priestley. . . . The existence of that part of the value of products which we now call surplus value had been ascertained long before Marx. It had also been stated with more or less precision what it consisted of. . . . But one did not get any further . . . [all economists] remained prisoners of the economic categories as they had come down to them. Now Marx appeared upon the scene. And he took a view directly opposite to that of all his predecessors. What they had regarded as a *solution*, he considered but a *problem*. He saw that he had to deal neither with dephlogisticated air nor with fireair, but with oxygen—that here it was not simply a matter of stating an economic fact or of pointing out the conflict between this fact and eternal justice and morality, but of explaining a fact which was destined to revolutionize all economics, and which offered to him who knew how to use it the key to an understanding of all capitalist production. With this fact as his starting point he examined all the economic categories which he found at hand, just as Lavoisier proceeding from oxygen had examined the categories of phlogistic chemistry." (Marx, *Capital* volume 2, 11–18.)

The Marxist theory was clearly dangerous in that it appeared to provide the key to understanding capitalist production from the position of those *not* in control of the means of production. Consequently, the categories, concepts, relationships and methods which had the potential to form a new paradigm were an enormous threat to the power structure of the capitalist world. The subsequent emergence of the marginal theory of value (especially among the Austrian school of economists such as Böhm-Bawerk and Menger) did away with many of the basics of Smith's and Ricardo's analysis (in particular the labour theory of value) and also, incidentally, served to turn back the Marxist challenge in economics. The counter-revolutionary cooptation of Marxist theory in Russia after Lenin's death, and a similar counter-revolutionary cooptation of much of the Marxist language into Western sociology (so much so that some sociologists suggest that we are all Marxists now) without conveying the essence of Marxist thinking, has effectively prevented the true flowering of Marxist thought and, concomitantly, the emergence of that humanistic society which Marx envisaged. Both the concepts and the projected social relationships embodied in the concepts were frustrated.

Revolution and counter-revolution in thought are therefore characteristic of the social sciences in a manner apparently not characteristic of the natural sciences. Revolutions in thought cannot ultimately be divorced from revolutions in practice. This may point to the conclusion that the social sciences are indeed in a pre-scientific state. The conclusion is ill-founded, however, since the natural sciences have never been wrested for any length of time out of the control of a restricted interest group. It is this fact, rather than anything inherent in the nature of natural science itself, that accounts for the lack of counter-revolutions in the natural sciences. In other words, those revolutions of thought which are accomplished in the natural sciences pose no threat to the existing order since they are constructed with the requirements of that existing order broadly in mind. This is not to say that there are not some uncomfortable social problems to resolve *en route*, for scientific discovery is not predictable and it can therefore be the source of social tension. What this does suggest, however, is that the natural sciences are in a pre-social state. Accordingly, questions of social action and social control, which the techniques of natural science frequently help to resolve, are not incorporated into natural science itself. In fact there is a certain fetishism about keeping social issues out of the natural sciences since incorporating them would supposedly "bias" research conducted at the behest of the existing social order. The consequent moral dilemmas for those scientists who take their social responsibility seriously are real indeed. Contrary to popular opinion, therefore, it seems appropriate to conclude that the philosophy of social science is *potentially* much superior to that of natural science and that the eventual fusion of the two fields of study will come about not through attempts to "scientize" social science but instead by the socialization of natural science (see Marx, *Economic and Philosophic Manuscripts of 1844*, 164). This may mean the replacement of manipulation and control with the realization of human potential as the basic criterion for paradigm acceptance. In such an event all aspects of science would experience both revolutionary and counter-revolutionary phases of thought which would undoubtedly be associated with revolutionary changes in social practice.

Let us return now to the initial question. How and why would we bring about a revolution in geographic thought? The quantitative revolution has run its course, and diminishing marginal returns are apparently setting in; yet another piece of factorial ecology, yet another attempt to measure the distance-decay effect, yet another attempt to identify the range of a good, serve to tell us less and less about anything of great relevance. In addition, there are younger geographers now, just as ambitious as the quantifiers were in the early sixties, a little hungry for recognition, and somewhat starved for interesting things to .do. So there are murmurs of discontent within the social structure of the discipline as the quantifiers establish a firm grip on the production of graduate students and on the curricula of various departments. This sociological condition within the discipline is not sufficient to justify a revolution in thought (nor should it), but the condition is there. More importantly, there is a clear disparity between the sophisticated theoretical and methodological framework which we are using and our ability to say anything really meaningful about events as they unfold around us. There are too many anomalies between what we purport to explain and manipulate and what actually happens.

There is an ecological problem, an urban problem, an international trade problem, and yet we seem incapable of saying
anything of depth or profundity about any of them. When we
do say something, it appears trite and rather ludicrous. In
short, our paradigm is not coping well. It is ripe for overthrow.
The objective social conditions demand that we say something
sensible or coherent or else forever (through lack of credibility
or, even worse, through the deterioration of the objective social
conditions) remain silent. It is the emerging objective social
conditions and our patent inability to cope with them which
essentially explains the necessity for a revolution in geographic
thought.

How should we accomplish such a revolution? There are a
number of paths we could take. We could, as some suggest,
abandon the positivist basis of the quantitative movement for an
abstract philosophical idealism and hope either that the objective social conditions will improve of their own accord, or that
concepts forged through idealist modes of thought will eventually achieve enough content to facilitate the creative change of
objective social conditions. It is, however, a characteristic of
idealism that it is forever doomed to search fruitlessly for real
content. We could also reject the positivist basis of the 1960s for
a phenomenological basis. This appears more attractive than
the idealists' course since it at least serves to keep us in contact
with the concept of man as a being in constant sensuous
interaction with the social and natural realities which surround
us. Yet phenomenological approaches can lead us into idealism or back into naïve positivist empiricism just as easily as they
can into a socially aware form of materialism. The so-called
behavioural revolution in geography points in both of these
directions. Therefore the most fruitful strategy at this juncture
is to explore that area of understanding in which certain aspects
of positivism, materialism and phenomenology overlap to
provide adequate interpretations of the social reality in which
we find ourselves. This overlap is most clearly explored in
Marxist thought. Marx, in the *Economic and Philosophic Manuscripts of 1844* and in the *German Ideology*, gave his system of
thought a powerful and appealing phenomenological basis.

There are also certain things which Marxism and positivism
have in common. They both have a materialist base and both
resort to an analytic method. The essential difference, of course,

is that positivism simply seeks to understand the world whereas Marxism seeks to change it. Put another way, positivism draws its categories and concepts from an existing reality with all of its defects while Marxist categories and concepts are formulated through the application of the dialectical method to history as it unfolds, here and now, through events and actions. The positivist method involves, for example, the application of traditional bi-valued Aristotelian logic to test hypotheses (the null hypothesis of statistical inference is a purely Aristotelian device): hypotheses are either true or false and once categorized remain ever so. The dialectic, on the other hand, proposes a process of understanding which allows the inter-penetration of opposites, incorporates contradictions and paradoxes, and points to the processes of resolution. Insofar as it is relevant to talk of truth and falsity, truth lies in the dialectical process rather than in the statements derived from the process. These statements can be designated as "true" only at a given point in time and, in any case, can be contradicted by other "true" statements. The dialectical method allows us to invert analyses if necessary, to regard solutions as problems, to regard questions as solutions.

And so at last I come to the question of ghetto formation. The reader may at present feel that the foregoing was an elaborate introduction which has only fringe relevance to the question of understanding ghetto formation and devising solutions to the ghetto problem. In fact, it is crucial to the case, for I shall argue that we are able to say something relevant to the problem only if we self-consciously seek, in the process, to establish a revolutionary geographical theory to deal with it. I shall also argue that we can devise this understanding using many of the tools which are currently available to us. However, we must be prepared to interpret those tools in a new and rather different way. In short, we need to think in terms of oxygen instead of in terms of dephlogisticated air.

The ghetto has attracted a good deal of attention as one of the major social problems of the American city. In British cities, fears of "polarization" and "ghettoization" are rising. It is generally held that ghettos are bad things and that it would be socially desirable to eliminate them, preferably without eliminating the populations they contain. (Banfield's position with respect to the latter question appears somewhat ambiguous.) The intention here is not to attempt a detailed analysis of the literature on the ghetto nor to become embroiled in definitions of it. Instead, examination shall be made of those geographical theories which appear to have some relevance for understanding ghetto formation and ghetto maintenance. The most obvious corpus of theory which calls for examination here is, of course, urban land-use theory.

One large segment of urban land-use theory in geography draws its inspiration from the Chicago school of sociologists. Park, Burgess and McKenzie (1925) wrote voluminously on the city and elaborated an interpretation of city form in ecological terms. They noted the concentration of low-income groups and various ethnic groups within particular sections of the city. They also discovered that cities exhibited a certain regularity of spatial form. From this, Burgess elaborated what came to be known as the concentric zone theory of the city. Park and Burgess both appeared to regard the city as a sort of man-produced, ecological complex within which the processes of social adaptation, specialization of function and of life style, competition for living space, and so on acted to produce a coherent spatial structure, the whole being held together by some culturally derived form of social solidarity which Park (1926) called "the moral order". The various groups and activities within the city system were essentially bound together by this moral order, and they merely jockeyed for position (both social and spatial) within the constraints imposed by the moral order. The main focus of interest was to find out who ended up where and what conditions were like when they got there. The main thrust of the Chicago school was necessarily descriptive. This tradition has had an extraordinarily powerful influence over geographic thinking and, although the techniques of description have changed somewhat (factorial ecology essentially replacing descriptive human ecology), the essential direction of the work has not changed greatly. The Chicago school of urban geographers is firmly derivative of the Chicago school of sociologists (see Berry and Horton, 1970). It is curious to note, however, that Park and Burgess did not pay a great deal of attention to the kind of social solidarity generated through the workings of the economic system nor to the social and economic relationships which derive from economic considerations. They did not ignore the issue, of course, but it was of secondary importance to them. As a result, the urban land-use theory which they developed has a critical flaw when it is used to explain the ghetto. It is interesting to observe that Engels, writing some eighty years before Park and Burgess, noted the phenomenon of concentric zoning in the city, but sought to interpret it in economic class terms. The passage is worth quoting, for it has several insights into the spatial structure of cities.

"Manchester contains, at its heart, a rather extended commercial district, perhaps half a mile long and about as broad, and consisting almost wholly of offices and warehouses. Nearly the whole district is abandoned by dwellers, and is lonely and deserted at night. . . . The district is cut through by certain main thoroughfares upon which the vast traffic concentrates, and in which the ground level is lined with brilliant shops. In these streets the upper floors are occupied, here and there, and there is a good deal of life upon them until late at night. With the exception of this commercial district, all Manchester proper, all Salford and Hulme . . . are all unmixed working people's quarters, stretching like a girdle, averaging a mile and a half in breadth, around the commercial district. Outside, beyond this girdle, lives the upper and middle bourgeoisie, the middle bourgeoisie in regularly laid out streets in the vicinity of working quarters . . . the upper bourgeoisie in remoter villas with gardens . . . in free, wholesome country air, in fine, comfortable homes, passed every half or quarter hour by omnibuses going into the city. And the finest part of the arrangement is this, that the members of the money aristocracy can take the shortest road through the middle of all the labouring districts without ever seeing that they are in the midst of the grimy misery that lurks to the right and left. For the thoroughfares leading from the Exchange in all directions out of the city are lined, on both sides, with an almost unbroken series of shops, and are so kept in the hands of the middle and lower bourgeoisie . . . [that] they suffice to conceal from the eyes of the wealthy men and women of strong stomachs and weak nerves the misery and grime which form the complement of their wealth. . . . I know very well that this hypocritical plan is more or less common to all great cities; I know, too, that the retail dealers are forced by the nature of their business to take possession of the great highways; I know that there are more good buildings than bad ones upon such streets everywhere, and that the value of land is greater near them than in remote districts, but at the same time I have never seen so systematic a shutting out of the working class from the thoroughfares, so tender a concealment of everything which might affront the eye and the nerves of the bourgeoisie, as in Manchester. And yet, in other respects, Manchester is less built according to plan, after official regulations, is more an outgrowth of accident, than any other city; and when I consider in this connection the eager assurances of the middle class, that the working class is doing famously, I cannot help feeling that the liberal manufacturers, the Big Wigs of Manchester, are not so innocent after all, in the matter of this sensitive method of construction." (Engels, *The Condition of the English Working Class in 1844*, 46–7.)

The line of approach adopted by Engels in 1844 was and still is far more consistent with hard economic and social realities than was the essentially cultural approach of Park and Burgess. In fact with certain obvious modifications, Engels's description could easily be made to fit the contemporary American city (concentric zoning with good transport facilities for the affluent who live on the outskirts, sheltering of commuters into the city from seeing the grime and misery which is the complement of their wealth, etc.). It seems a pity that contemporary geographers have looked to Park and Burgess rather than to Engels for their inspiration. The social solidarity which Engels noted was not generated by any superordinate "moral order". Instead, the miseries of the city were an inevitable concomitant to an evil and avaricious capitalist system. Social solidarity was enforced through the operation of the market exchange system. Engels reacted to London thus:

"These Londoners have been forced to sacrifice the best qualities of their human nature, to bring to pass all the marvels of civilization which crowd their city, a hundred powers which slumbered within them have remained inactive, have been suppressed in order that a few might be developed more fully and multiply through union with those of others. . . . The brutal indifference, the unfeeling isolation of each in his private interest becomes the more repellent and offensive, the more these individuals are crowded together within a limited space. . . . The dissolution of mankind into monads, of which each

133

one has a separate principle, the world of atoms, is here carried
out to its utmost extreme. . . . Hence it comes too, that the
social war, the war of each against all, is here openly declared
. . . people regard each other only as useful objects; each
exploits the other, and the end of it all is, that the stronger
treads the weaker under foot, and that the powerful few, the
capitalists, seize everything for themselves, while to the weak
many, the poor, scarcely a bare existence remains. . . . Everywhere barbarous indifference, hard egotism on one hand, and
nameless misery on the other, everywhere social warfare, every
man's house in a state of siege, everywhere reciprocal plunder-
ing under the protection of the law, and all so shameless, so
openly avowed that one shrinks before the consequences of our
social state as they manifest themselves here undisguised, and
can only wonder that the whole crazy fabric still hangs together." (*op. cit.*, 23–5.)
If we cleaned up the language a bit (by eliminating the references to capitalism, for example), we would have a description
worthy of the Kerner Commission Report (1968).

The common spatial structure of cities noted by Engels and
by Park and Burgess, can thus be analysed from economic and
cultural points of view. The question which Engels posed,
concerning the way in which such a system could evolve
without guidance from the "Big Wigs" and yet be to their clear
advantage, has subsequently been the subject of detailed
economic analysis. The possibility of using marginalist economic principles to explain this phenomenon was initially indicated in the work of von Thünen in an agricultural context. This
laid the basis for an economic theory of the urban land-market
in the relatively recent work of Alonso (1964) and Muth (1969).
The details of this theory need not detain us (though see chapter
5), but it is worth examining its contribution to an understanding of ghetto formation. Urban land use, it is argued, is
determined through a process of competitive bidding for the use
of the land. The competitive bidding proceeds so that land
rents are higher nearer the centre of activity (in the theory it is
usually assumed that all employment is concentrated in one
central location). If we now consider the residential choice
open to two groups in the population (one rich and one poor)
with respect to one employment centre, we can predict where
each must live by examining the structure of their bid rent

curves. For the poor group the bid rent curve is characteristically steep since the poor have very little money to spend on transportation; and therefore their ability to bid for the use of the land declines rapidly with distance from the place of employment. The rich group, on the other hand, characteristically has a shallow bid rent curve since its ability to bid is not greatly affected by the amount of money spent on transportation. When put in competition with each other, we find the poor group forced to live in the centre of the city, and the rich group living outside (just as Engels described it). This means that the poor are forced to live on high rent land. The only way they can adjust to this, of course, is to save on the quantity of space they consume and crowd into a very small area. The logic of the model indicates that poor groups will be concentrated in high rent areas close to the city centre in overcrowded conditions. Now, it is possible to construct a number of variants to the model, since the shape of the bid rent curve of the rich is really a function of their preference for space relative to transportation cost. Lave (1970) points out that the spatial structure of the city will change if the preferences of the rich group change. If congestion costs increase in the central city, for example, and the rich decide that the time and frustration are not worth it, then they can with ease alter their bid rent function and move back into the centre of the city. Various city structures can be predicted depending on the shape of the bid rent curves, and it is perfectly feasible to find the rich living in the centre of the city and the poor located on the outskirts. In this case, the poor are forced to adjust, for example, by exchanging time for cost distance so that they expend large quantities of time walking to work in order to save on transport costs (a condition not unknown in Latin American cities). All this actually means is that the rich group can always enforce its preferences over a poor group because it has more resources to apply either to transport costs or to obtaining land in whatever location it chooses. This is the natural consequence derived from applying marginalist economic principles (the bid rent curve being a typical marginalist device) to a situation in which income differences are substantial. The theory rests on the achievement of what is usually called "Pareto optimality" in the housing market.

It is possible to use theoretical formulations of this sort to analyse disequilibrium in a city system and to devise policies which will serve to bring conditions back into equilibrium. With the rapid suburbanization of employment in the United States since 1950, we would anticipate an outward shift of poor populations (given their bid rent functions) as they attempt to locate nearer their employment centres. This shift has *not* occurred because of the exclusive residential zoning in suburban areas. We may thus attribute the seriousness of the ghetto problem in modern society to a function of those institutions which prevent the achievement of equilibrium. We may, through court suits and the like, challenge the legality and constitutionality of exclusive zoning. (Interestingly enough, this effort is supported both by civil rights groups and corporations, since the former regard suburban zoning as discriminatory whereas the latter are concerned by the lack of low-income labour in suburban locations.) We may also try to modify land-use controls so that the kind of situation reported for some twenty communities in the Princeton, New Jersey, area, in which there is industrial and commercial zoning for 1.2 million jobs and residential zoning adequate for 144,000 workers, would be avoided (Wall Street Journal, 27 November, 1970). We might also try to overcome the problem of insufficient transportation from inner city areas to outer suburbs by subsidizing transport systems or organizing special transport facilities to get ghetto residents out to suburban employment. Of necessity, this requires the ghetto resident to substitute time for cost (if service is subsidized). Most of these programmes have been failures. We might also try to get back into equilibrium by attracting employment back into the city centre by urban renewal projects, support of Black capitalism, and the like. All of these solutions have as their basis the tacit assumption that there is disequilibrium in urban land use and that policy should be directed towards getting urban land use back into balance. These solutions are liberal in that they recognize inequity but seek to cure that inequity within an existing set of social mechanisms (in this case, mechanisms which are consistent with the von Thünen theory of urban land use).

How can we identify more revolutionary solutions? Let us go back to Muth's (1969) presentation of the von Thünen theory.

After an analytic presentation of the theory, Muth seeks to evaluate the empirical relevance of the theory by testing it against the existing structure of residential land use in Chicago. His tests indicate that the theory is broadly correct, with, however, certain deviations explicable by such things as racial discrimination in the housing market. We may thus infer that the theory is a true theory. This truth, arrived at by classical positivist means, can be used to help us identify the problem. What for Muth was a successful test of a social theory becomes for us an indicator of what the problem is. The theory predicts that poor groups must, of necessity, live where they can least afford to live.

Our objective is to eliminate ghettos. Therefore, the only valid policy with respect to this objective is to eliminate the conditions which give rise to the truth of the theory. In other words, we wish the von Thünen theory of the urban land market to become *not* true. The simplest approach here is to eliminate those mechanisms which serve to generate the theory. The mechanism in this case is very simple—competitive bidding for the use of the land. If we eliminate this mechanism, we will presumably eliminate the result. This is immediately suggestive of a policy for eliminating ghettos, which would presumably supplant competitive bidding with a socially controlled urban land market and socialized control of the housing sector. Under such a system, the von Thünen theory (which is a normative theory anyway) would become empirically irrelevant to our understanding of the spatial structure of residential land use. This approach has been tried in a number of countries. In Cuba, for example, all urban flats were expropriated in 1960. Rents were paid to the government "and were considered as amortization towards ownership by the occupants, who must pay promptly and regularly and maintain the premises" (Valdès, 1971). Change of occupancy could occur only through a state institution.

"Those living in homes built in or prior to 1940 were to cease payment in 1965 if rent had been paid punctually since 1959. And after May 1961, all new vacant units were distributed to families who had to pay rent equal to ten per cent of the family income. Moreover, in mid-1966, the right to live rent free for the rest of their lives was granted to all occupants of run-down tenements who had made at least 60 months payment. A total

137

Socialist Formulations

of 268,089 families no longer were paying rent in 1969."
(Valdès, 1971, 320.)

Obviously, a small country, such as Cuba, in a fairly primitive stage of economic development is going to suffer chronic housing shortages, and poor housing per se cannot be eliminated through such action. However, the solutions adopted are interesting in that they will ultimately render the Alonso–Muth theory of the urban land market irrelevant to an understanding of residential spatial structure, and this, presumably, is what might happen if we succeed in eliminating the ghetto.

This approach to the ghetto land and housing market is suggestive of a different framework for analysing problems and devising solutions. Notice, for example, that all old housing became rent free. If we regard the total housing stock of an urban area as a social (as opposed to a private) good, then obviously the community has already paid for the old housing. By this calculus, all housing in an urban area built before, say, 1940 (and some of it built since) has been paid for. The debt on it has been amortized and retired. The only costs attached to it are maintenance and service charges. We have an enormous quantity of social capital locked up in the housing stock, but in a private market system for land and housing, the value of the housing is not always measured in terms of its use as shelter and residence, but in terms of the amount received in market exchange, which may be affected by external factors such as speculation. In many inner city areas at the present time, houses patently possess little or no exchange value. This does not mean, however, that they have no use value. As a consequence, we are throwing away use value because we cannot establish exchange values (see chapter 5). This waste would not occur under a socialized housing market system and it is one of the costs we bear for clinging tenaciously to the notion of private property. It has, of course, been an assumption of economic theory for some time that use value is embodied in exchange value. While the two are obviously related, the nature of the relationship depends upon who is doing the using. In the inner city housing market we get quite different use values when we contrast the landlord, who uses the house as a source of income, and a tenant, who is interested in shelter.

This argument with respect to the Alonso–Muth residential land-use theory is over-simplistic. Since it is frequently the case

138

that a mechanism which is assumed for the purposes of the theory is not necessarily the same as the real mechanisms which generate results in accordance with the theory, it would be dangerous indeed to point immediately to competitive market processes as being the root cause of ghetto formation. All a successful test of the theory should do, therefore, is to alert us to the possibility that it is the competitive market mechanism which is at fault. We need to examine this mechanism in some detail.

A market functions under conditions of scarcity. Put another way, the allocation of scarce resources is the foundation for the market economy. It is thus important for us to look again (see above pp. 80–86; 114) at the content of the two concepts "resource" and "scarcity". Geographers have long recognized that a resource is a technical and social appraisal (Spoehr, 1956). This means that materials and people become natural and human resources only when we possess the appropriate technology and social form to be able to make use of them. Uranium became a resource with technological advances in nuclear physics, and people become resources when they are forced to sell their labour on the market in order to survive (this is the real content of the term human resources). The concept of scarcity, likewise, does not arise naturally, but becomes relevant only in terms of social action and social objectives, (Pearson, 1957). Scarcity is socially defined and not naturally determined. A market system becomes possible under conditions of resource scarcity, for only under these conditions can price-fixing commodity exchange markets arise. The market system is a highly decentralized control device for the coordination and integration of economic action. The extension of this coordinative ability has historically allowed an immense increase in the production of wealth. We therefore find a paradox, namely that wealth is produced under a system which relies upon scarcity for its functioning. It follows that if scarcity is eliminated, the market economy, which is the source of productive wealth under capitalism, will collapse. Yet capitalism is forever increasing its productive capacity. To resolve this dilemma many institutions and mechanisms are formed to ensure that scarcity does not disappear. In fact many institutions are geared to the maintenance of scarcity (universities being a prime example, although this is always done in the name of "quality"). Other

139

mechanisms ensure control over the flow of other factors of production. Meanwhile, the increasing productive power has to find an outlet and hence the process of waste (on military ventures, space programmes, and the like) and the process of need creation. What this suggests, of course, is that scarcity cannot be eliminated without also eliminating the market economy. In an advanced productive society, such as the United States, the major barrier to eliminating scarcity lies in the complicated set of interlocking institutions (financial, judicial, political, educational, and so on) which support the market process. Let us examine how this situation is revealed in the inner city housing market.

There are some curious features about ghetto housing. One paradox is that the areas of greatest overcrowding are also the areas with the largest number of vacant houses. There are about 5,000 vacant structures in Baltimore—a good many of which are in reasonable condition—and they are all located in areas of greatest overcrowding. Other cities are experiencing something similar. The same areas are characterized by a large proportion of houses being let go in lieu of property taxes. Landlords in the inner-city housing market, contrary to popular opinion, are not making huge profits. In fact, the evidence suggests that they are making less than they would elsewhere in the housing market (see Sternlieb, 1966; Grigsby *et al.*, 1971) Some are unethical, of course, but good, rational, ethical landlord behaviour provides a relatively low rate of return. Yet the rents such landlords charge are very high relative to the quality of the accommodations, while properties, if they do change hands, do so at negligible prices. The banks, naturally, have good rational business reasons for not financing mortgages in inner city areas. There is a greater uncertainty in the inner city and the land is, in any case, frequently regarded as "ripe" for redevelopment. The fact that failure to finance mortgages makes it even riper is undoubtedly understood by the banking institutions, since there are good profits to be reaped by redevelopment under commercial uses. Given the drive to maximize profits, this decision cannot be regarded as unethical. In fact, it is a general characteristic of ghetto housing that if we accept the mores of normal, ethical, entrepreneurial behaviour, there is no way in which we can blame anyone for the objective social conditions which all are willing to characterize as appalling and wasteful of potential housing resources. It is a situation in which we can find all kinds of contradictory statements "true". Consequently, it seems impossible to find a policy within the existing economic and institutional framework which is capable of rectifying these conditions. Federal subsidies to private housing fail; rent subsidies are quickly absorbed by market adjustments; and public housing has little impact because it is too small in quantity, too localized in distribution (usually in those areas where the poor are forced to live anyway) and devised for use by the lowest classes in society only. Urban renewal merely moves the problem around and in some cases does more harm than good.

Engels, in a set of essays entitled *The Housing Question*, published in 1872, predicted that this was the impasse into which capitalist solutions to housing problems would inevitably lead. Theoretically, his prediction can be derived from criticizing von Thünen's analysis in exactly the same way as Marx criticized Ricardo's. Since the conceptualization of rent in von Thünen's model (and in the Alonso–Muth model) is essentially the same as Ricardo's (it merely arises under somewhat different circumstances), we can use Marx's (*Capital* volume 3; *Theories of Surplus Value* Part 2) arguments with respect to it directly. Rent according to Marx, was but one manifestation of surplus value under capitalist institutions (such as private property), and the nature of rent could not be understood independently of this fact. To regard rent as something "in itself", independent of other facets of the mode of production and independent of capitalist institutions is to commit a conceptual error. It is precisely this error which is committed in the Alonso–Muth formulations. Further, this "error" is manifest in the capitalist market process itself, for it requires that rents (or return on capital) be maximized rather than realizing a maximum social surplus value. Since rent is merely one possible and partial manifestation of surplus value, the drive to maximize rent rather than the surplus value which gives rise to it is bound to create tensions in the capitalist economy. In fact it sets in motion forces which are antagonistic to the realization of surplus value itself—hence, the decline in production which results as potential work forces are separated from work places by land-use changes brought about both by commercial interests seeking to maximize the return on the land under their control, and by communities' seeking to maximize their available tax bases. Engels, in *The Housing Question* (1872), pointed to the whole gamut of consequences which flowed from this sort of competitive market process.

"The growth of the big modern cities gives the land in certain areas, particularly in those which are centrally situated, an artificial and colossally increasing value; the buildings erected on these areas depress this value, instead of increasing it, because they no longer correspond to the changed circumstances. They are pulled down and replaced by others. This takes place above all with worker's houses which are situated centrally and whose rents, even with the greatest overcrowding, can never, or only very slowly, increase above a certain maximum. They are pulled down and in their stead shops, warehouses and public buildings are erected." (p. 23.)

This process (which is clearly apparent in every contemporary city) results from the necessity to realize a rate of return on a parcel of land which is consistent with its location rent. It does not necessarily have anything to do with facilitating production. The process is also consistent with certain other pressures.

"Modern natural science has proved that so-called 'poor districts' in which the workers are crowded together are the breeding places of all those epidemics which from time to time afflict our towns. . . . Capitalist rule cannot allow itself the pleasure of creating epidemic diseases among the working class with impunity; the consequences fall back on it and the angel of death rages in its ranks as ruthlessly as in the ranks of the workers. As soon as this fact had been scientifically established the philanthropic bourgeoisie began to compete with one another in noble efforts on behalf of the health of their workers. Societies were founded, books were written, proposals drawn up, laws debated and passed, in order to close the sources of the ever-recurring epidemics. The housing conditions of the workers were examined and attempts were made to remedy the most crying evils. . . . Government Commissions were appointed to inquire into the hygienic conditions of the working classes." (p. 43.)

Today it is social pathology—drugs and crime—which is important, but the problem does not seem essentially different. The solutions devised still have the same characteristics. Engels states:

"In reality the bourgeoisie has only one method of solving the housing question after *its* fashion—that is to say, of solving it in such a way that the solution continually reproduces the question anew. This method is called 'Haussmann'. . . . By 'Haussmann' I mean the practice which has now become general of making breaches in the working class quarters of our big towns, and particularly in areas which are centrally situated, quite apart from whether this is done from considerations of public health and for beautifying the town, or owing to the demand for big centrally situated business premises, or owing to traffic requirements, such as the laying down of railways, streets (which sometimes appear to have the strategic aim of making barricade fighting more difficult). . . . No matter how different the reasons may be, the result is everywhere the same; the scandalous alleys disappear to the accompaniment of lavish self-praise from the bourgeoisie on account of this tremendous success, but they appear again immediately somewhere else and often in the immediate neighborhood! . . . The breeding places of disease, the infamous holes and cellars in which the capitalist mode of production confines our workers night after night, are not abolished; they are merely *shifted elsewhere*! The same economic necessity which produced them in the first place, produces them in the next place also. As long as the capitalist mode of production continues to exist, it is folly to hope for an isolated solution of the housing question or of any other social question affecting the fate of the workers. The solution lies in the abolition of the capitalist mode of production and the appropriation of all the means of life and labour by the working class itself." (pp. 74–7.)

The experience gained from implementing urban policies in contemporary American cities indicates some disturbing similarities to Engels's account, and it is difficult to avoid concluding that the inherent contradiction in the capitalist market mechanism contributes to it. Therefore, there is good reason to believe that our initial suspicion is correct and that the market mechanism is the culprit in a sordid drama. If we think in these terms, we can explain why almost all policies devised for the inner city have both desirable and undesirable outcomes. If we "urban renew", we merely move the poverty around; if we don't, we merely sit by and watch decay. If we prevent block-busting, we also prevent Blacks from getting housing. The frustration consequent upon such a situation can easily lead to contradictory conclusions. The poor can be blamed for conditions (a conclusion which Banfield finds appropriate), and we can institute policies based on "benign neglect" which will at least not provoke the kinds of questions which policy failures inevitably raise. It is therefore interesting to note that urban policy at the present time appears to involve a shift in emphasis from trying to save the inner cities (where programmes are doomed to failure) to trying to preserve the "gray areas" where the market system is still sufficiently vigorous to make it possible to achieve some degree of success. Whether such a policy will prevent disaffection and the spread of decay may be doubted. However, unfortunately it also entails writing off the accumulated use values in the inner cities as well as the fates and lives of those 15–25 million people who are currently condemned to live out their existence in such locations. This seems a high price to pay for merely avoiding a realistic consideration of both the conclusion which Engels reached and the theoretical basis upon which that conclusion rests. The point I am working towards is that although all serious analysts concede the seriousness of the ghetto problem, few call into question the forces which rule the very heart of our economic system. Thus we discuss everything except the basic characteristics of a capitalist market economy. We devise all manner of solutions except those which might challenge the continuance of that economy. Such discussions and solutions serve only to make us look foolish, since they eventually lead us to discover what Engels was only too aware of in 1872—that capitalist solutions provide no foundation for dealing with deteriorated social conditions. They are merely "de-phlogisticated air". We can, if we will, discover oxygen and all that goes with it by subjecting the very basis of our society to a rigorous and critical examination. It is this task which a revolutionary approach to theory must first accomplish. What does this task entail?

Let me say first what it does not entail. It does not entail yet another empirical investigation of the social conditions in the ghettos. In fact, mapping even more evidence of man's patent inhumanity to man is counter-revolutionary in the sense that it allows the bleeding-heart liberal in us to pretend we are contributing to a solution when in fact we are not. This kind of empiricism is irrelevant. There is already enough information in congressional reports, newspapers, books, articles and so on to provide us with all the evidence we need. Our task does not lie here. Nor does it lie in what can only be termed "moral masturbation" of the sort which accompanies the masochistic assemblage of some huge dossier on the daily injustices to the populace of the ghetto, over which we beat our breasts and commiserate with each other before retiring to our fireside comforts. This, too, is counter-revolutionary for it merely serves to expiate guilt without our ever being forced to face the fundamental issues, let alone do anything about them. Nor is it a solution to indulge in that emotional tourism which attracts us to live and work with the poor "for a while" in the hope that we can really help them improve their lot. This, too, is counter-revolutionary—so what if we help a community win a playground in one summer of work to find that the school deteriorates in the fall? These are the paths we should *not* take. They merely serve to divert us from the essential task at hand.

This immediate task is nothing more nor less than the self-conscious and aware construction of a new paradigm for social geographic thought through a deep and profound critique of our existing analytical constructs. This is what we are best equipped to do. We are academics, after all, working with the tools of the academic trade. As such, our task is to mobilize our powers of thought to formulate concepts and categories, theories and arguments, which we can apply to the task of bringing about a humanizing social change. These concepts and categories cannot be formulated in abstraction. They must be forged realistically with respect to the events and actions as they unfold around us. Empirical evidence, the already assembled dossiers, and the experiences gained in the community can and must be used here. But all of those experiences and all of that information means little unless we synthesize it into powerful patterns of thought.

However, our thought cannot rest merely on existing reality. It has to embrace alternatives creatively. We cannot afford to plan for the future on the basis of positivist theory, for to do so would merely reinforce the status quo. Yet, as in the formation of any new paradigm, we must be prepared to incorporate and reassemble all that is useful and valuable within that corpus of theory. We can restructure the formulation of existing theory in the light of possible lines of future action. We can criticize existing theories as "mere apologetics" for the dominant force in our society—the capitalist market system and all its concomitant institutions. In this manner we will be able to establish both the circumstances under which location theory can be used to create better futures, and the circumstances in which it reinforces modes of thought conducive to the maintenance of the status quo. The problem in many cases is not the marginalist method *per se* nor optimizing techniques *per se*, but that these methods are being applied in the wrong context. Pareto optimality as it enters location theory is a counter-revolutionary concept, as is any formulation which calls for the maximization of any one of the partial manifestations of surplus value (such as rent or return on capital investment). Yet programming solutions are clearly extremely relevant devices for understanding how resources can best be mobilized for the production of surplus value. Formulations based on the achievement of equality in distribution are also counter-revolutionary unless they are derived from an understanding of how production is organized to create surplus value. By examining questions such as these, we can at least begin to evaluate existing theory and in the process (who knows?) perhaps begin to derive the lineaments of new theory.

A revolution in scientific thought is accomplished by marshalling concepts and ideas, categories and relationships into such a superior system of thought when judged against the realities which require explanation that we succeed in making all opposition to that system of thought look ludicrous. Since we are, for the most part, our own chief opponents in this matter, many of us will find that a first initial step on this path will be to discomfort ourselves, to make ourselves look ludicrous to ourselves. This is not easy, particularly if we are possessed of intellectual pride. Further, the emergence of a true revolution in geographic thought is bound to be tempered by commitment to revolutionary practice. Certainly, the general acceptance of revolutionary theory will depend upon the strengths and accomplishments of revolutionary practice. There will be many hard personal decisions to make—decisions that require "real" as opposed to "mere liberal" commitment. Many of us will undoubtedly flinch before making such a commitment, for it is indeed very comfortable to be a mere liberal. However, if conditions are as serious as many of us believe, then we will increasingly come to recognize that nothing much can be lost by that kind of commitment and that almost everything stands to be gained should we make it and succeed.

A FURTHER COMMENT ON REVOLUTIONARY AND COUNTER-REVOLUTIONARY THEORIES

Reaction to a circulated version of this paper had indicated a certain ambiguity in the presentation concerning the relationship between disciplinary endeavours and social revolutions in general. This ambiguity requires clarification.

I accept the proposition, put forward by Marx and Engels in *The German Ideology*, that the ruling class produces the ruling ideas in society. This production is not a simple process, of course, but by and large the ideas generated in society are those which are consistent with the interests of those who are in control of the means of production. There is no necessary plot involved (although the control of the media, indoctrination and propaganda often suppress potentially revolutionary ideas). The "hidden hand" is fairly effective at ruling our thoughts as well as our economy. It is not merely ideas and concepts which are produced, however. The whole organization of knowledge (the organization of the learning process, the structure of the educational system, the division of knowledge into distinctive disciplines, and so on) also reflects the ruling interests in society, for these are all part of the process which contributes to the reproduction of society. Graduate students are thus "produced", as are geographers, planners, chemists, doctors, teachers, and the like. This is not to say that there cannot be considerable diversity in the particular forms of academic organization or in the sentiments expressed. But it is to say that whatever the form it must be such that it satisfies the primary need to perpetuate society in its existing state. This means that *in general* all knowledge is suffused with apologetics for the *status quo* and with counter-revolutionary formulations which function to frustrate the investigation of alternatives. It also means that the organization of knowledge (including the disciplinary divisions) has an inherently *status quo* or counter-revolutionary posture. The pursuit of knowledge and the organization and dissemination of it are inherently conservative.

Within disciplines we must therefore expect that most theoretical formulations will be *status quo* or counter-revolutionary. These formulations characteristically reify (and thereby tacitly legitimize) an existing situation in concept form or else (whenever appropriate) divert attention from real issues to issues which are irrelevant or of minor significance. The latter tactic gives a certain unreal quality to theory—a quality which is particularly marked in many of the theories in the contemporary social sciences. It consequently takes an act of revolutionary consciousness for the academic to divest himself or herself of counter-revolutionary presuppositions in order to catch up with the realities we are purportedly trying to analyse and understand. It takes a similar effort to recognize the apologetic quality of much of our theory or to adapt *status quo* theory to deal with changed circumstances. Such acts of revolutionary consciousness are capable of generating revolutions in thought within a discipline. It is instructive to recall, for example, that the fundamental and quite revolutionary formulations of August Lösch in the field of location theory sprang from his sense of "real duty . . . not to explain our sorry reality, but to improve it" (1954, 4).

Revolutions in thought are also necessary to maintain manipulation and control under changed circumstances for those in control of the means of production. The Keynesian revolution was necessary because the *status quo* theories of the preceding generation were no longer effective tools for use under changed circumstances. Revolutions in thought are thus possible and necessary without real revolutions in social practice. I do not want to minimize the effort involved in or the significance of internally generated revolutions in disciplinary thought. But, if such revolutions in thought are to be anything more than adaptations whereby those in control in society perpetuate their ability to control, they must be viewed as the beginning of a struggle to bring into being a more complete revolutionary theory which can be validated through revolutionary practice. In this it has first to be recognized that *all* disciplinary boundaries are themselves counter-revolutionary. The division of knowledge allows the body politic to divide and rule as far as the application of knowledge is concerned. It also renders much of the academic community impotent, for it traps us into thinking that we can understand reality only through a synthesis of what each discipline has to say about its particular segment and we quickly shrink away from what is so clearly an impossible task. Inter-, multi-, and cross-disciplinary studies are potentially revolutionary, but never really succeed—the odds against them working are just too great. Reality has, therefore, to be approached directly rather than through the formulations of academic disciplines. We have to think in non- or meta-disciplinary terms if we are to think academically about our problems at all. Genuine revolutionary formulations cannot have a specific disciplinary basis—they must be located with respect to all relevant aspects of material reality. Unfortunately, most of us in academia have been trained to think in terms of (and to locate our identity with respect to) specific disciplines. Geography has less of a problem than most in this regard since most geographers fortunately have little idea as to what geography is and are forced to make heavy use of other disciplines in the course of their work. However, all academics have to "untrain" themselves in some sense before they are really in a position to confront the realities around them in any direct way.

By confronting our situation directly we become active participants in the social process. The intellectual task is to identify real choices as they are immanent in an existing situation and to devise ways of validating or invalidating these choices through action. This intellectual task is not a task specific to a group of people called "intellectuals", for all individuals are capable of thought and all individuals think about their situation. A social movement becomes an academic movement and an academic movement becomes a social movement when all elements in the population recognize the need to reconcile analysis and action. Gramsci (in *Selections from Prison Notebooks*) provides an excellent analysis of the role of intellectual activity in revolutionary movements.

It is realistic, however, to accept that there is an immediate task within geography. This task is to abjure and reject *status quo* and counter-revolutionary formulations. We are scarcely in a position to identify wheat from chaff in our thought and it will take some effort a-winnowing to do so. But it makes sense to pursue this task only if we bear in mind the broader context of social movement and macro-change in which we are working.

What we do in geography is ultimately irrelevant and it is therefore unnecessary to be concerned with some parochialist struggle for power within a particular discipline. My appeal for a revolution in geographic thought must therefore be interpreted as an appeal for a reformulation of geographic theory designed to "bring us up to date" with the realities we seek to understand, as well as to help with the broader social task of stimulating a political awareness in that segment of the population called "geographers". My comments on social revolution were designed to point out that within-disciplinary activity must be formulated in the broader social context and that it must also ultimately be replaced by a real social movement. I regret that this distinction may not be clear in the original presentation.

I contend that there are a number of positive tasks to be performed *within* our discipline. We have to clear away the counter-revolutionary clutter that surrounds us. We also have to recognize the *status quo* apologetic quality of the rest of our theory. These two tasks can in fact be derived by setting out a number of propositions about the nature of theory. Let me set these down as well as I can:

1   Each discipline locates problems and solutions through a study of real conditions mediated through a theoretical framework consisting of categorizations, propositions, suggested relationships and general conclusions.

2   There are three kinds of theory:

(i) *Status quo theory*—a theory which is grounded in the reality it seeks to portray and which accurately represents the phenomena with which it deals at a particular moment in time. But, by having ascribed a universal truth status to the propositions it contains, it is capable of yielding prescriptive policies which can result only in the perpetuation of the *status quo*.

(ii) *Counter-revolutionary theory*—a theory which may or may not *appear* grounded in the reality it seeks to portray, but which obscures, be-clouds and generally obfuscates (either by design or accident) our ability to comprehend that reality. Such a theory is usually attractive and hence gains general currency because it is logically coherent, easily manipulable, aesthetically appealing, or just new and fashionable; but it is in some way quite divorced from the reality it purports to represent. A counter-revolutionary theory automatically frustrates either the creation or the implementation of viable policies. It is therefore a perfect device for non-decision making, for it diverts attention from fundamental issues to superficial or non-existent issues. It can also function as spurious support and legitimization for counter-revolutionary actions designed to frustrate needed change.

(*iii*) *Revolutionary theory*—a theory which is firmly grounded in the reality it seeks to represent, the individual propositions of which are ascribed a contingent truth status (they are in the process of becoming true or false dependent upon the circumstances). A revolutionary theory is dialectically formulated and it can encompass conflict and contradiction within itself. A revolutionary theory offers real choices for future moments in the social process by identifying immanent choices in an existing situation. The implementation of these choices serves to validate the theory and to provide the grounds for the formulation of new theory. A revolutionary theory consequently holds out the prospect for creating truth rather than finding it.

3   Individual propositions and, indeed, whole theoretical structures are not necessarily *in themselves* in any one of the above categories. They only enter a category in the process of use in a particular social situation. Otherwise propositions and theories remain abstracted, idealized and ethereal formulations which possess form but not content (they are words and symbols merely). Counter-revolutionary formulations are frequently kept permanently in this content-less state.

4   A theoretical formulation can, as circumstances change and depending upon its application, move or be moved from one category to another. This suggests two dangers which must be avoided:

(*i*) *Counter-revolutionary cooptation*—the perversion of a theory from a revolutionary to a counter-revolutionary state.

(*ii*) *Counter-revolutionary stagnation*—the stagnation of a revolutionary theory through failure to reformulate it in the light of new circumstances and situations—by this means a revolutionary theory may become a *status quo* theory.

But there are also two important revolutionary tasks:

(*iii*) *Revolutionary negation*—taking counter-revolutionary theory and exposing it for what if really is.

(*iv*) *Revolutionary reformulation*—taking *status quo* or *counter-revolutionary* formulations, setting them into motion or providing them with real content, and using them to identify real choices immanent in the present.

5   These tasks can be pursued and these dangers can be avoided only if the counter-revolutionary posture of the organized pursuit of knowledge (and in particular disciplinary division) is recognized and reality is confronted directly.

Chapter 5

Use Value, Exchange Value and the Theory of Urban Land Use

"The word VALUE, it is to be observed, has two different meanings, and sometimes expresses the utility of some particular object, and sometimes the power of purchasing other goods which the possession of that object conveys. The one may be called 'value in use', the other, 'value in exchange'. The things which have the greatest value in use have frequently little or no value in exchange; and on the contrary, those which have the greatest value in exchange have frequently little or no value in use." (Adam Smith, *The Wealth of Nations*, 1776, 28.)

The distinction between use value and exchange value was a prevailing source of concern for the political economists of the nineteenth century. It provides the starting point for Ricardo's *Principles of Political Economy and Taxation* as well as for Marx's *Capital*. Jevons (1871, 128-44) set out to clarify what he correctly perceived as certain ambiguities and inconsistencies in both Smith's and Ricardo's discussions on the matter, but in the process he eliminated many of the interesting and socially relevant issues which attached to it. He equated use value to "total utility" and exchange value to "the ratio of exchange". The latter then was related to the former via a formal definition— a definition which Jevons regarded as the "keystone" for all economic thought:

"The ratio of exchange of any two commodities will be the reciprocal of the ratio of the final degrees of utility of the quantities of commodity available for consumption after the exchange is completed."

And so Jevons transformed political economy into economics with its emphasis on sophisticated theoretical devices for marginal analysis. These sophisticated devices, insightful as they

153

may prove in certain respects, turn out to be weak tools for handling some of the important and relevant problems posed in classical political economy. Consequently, these problems have the awkward habit of arising again in new guises. They permeate much of welfare economics and take on quite specific form in arguments over the specification of social welfare, the provision of public goods, the nature of consumers' and producers' surpluses, the nature and appropriate measure of capital, etc. They also arise in the policy arena. It is evident, for example, that the social concept of need and the economic concept of demand are two quite different things and that they exist in a peculiar relationship to each other. It seems relevant, therefore, to resurrect the distinction between use value and exchange value in its original form and to enquire whether the classical debate can provide any enlightenment with respect to contemporary urban problems.

Marx made several significant contributions to the classical debate. These contributions effectively resolve the ambiguities found in the discussions by Smith and Ricardo, but indicate a path for economic analysis quite different from that laid out by Jevons. Part of the difficulty posed by Marx's analysis lies in his highly original way of using words. Ollman (1971) has recently provided a detailed discussion on this topic. The difficulty arises because Marx uses words in a relational and dialectical way. Use value and exchange have no meaning in and of themselves. They do not refer, as they appear to in other discussions of the time, to two fixed but separate scaling systems (possessing universal attributes) which either "exist" in some *a priori* Kantian sense or can be discovered through an empirical investigation of human behaviour. For Marx, they take on meaning (come into existence if you will) through their relationship to each other (and to other concepts) and through their relationship to the situations and circumstances under discussion (Ollman, 1971, 179–89). The term "use value" can thus be applied to all manner of objects, activities and events in particular social and natural settings. It can refer to religious ideology, social institutions, work, language, commodities, recreation, and so on. It is even reasonable to consider the use value of the concept "use value"—indeed, this is what this essay is partly about.

Marx paid greatest attention to the meaning of use value and exchange value in capitalist society. In both the opening chapters of *Capital* and in *A Contribution to the Critique of Political Economy* he details the meaning of these concepts in the capitalist context. In the latter work (which we will draw upon here) Marx begins by accepting the proposition that every commodity has a two-fold aspect in bourgeois capitalist society—use value and exchange value. He then asserts that "a use value has value only in use and is realized in the process of consumption." Use values consequently "serve directly as means of existence." Employed in this manner, however, "use value as such lies outside the sphere of investigation of political economy." Marx then goes on to consider exchange value. This, he suggests, at first sight appears as a "quantitative relation, the proportion in which use values are exchanged for each other." But, in the manner typical of Marx, he then goes on to enquire as to the forces that yield up exchange value in capitalist society. He concludes that the creation of exchange value resides in the social process of applying socially necessary labour to objects of nature to yield up material objects (commodities) suitable for consumption (use) by man. Marx then brings use value and exchange value into a relationship with each other. It is interesting to contrast this method with that of Jevons who appealed to the marginalist assumption. Marx writes:

"So far, two aspects of the commodity—use value and exchange value—have been examined, but each one separately. The commodity, however, is the direct unity of use value and exchange value, and at the same time it is a commodity only in relation to other commodities. The *exchange process* of commodities is the *real* relation that exists between them. This is the social process which is carried on by individuals independently of one another, but they take part in it only as commodity owners. . . . The commodity *is* a use value, but as a commodity it is simultaneously *not* a use value. It would not be a commodity if it were a use value for its owner, that is, a direct means for the satisfaction of his own needs. For its owner it is on the contrary a *non-use value*, that is merely the physical depository of exchange value or simply a *means of exchange*. Use value as an active carrier of exchange value becomes a means of exchange. The commodity is a use value for its owner only so far as it is an exchange value. The commodity therefore has still to become a use value . . . a use value for others. Since it is not a use value to its owner, it must be a use value to other owners of commodities. If this is not the case, then the labour expended on it was useless labour and the result accordingly is not a commodity. . . . To become a use value, the commodity must encounter the particular need which it can satisfy. Thus the use values of commodities become use values by a mutual exchange of places: they pass from the hands of those for whom they were means of exchange into the hands of those for whom they serve as consumer goods. Only as a result of the universal alienation of commodities does the labour contained in them become useful labour. . . . To become use values commodities must be altogether alienated; they must enter into the exchange process; exchange however is concerned merely with their aspect as exchange values. Hence, only by being realized as exchange values can they be realized as use values." (*A Contribution to the Critique of Political Economy*, 41–3.)

Marx's technique here is to bring use value and exchange value into a dialectical relationship with each other through the form they assume in the commodity. The commodity also expresses a set of social relationships. The "universal alienation" of which Marx writes is explained in greater detail in *The Economic and Philosophic Manuscripts of 1844* (pp. 106–19). Marx there argues that human beings have, through history, become progressively more alienated (1) from the product of labour (from the world of objects and from nature), (2) from the activity of production (as control is lost over the means of production), (3) from their own inherent "species being" (which stems from the sense in which human beings are a part of nature and therefore have a human nature) and (4) from each other (as each individual assumes an identity and is forced to compete rather than to cooperate with others). These aspects of "universal alienation" are all present in the commodity. The commodity as a simple object or "thing in itself" is replaced in Marx's analysis by the commodity as an expression of innumerable social relationships which, through a simple changing of hands, can undergo a radical transformation of meaning. The "commodity" subsumes within itself everything else that is happening in the social situation in which it is produced and consumed. It is in this dialectical and relational style of analysis that Marx parts company from traditional analyses. There is undoubtedly both resistance to and resentment at this mode of approach: Joan Robinson (quoted by Ollman, 1971, 188) complains, for example, at "Hegel putting his nose between me and Ricardo." But a careful reading of the above passage suggests that Marx's formulation is not unreasonable. It yields more adequate insights in certain respects than does the stratagem devised by Jevons. The latter supposes two separate value systems which can be brought into a functional relationship with each other by a theoretical device. This supposition has yielded important results (particularly in marginalist economic theory), but in the context of use value and exchange value it has led economic theory into either somewhat arid discussions on the mathematical properties of utility functions or into reliance on the rather unrevealing notion of "revealed preference" which simply allows that people behave in the way they behave. Geographers, planners and sociologists, on the other hand, have treated of commodities in their use value aspects only or, if they sought for analytical enlightenment, have borrowed unquestioningly from the marginal analytics. Use value provides the conceptual underpinning of traditional geographical and sociological treatments of land-use problems, but it is used in such a way that land-use studies lie "outside of the sphere of investigation of political economy". The Marxist device for bringing use value and exchange value into a dialectical relationship with each other demands consideration for it offers the dual prospect of breathing new life into geographical and sociological studies of land use, and of building a bridge between spatial and economic approaches to urban land-use problems. The latter prospect may be as beneficial to contemporary economics as it is to contemporary spatial analysis.

THE USE VALUE AND EXCHANGE VALUE OF LAND AND
IMPROVEMENTS

Land and the improvements thereon are, in the contemporary capitalist economy, commodities. But land and improvements are not ordinary commodities: thus the concepts of use value and exchange value take on their meaning in a rather special situation. Six features require particular attention.

(i) Land and improvements cannot be moved around at

will and this differentiates them from other commodities such as wheat, automobiles, and the like. Land and improvements have a fixed location. Absolute location confers monopoly privileges upon the person who has the rights to determine use at that location. It is an important attribute of physical space that no two people or things can occupy exactly the same location and this principle when institutionalized as private property, has very important ramifications for urban land-use theory and for the meaning of value in use and value in exchange.

(ii) Land and improvements are commodities which no individual can do without. I cannot exist without occupying space; I cannot work without occupying a location and making use of material objects located there; and I cannot live without a dwelling of some sort. It is impossible to do without some quantity of these commodities and this places strong constraints upon consumer choice with respect to them.

(iii) Land and improvements change hands relatively infrequently. In certain types of business operation (particularly when heavy fixed capital investment is involved), in the layout of many public facilities (roads, schools, hospitals, etc.), and in stable sectors of the owner-occupier housing market, land and improvements take on the commodity form very infrequently even though they are constantly in use. In the rental sector of the housing market, in unstable owner-occupied areas, and in the retail sector, land and improvements take on the commodity form much more frequently. The dialectical interpenetration of use value and exchange value in commodity form is not manifest to the same degree nor does it occur with the same frequency in all sections of the urban economy.

(iv) Land is something permanent and the life-expectancy of improvements is often considerable. Land and improvements, and the rights of use attached to them, therefore provide the opportunity to store wealth (both for individuals and for society). Many capital goods have this quality to them, but land and structures have historically been the single most important repository of stored assets. Land is peculiar in a separate respect, however, for it does not require upkeep in

158

order to continue its potential for use; there is, as Ricardo pointed out, something "original and indestructible" about it. It is therefore difficult to analyse current land-use patterns without taking this feature into account. In a capitalist economy an individual has a dual interest in property both as current and future use value and as potential or actual exchange value both now and in the future.

(v) Market exchange occurs at an instant in time, but use extends over a period of time. This aspect of the commodity is not unique to land and improvements, but the ratio of frequency of exchange to duration of use is peculiarly low. Consumption rights for a relatively long period of time are purchased by a large outlay at one point in time. Consequently, financial institutions must play a very important role in the functioning of the market for urban land and property in a capitalist economy.

(vi) Land and improvements have numerous different uses which are not mutually exclusive for the user. A house, for example, can be used in many different ways simultaneously. It provides

1 shelter
2 a quantity of space for exclusive use by the occupants
3 privacy
4 a relative location which is accessible to work places, retail opportunities, social services, family and friends, and so on (and this includes the possibility for place of work etc., to be actually in the house)
5 a relative location which is proximate to sources of pollution, areas of congestion, sources of crime and hazard, people viewed with distaste, and so on
6 a neighbourhood location that has physical, social and symbolic (status) characteristics
7 a means for storing and enhancing wealth.

All of these uses, when taken together, constitute the use value of the house for the occupant(s). This use value is not the same for all people in comparable dwellings, nor is it constant over time for the same person in the same dwelling. Swinging singles, young married couples with children, old retired people, sick people, sports buffs and gardeners, all have different needs and consume different aspects of housing in different quantities in their daily lives. Each individual and group will determine use value differently. It is only when the characteristics of people are brought together with the characteristics of housing that use value takes on its real meaning.

Use values reflect a mix of social needs and requirements, personal idiosyncracies, cultural habits, life-style habits, and the like, which is not to say that they are arbitrarily established through "pure" consumer sovereignty. But use values are basically formed with respect to what might be called the "life support system" of the individual. Use value, conceived of in this everyday sense, "lies outside of the sphere of political economy". It is essential to grasp how this life support system works. But no matter how sophisticated our understanding of it, we cannot generate an adequate theory of urban land use out of it. For this to emerge we must focus attention on those catalytic moments in the urban land-use decision process when use value and exchange value collide to make commodities out of the land and the improvements thereon. At these moments decisions concerning the allocation of activities and resources to land are made. And it is particularly important to an understanding of what happens at those moments to bear in mind the very special characteristics of both land and the improvements with which that land is blessed.

URBAN LAND-USE THEORY

Contemporary urban land-use theory is in a peculiar state. Analysis typically concentrates either on use value characteristics (through the study of the life-support system) or on exchange value characteristics (the market exchange system), but there is little or no conception as to how the two may be related to each other.

Geographers and sociologists, for example, have evolved a variety of land-use theories which focus on patterns of use. The concentric zone, multiple nuclei and sectoral "theories" are nothing more than generalized descriptions of patterns of use in the urban space economy. The tradition of research in factorial ecology attempts the same thing with much greater sophistication (and some enlightenment), while the work of other sociologists such as Gans (1970) and Suttles (1968) brings a certain amount of realism to the somewhat arid statistical summaries of factorial ecology. Various other devices exist for generalizing statistically about the macro-patterns of urban land use. The negative exponential "model" of population-density (and land-rent) decline with distance from the urban centre has been investigated in some detail. Various models out of the social physics tradition—of which Wilson's (1970) formulations are surely the most sophisticated to date—have also been used to characterize the macro-characteristics of activities and uses in the urban system. All these formulations, however, amount to sophisticated analyses of patterns of use which differ in degree, but not in kind, to those expressed in a land-use map or in a description of daily activity as it unfolds in the life-support system that is the city. A great deal can be gained by such descriptions. But studies such as this cannot yield up a theory of urban land use.

By way of contrast, land-use theories generated out of neo-classical micro-economics focus upon exchange value, although in so doing they appeal explicitly to the strategy pioneered by Jevons through which use value (utility) is equated to exchange value at the margin. Alonso (1964), Beckmann (1969), Mills (1967; 1969) and Muth (1969) presume utility-maximizing behaviour on the part of individuals. In the housing market this is taken to mean that individuals trade off the quantity of housing (usually conceived of as space), accessibility (usually cost of transport to place of employment), and the need for all other goods and services, within an overall budget constraint. It is presumed that consumers are indifferent with respect to certain combinations of space and accessibility. It is also presumed that individuals bid for housing at a location up until the point where the extra amount of "satisfaction" gained from a move is exactly equal to the marginal utility of laying out an extra quantity of money. From this conceptualization it is possible to derive equilibrium conditions in the urban housing market—conditions which are held to be Pareto opti-mal. This process can be modelled in a variety of ways. Herbert and Stevens (1960) formulate it as a programming problem in which households seek their best "residential bundle" of goods out of a general market basket of all goods subject to cost and budget constraints. Muth (1969) provides particularly sophisticated formulations in which he attempts to bring together analyses of the production of housing, the allocation of existing housing stock, the allocation of land to uses, and utility-maximizing behaviour on the part of individual consumers with different income characteristics and diverse preferences for housing. Other writers have examined the competition for space and location among different uses (commercial, industrial, residential, etc.).

It is tempting to view this corpus of urban land-use theory as providing an adequate framework for analysing the market forces shaping urban land use. Unfortunately these theories abstract from questions of use value and do as little to bring use and exchange value together as do the formulations of geographers and sociologists, who start with use value as their basic consideration. The fact that utility-maximizing models contain a crude assumption concerning the relationship between use value and exchange value should not deceive us into thinking that real problems have been resolved. This is not to condemn the models derived out of micro-economics as useless. They shed light on the exchange value aspect of urban land-use theory in much the same way that geographers and sociologists have shed light on the use value aspects. But an adequate urban land-use theory requires a synthesis of both these two aspects in such a way that we grasp the social process of commodity exchange in the sense that Marx conceived of it. This theory will not be easy to construct, particularly in view of the peculiar qualities of land and improvements and the diverse uses to which these may be put.

MICRO-ECONOMIC URBAN LAND-USE THEORY

A critical appraisal of the micro-economic approach will help us to identify what the problem is. Kirwan and Martin (1971) have recently reviewed the contribution of this approach to our understanding of residential land uses, and for the sake of brevity I will concentrate on this aspect of urban land-use theory. It should be evident that my remarks can in principle be generalized to all other aspects of urban land use.

The assumptions typically built into the micro-economic approach are obviously unrealistic, and are generally admitted to be so. But then this is true of all micro-economic models of this sort. The question is, how and to what degree is the general conceptualization unrealistic? We can start to answer this by comparing the general nature of the results with the reality we are seeking to understand. The remarkable fact here is that although the theories derived analytically out of the micro-economic framework cannot be regarded as "true" in the sense that they have been subjected to rigorous empirical testing, these theories of urban land use (although normative) yield results which are not too much at variance with the realities of city structure. Put another way, the case for regarding them as empirically relevant devices may not have been proved, but it has not been disproved either. These theories may thus be regarded as perhaps not unreasonable general characterizations of the forces shaping urban land use. There are, however, grounds upon which this interim conclusion may be criticized: we will now explore them.

There are numerous and diverse actors in the housing market and each group has a distinctive way of determining use value and exchange value. Let us consider the perspective of each of the main groups operating in the housing market.

(i) The *occupiers* of housing consume the various facets of housing according to their desires and needs. The use value of the house is determined by the coming together of a personal or household situation and a particular house in a particular location. Owner-occupiers are basically concerned with use values and act accordingly. But, insofar as the house has a use in storing equity, exchange value may become a consideration. We may fix our house up so that we can use it better, or we may modify it with an idea of increasing its exchange value. Owner-occupiers typically become concerned with exchange value at two points—at the time of purchase and when major repairs force them to look to their budget constraints. Renters (and other kinds of tenant) are in a rather different position in that use value provides only limited rationale for action when exchange value goes to the landlord. But all occupiers of housing have a similar concern—to procure use values through laying out exchange value.

(ii) *Realtors* (estate agents) operate in the housing market to obtain exchange value. They realize a profit through buying and selling or through charging transaction costs for their services as intermediaries. Realtors rarely contribute much to the use value of the house (although they may undertake some improvements in certain cases). To realtors the use value of housing lies in the volume of transactions, for it is from these that they gain exchange value. They operate as coordinating entrepreneurs in the housing market, work under competitive pressure and need to reap a certain level of profit. They have an incentive to increase turnover in the housing stock for this leads to an expansion of business. Turnover may be stimulated by ethical or unethical means (blockbusting being a good example of the latter). Realtors can thus play a role on a continuum between passive coordinator of the market through encouraging market activity to forcing it.

(iii) *Landlords* operate, for the most part, with exchange value as their objective. Owner-occupiers who rent out a portion of their house have a dual objective of course, and may be as much motivated by considerations of use value as those who occupy the whole of their property. But professional landlords regard the house as a means of exchange—housing services are exchanged for money. The landlord has two strategies. The first to purchase a property outright and then to rent it out in order to obtain an income from the capital invested in it. The second strategy involves the purchase of a property through mortgage financing: the application of the rental income to servicing the mortgage (together with depreciation allowances and tax breaks) then allows the landlord to increase the net worth of his or her holdings. The first strategy maximizes current income (usually over a short-term time horizon), while the second maximizes the increase in wealth. The choice of strategy has an important impact upon the management of the housing stock, the first strategy tending to lead to rapid obsolescence, the second to good upkeep and maintenance. The choice depends upon the circumstances—the opportunity cost of capital invested in housing as opposed to all other forms of investment, the availability of mortgage financing, and so on. Whatever the strategy, it still remains the case that professional landlords treat housing as a means of exchange and not as a use value for themselves.

(iv) *Developers* and the housing construction industry are involved in the process of creating new use values for others in order to realize exchange values for themselves. The purchase of the land, the preparation of it (particularly the provision of public utilities), and the construction of the housing, require considerable capital outlay in advance of exchange. Firms involved in this process are subject to competitive pressure, and must realize a profit. They therefore have a strong vested interest in bringing into being the use values necessary to sustain their exchange value benefits. There are numerous ways (both legal and illegal) for accomplishing this, and certainly this group in the housing market has a strong vested interest in the process of suburbanization and, to a lesser degree, in processes of rehabilitation and redevelopment. In much the same way that realtors are interested in increased turnover, so developers and construction firms are interested in growth, reconstruction and rehabilitation. Both these groups are interested in use values for others, only in so far as they yield exchange values to themselves.

(v) Financial institutions play an important role in the housing market owing to the particular characteristics of housing. The financing of owner-occupancy, landlord operations, development and new construction, draws heavily upon the resources of banks, insurance companies, building societies and other financial institutions. Some of these institutions are locked into financing in the housing market (the Savings and Loan Associations in the United States for example). But others service all sectors and they tend to allocate their funds to housing insofar as housing yields opportunities for profitable and secure investment relative to other investment opportunities. Fundamentally, the financial institutions are interested in gaining exchange values through financing opportunities for the creation or procurement of use values. But financial institutions as a whole are involved in all aspects of real estate development (industrial, commercial, residential, etc.) and they therefore help to allocate land to uses through their control over financing. Decisions of this sort are plainly geared to profitability and risk-avoidance.

(vi) *Government institutions*—usually called into existence by political processes stemming from the lack of use values available to the consumers of housing—frequently interfere in the housing market. Production of use values through public action (the provision of public housing for example) is a direct form of intervention; but intervention is frequently indirect (particularly in the United States). The latter might take the form of helping the financial institutions, the developers and construction industry to gain exchange values by government action to provide tax shelter, to guarantee profits, or to eliminate risk. It is argued that supporting the market is one way of ensuring the production of use values—unfortunately it does not always work out that way. Government also imposes and administers a variety of institutional constraints on the operation of the housing market (zoning and land-use planning controls being the most conspicuous). Insofar as government allocates many of the services, facilities and access routes, it also contributes indirectly to the use value of housing by shaping the surrounding environment (see chapter 2).

The operations of all these diverse groups in the housing market cannot easily be brought together into one comprehensive framework for analysis. What is a use value for one is an exchange value for another, and each conceives use value differently. The same house can take on a different meaning depending upon the social relationships which individuals, organizations and institutions express in it. A model of the housing market which presumes all housing stock to be allocated among users (whose only differentiating characteristics are income and housing preferences) through utility-maximizing behaviour appears peculiarly restricted in its applicability. Realistic analyses of how urban land-use decisions are made— dating from Hurd's (1903) perceptive analysis—have consequently led Wallace Smith (1970, 40), for example, to conclude that "the traditional concept of 'supply-and-demand equilibrium' is not very relevant to most of the problems or issues which are associated with the housing sector of the economy." It is difficult not to concur with this opinion, for if a commodity depends upon the coming together of use value and exchange value in the social act of exchange, then the things we call land

and housing are apparently very different commodities depending upon the particular interest-group operating in the market. When we introduce the further complexity generated by competition among diverse uses, we may be inclined to extend Wallace Smith's conclusion to urban land-use theory as a whole.

Another general line of criticism of the micro-economic approach to urban land-use theory stems from the fact that it is formulated in a static equilibrium framework. This would be mere churlish criticism, however, if it were only pointed out that the urban land-use system rarely approaches anything like an equilibrium posture and that Pareto optimality is likely never to be achieved. Differential disequilibrium is everywhere evident (see above, chapter 2) and there are too many imperfections, rigidities, and immobilities for the market to work well as a coordinating device. But there is a point of substance here that requires examination. The urban area is built up sequentially over a long period of time and activities and people take up their positions in the urban system sequentially. Once located, activities and people tend to be particularly difficult to move. The simultaneity presupposed in the micro-economic models runs counter to what is in fact a very strong process. This indicates a fatal flaw in the micro-economic formulations—their inability to handle the absolute quality of space which makes land and improvements such peculiar commodities. Most writers either ignore this issue or dismiss it. Muth (1969, 47), for example, holds that:

"Many of the features of city structure and urban land use can be explained without reference to the heritage of the past. To the extent that there is any distinction between land, especially urban land, and other factors of production, such a distinction would seem to arise chiefly from the fact of spatial uniqueness. In fact spatial uniqueness is not as clearly a distinction in kind as one might initially suppose. If labour were not sometimes highly immobile, and hence spatially unique, there would probably be no depressed area or farm problems. And the supply of land with certain spatial characteristics is sometimes increased by filling in areas along waterfronts and more frequently through investment in transport facilities."

This treatment of spatial uniqueness (or absolute space) plainly will not do. Spatial uniqueness cannot be reduced to mere immobility nor to a question merely of transport access.

To say that space has absolute properties is to say that structures, people and land parcels exist in a manner that is mutually exclusive each of the other in a three-dimensional, physical (Euclidean) space. This concept is not *in itself* an adequate conceptualization of space for formulating urban land-use theory. The distance between points is *relative* because it depends upon the means of transportation, on the perception of distance by actors in the urban scene, and so on (see chapter 1). We also have to think *relationally* about space for there is an important sense in which a point in space "contains" all other points (this is the case in the analysis of demographic and retail potential for example and it is also crucial for understanding the determination of land value, as we shall later see). But we cannot ever afford to forget that there cannot be more than one land parcel in *exactly* the same location. This means that all spatial problems have an inherent monopolistic quality to them. Monopoly in absolute space is a condition of existence not something experienced as a deviation from the spaceless world of perfect competition. In capitalist society this characteristic of absolute space is institutionalized through the private property relation, so that "owners" possess monopoly privileges over "pieces" of space. Our attention has therefore to focus on "the realization of this monopoly on the basis of capitalist production" (Marx, *Capital* volume 3, 615–16). The Muth–Alonso models discount the monopoly qualities of space in certain important respects—the analytics in fact depend upon a particular view of space and time as well as on certain abstractions from the institutional setting of a capitalist economy.

We can begin to incorporate considerations stemming from the conception of absolute space if we envision allocation occurring in a sequential manner across an urban space divided into a large but finite number of land parcels. Land-use theory then appears as a sequential space-packing problem (with the possibility of adding space at the periphery). In the housing market with a fixed housing stock the process is analogous to filling up seats sequentially in an empty theatre. The first who enters has n choices, the second has $n-1$, and so on, with the last having no choice. If those who enter do so in order of their bidding power then those with money have more choices, while the poorest take up whatever is left after everyone else has exercised choice. This conceptualization is suggestive—

particularly if it is brought together with the concept of consumers' surplus.

Consumers' surplus is the difference between what an individual actually pays for a good and what he or she would be willing to pay rather than go without it (Hicks, 1941; 1944; Mishan, 1971). This concept does something to retrieve the lost distinction between value in use and value in exchange, although it does so by way of an assumption which allows use value to be estimated in exchange value terms (it is a non-Marxist conceptualization of the matter). Consumers' surplus provides a fundamental but largely unexplored link between locational analysis and welfare economics (Gaffney, 1961; Alonso, 1967, Denike and Parr, 1970). That there are consumers' surpluses in the housing market, for example, is beyond question. The interesting task is to determine how they may be estimated and how the collective consumers' surplus (defined by Hicks as the "amount of money which consumers as a body would have to lose in order to make each of them as badly off as he would be if the commodity disappeared") is distributed among individuals and groups. A differential distribution arises partly because benefits, costs, opportunities, accessibilities and the like, are differentially distributed throughout the man-made resource system that is the city (see chapter 2). Land parcels capture external benefits generated elsewhere and housing occupancy translates these benefits into consumers' surpluses (we are here thinking relationally about land parcels in an absolute space). We will confine attention, however, to the manner in which competitive bidding contributes to the differential distribution of the consumers' surplus.

The simplest way to estimate the consumers' surplus is to equate it with the area under the demand curve and above the competitive equilibrium price line. This estimate is realistic only under certain assumptions (Hicks, 1944), but it will suffice for our purpose. Let us proceed as if there are distinctive income groups in society with all groups having a homogeneous taste with respect to housing services. If the marginal utility of housing to all consumers remains constant, then the demand curve will push outwards from the origin with increasing income—in other words, the consumers' surplus will increase with increasing income of the group. The consumers' surplus may also increase disproportionately with increasing ability to bid. The richest group has to bid only a small amount more than the next richest to obtain the rights to occupancy in the prime location and the best housing. Since income distribution is highly skewed in capitalist societies and the number of good locations is presumably limited, it is very possible that the quantity of consumers' surplus will decline disproportionately with a declining income of the group. Also, since ability to bid depends on credit rating, there is a definite decline in that ability with declining collateral. As a consequence we may find the richest group in the United States paying on average say, $50,000 for houses that they would be prepared (on average) to bid $75,000 for rather than do without, while poorer groups may be paying $5,000 for housing that they might each be prepared to pay $6,000 for (yielding a consumer's surplus of $25,000 in the first case and a mere $1,000 in the second). Whether the rich groups gain more consumers' surplus per dollar of outlay on housing than do the poor is a matter for empirical investigation.

In a sequential allocation of a fixed housing stock in order of competitive bidding power, the poorest group, because it enters the housing market last, has to face producers of housing services who are in a quasi-monopolistic position. Those who arrive last in the bidding process can therefore be forced to yield up part of their consumers' surplus as producers' surplus to realtors, landlords, and the like. Lack of choice makes the poor more prone to being squeezed by quasi-monopolistic policies (a process which is not confined to the housing market but which extends to job and retail opportunities, and so on). If producers' surpluses can simply be interpreted as rents or profits, as Mishan (1968) suggests, then excess profits and excess rents can accrue more easily in this sector of the housing market. These excess rents and profits may be reduced by competition, but for the consumer the result is the same—the consumers' surplus is diminished. In this manner we may anticipate realtor exploitation (excessive mark-ups on house sales) and landlord exploitation (excessively high rents) in the poorest areas even if the realtors and landlords themselves do not individually make excessive profits. This peculiar condition can arise when producers compete with each other over space for the custom of consumers trapped in space; in other words we are dealing with a class monopoly of landlords with respect to housing provision for a class of low-income tenants. The phenomenon of class monopoly is very important in explaining urban structure and it therefore requires elucidation. There is a class of housing consumers who have no credit rating and who have no choice but to rent wherever they can. A class of landlords emerges to provide for the needs of those consumers but since the consumers have no choice the landlords, as a class, have monopoly power. Individual landlords compete with each other but as a class they exhibit a certain common patterning in behaviour—they will withdraw housing from the market, for example, if the rate of return on capital falls below a certain level. Arriving last in the market in an economic sense has to be differentiated from arriving last for other reasons. New households as they form, also have to face this problem in a way, but in a market where new construction is possible the rich groups always have the option to take up new construction. The main conclusion to be drawn, however, is that in a capitalist market exchange economy it is possible to realize more gains as the result of the inherent monopolistic quality of space in some situations than it is in others. Individual monopolists maximize profit by producing to the point where marginal cost equals marginal revenue rather than price (as would be the case under pure competition). This means lower output, higher price and higher profit under both individual and class monopoly. The rich, who have plenty of economic choice, are more able to escape such consequences of monopoly, than are the poor whose choices are exceedingly limited. We therefore arrive at the fundamental conclusion that the rich can command space whereas the poor are trapped in it (see above p. 83).

The argument constructed above is informal and incomplete. But it provides a useful foil against which to compare the utility-maximizing models of Alonso, Muth, Beckmann and Mills. Insofar as these models are formulated in relative space in a manner which discounts the monopoly characteristics of absolute space, they appear most appropriate as arguments governing what happens to affluent groups who are in a position to escape the consequences of monopoly in space; the formulations are therefore income-biased. The criterion of Pareto-optimality also appears irrelevant (if not downright misleading) in any analysis of the urban housing market. The differential distribution of the collective consumers' surplus according to the first-come-first-served principle with the rich at the head of the queue, almost certainly has a differential income effect in which the rich are destined to gain more than the poor in most situations. Sequential occupancy in urban land-use of the type we are here hypothesizing does not yield Pareto optimality, but a redistribution of imputed income (which is what consumers' surplus really amounts to). Even if we take into account that new construction is possible (i.e. the housing stock is not fixed), this condition is unlikely to change, for the poor certainly are in no condition to generate activity in the private sector because of the weak effective demand for housing which they are capable of expressing in the market place.

The absolute space constraint provides some interesting insights into the processes of land-use change. Let us suppose, for convenience, that occupants are geographically ordered according to their income characteristics. How do positions change in this ordered situation? It is frequently assumed (without any evidence being produced to support the assertion) that consumers have an insatiable desire for housing (the desire for use values is never satisfied) and that all will strive to procure better housing in a better location. The richest, because they have the most resources, can most easily move and if they do so they leave behind good quality housing which can be taken up by others. By a "filtering" process the poorest groups eventually achieve better housing. This "filter down" theory has been much considered, but little evidence has been produced for it (Lowry, 1960; Douglas Commission, 1968). Yet certain processes of land-use transformation and residential mobility can be observed. If we resort to the "space-packing model" set up above, we can guess at something. The poorest groups, who have the greatest latent demand for housing and the least resources to procure it, cannot afford new housing. Yet poor groups have a singular power (a power which many of them probably wish they were not blessed with) in that richer groups in contemporary society do not take easily to living in close geographical proximity to them. The poor therefore exert a social pressure which can vary in its form from a mere felt presence, through a gross exhibition of all those social pathologies associated with poverty, to a fully fledged riot. The latter helps to open up the housing market to the poor most marvellously. Instead of a "filter down" theory, therefore, it might be more interesting to examine a "blow out" theory. Social and physical pressure is exerted at the bottom end of the housing market and this is transmitted up the socioeconomic scale until the richest are pressured to move (we are leaving out of the picture, of course, the problem of new household formation, in-migration and so on). This formulation is, however, clearly unrealistic for the rich possess the political and economic power to resist encroachment, while the socioeconomic group immediately below them is unlikely to be as unacceptable in its behaviour as is the poorest group. The richest of all will probably not move unless they prefer to, which leaves the various intermediate groups squeezed between a social pressure emanating from below and an immoveable political and economic force above. Depending upon the relative pressure exerted at different points in this system, different groups may "blow out": middle-income groups may be forced out to new suburban construction locations—a process which may well diminish their consumers' surplus. This kind of behaviour is evident in the housing market—Wallace Smith (1966) found, for example, that it was middle and lower income groups who took up new housing in Los Angeles while the upper income groups remained stationary or "filtered in" to older housing in good locations. The exact manner in which such a process unfolds depends very much upon the circumstances of the time. The social unrest of the late 1960s in many American cities led many intermediate groups to flee outwards very rapidly, leaving behind a substantial housing stock which, given the economics of the situation, has often been abandoned, rather than used. In practice, the dynamics of the housing market can probably best be viewed as a combination of "blow out" and "filter down".

It is also as well to recognize that land-use changes in the housing sector are not independent of the prospects for gain under other kinds of land use. Poor groups are typically subject to pressure from this source. Hawley suggests for example that:

"The residential property on high priced land is usually in a deteriorated condition, for since it is close to business and industrial areas it is being held speculatively in anticipation of

173

its acquisition by more intensive and therefore more remunerative land use. In view of that probability owners of such property are not disposed to spend heavily for maintenance or to engage in new residential construction." (1950, 280.)

Deteriorated housing is typically subject to speculative pressure—a pressure which may lead to urban renewal under a different kind of housing or a transformation in the use of the land. Engels recognized the significance of the process described by Hawley as long ago as 1872:

"The growth of the big modern cities gives the land in certain areas, particularly those which are centrally situated, an artificial and often colossally increasing value; the buildings erected on these areas depress this value, instead of increasing it, because they no longer conform to the changed circumstances. They are pulled down and replaced by others. This takes place above all with workers' houses which are situated centrally and whose rents, even with the greatest overcrowding, can never, or only very slowly, increase above a certain maximum. They are pulled down and in their stead shops, warehouses and public buildings are erected. . . . The result is that the workers are forced out of the centre of the towns towards the outskirts; that workers' dwellings in general, become rare and expensive and often altogether unobtainable, for under these circumstances the building industry, which is offered a much better field for speculation by more expensive houses, builds workers' houses only by way of exception." (*The Housing Question*, 23.)

The evidence from the contemporary American city suggests that the dynamics of land-use change remains fairly constant under the capitalist mode of production. The consumers' surplus of the poorest groups is diminished by producers of housing services transforming it into producers' surplus through quasi-monopolistic practices (usually exercised on the basis of class monopoly power). Also the poorest groups generally live in locations subject to the greatest speculative pressure from land-use change. In order to realize an adequate future return on investment in existing commercial urban renewal schemes, for example, financial institutions have a vested interest in expanding commercial development geographically; by this process spatial externalities are created through which new commercial development enhances the value of the old. New commercial development will usually have to take place over land already in housing. Housing in these areas can be deliberately economically run down by the withdrawal of financial support for the housing market—"red-lining" by financial institutions is a common practice in the United States, although it is generally explained away as risk aversion: this is but a part of the story, however. Landlords are forced under these conditions to maximize current income over a short-term time horizon, which means a rational business-like milking of a property for all it is worth. The physical obsolescence, generated out of this economic obsolescence, results in social and economic pressures which build up in the worst sections of the housing market and which have to be relieved, at some stage or other, by a "blow out" somewhere. This "blow out" results in new construction and the taking up of new land at the urban fringes or in urban redevelopment—processes which are both subject to intense speculative pressure. New household formation and in-migration supplement this dynamic.

The same financial institutions which deny funds to one sector of the housing market stand to gain from the realization of speculative gains in another, as land use is subsequently transformed or as suburbanization proceeds. The impulses which are transmitted throughout the urban land-use system are not unconnected. The diversity of actors and institutions involved makes a conspiracy theory of urban land-use change unlikely (which is not to say that conspiracy never occurs). The processes are strongly structured through the market exchange system so that individuals, groups and organizations operating self-interestedly in terms of exchange value can, with the help of the "hidden hand", produce the requisite result. It is argued by some that this system produces the best possible distribution of use values. This is a presumption which casual observation suggests is wrong: the maximization of exchange values by diverse actors produces disproportionate benefits to some groups and diminishes the opportunities for others. The gap between the proper production and distribution of use values and a system of allocation that rests on the concept of exchange value cannot easily be glossed over.

The diversity of actors operating in a land-use system and the monopolistic quality inherent in absolute space render the micro-economic theories of urban land use inadequate as describers of the mechanisms of allocation when judged against alternative formulations in which exchange value predominates. If we drop the assumption that individuals and groups have homogeneous tastes with respect to housing and allow the great diversity of needs and tastes to play its part, then we stray even further from the framework encompassed in microeconomic theory—and it is thus far that we ought to stray if we are to construct a realistic theory of the forces shaping urban land use. Yet there is something disconcerting about this conclusion, for the micro-economic theories do indeed produce results which are reasonably consistent with the actual results of diverse social processes governing land-use allocation. Alonso (1964, 11) addresses himself directly to this point; he suggests that the micro-economic theories can succeed in doing much more simply what the more elaborate conceptualizations of workers such as Hawley (1950) do more realistically but with less analytic power. We therefore have to consider what it is that makes micro-economic theory so successful (relatively speaking) in the modelling of urban land-use patterns, when it is so obviously wide of the mark when it comes to modelling the real processes that produce these patterns. The solution to this problem may be sought by investigating the meaning and role of rent as an allocative device in the urban system.

RENT AND THE ALLOCATION OF URBAN LAND TO USES

The rental concept occupies a critical position in theories of urban land use. It is explicitly set forth in the Alonso–Muth–Mills formulations and it emerges in the form of shadow prices on land and resources in the programming versions of other location theories. The suspicion lurks that the general spatial equilibrium theory, which is the holy grail for many location theorists, might be reached through a fusion of rent and location theory. "It has long been recognized," Alonso (1967, 39) writes, "that rent and location theories are twins, but the linkages are elusive." Rent functions as a rationing device which sorts land uses into locations usually, it is presumed, via competitive bidding. All actors in the housing drama are affected by it at some stage; it provides a common standard in terms of which all actors must measure their aspirations if they are to achieve their disparate objectives. It is because all calculations are based on this common yardstick that diverse activities appear coordinated in the land and property market to produce the patterning of land uses which is so evident in the contemporary metropolis.

The concept of rent has a long and controversial history in political economic thought (Keiper *et al.*, 1961, provide a very thorough survey; see also Bye, 1940). Yet rent enters into urban land-use theory in an innocent state as if there were no serious problems attached to its interpretation. This fact may be accounted for by the pervasive and complete acceptance in micro-economic urban land-use theory of the neo-classical view that rent is the return to a scarce factor of production and that land is in essence no different from labour and capital. The consequences of this view for the conception of urban rent are spelled out by Mills:

"Urban land rents are determined by the value of the land's marginal productivity. And, as in agriculture, the land's productivity is determined by the characteristics of the land itself and by transportation costs to relevant markets. . . . These basic ideas are now well understood by economists. And the process of sorting them out has been a notable accomplishment in the development of economic doctrine. By themselves, they do not, of course, provide us with a model of urban land values. For that purpose it is necessary to incorporate land rents into a model that describes the demand and supply of urban land for all uses. The crucial characteristics of urban land is the great complexity resulting from the fact that supply and demand for different parcels of land are related in significant and poorly understood ways. In other words, an urban economy is a complicated general equilibrium system." (1969, 233.)

That all is not well with this "received and embellished wisdom" of location theory has been signalled by Gaffney (1961; 1969). Ground rent, he observes, is a surplus "differentiated from other distributive shares in lacking the function of eliciting aggregate supply" (1961, 147)—the assumed symmetry between land and other factors of production cannot be accepted. Gaffney also takes welfare economics to task:

"For all its ecumenical purport, most of 'pure' welfare economics is both spaceless and timeless. It is all very well to abstract from localisms, but space and time are absolute universals.

It is welfare economics that preaches against piecemeal optimizing. Economizing at dimensionless points in space and time is piecemealism beyond sufferance." (1961, 142–3.)
Land is fixed in both location and aggregate supply, and the neo-classical fiction that it is neither (accepted completely by Muth, for example) is an innocent trap which can easily lead us into a misinterpretation of the forces determining urban land use. We neglect the realities of absolute, relative and relationally determined space and time at our peril. As Lösch (1954, 508) has it: "particularity is the price of our existence".

It is useful, therefore, to turn to the earthy richness of classical political economy to elucidate the nature of rent, for the neo-classical achievement, which is elegant and very useful for certain purposes, succeeds in burying some of the more relevant technical and ethical issues which attach to rent as it functions in the urban land market. The classical writings were largely devoted, however, to the rent of agricultural land and the particularities of the argument are cast in these rather than in urban land-use terms. This ought not to deter us, for the translation to the urban context is relatively easy provided we can garner a general enough concept of rent from the classical debate. Marx provides a lengthy generalization and synthesis of the argument surrounding the rental concept in *Capital* (volume 3) and in *Theories of Surplus Value* (particularly Part 2). It was Marx's peculiar strength to look for the hidden connections between things and not to remain content with superficial appearances. He regards rent as something which can emerge in a variety of ways out of all manner of initial conditions. The feature common to all cases, however, is the institution of private property in the land.

"Landed property is based on the monopoly by certain persons over definite portions of the globe, as exclusive spheres of their private will to the exclusion of others. With this in mind, the problem is to ascertain the economic value, that is, the realization of this monopoly on the basis of capitalist production. With the legal power to use or misuse certain portions of the globe, nothing is decided. The use of this power depends wholly upon economic conditions, which are independent of their will. . . . Whatever the specific form of rent may be, all types have this in common: the appropriation of rent is that economic form in which landed property is realized. . . . This common element in the various forms of rent makes it possible for the differences to escape detection." (*Capital* volume 3, 615, 634.)

Landowners thus possess a class monopoly over land use. Within this general conception, Marx sets out to uncover the "differences" that might otherwise escape detection. He shows in *Capital* (volume 3, chapter 47) how rent can arise in a variety of ways depending on the dominant mode of production and he assembles some historical evidence to illustrate his argument. Much of Part 2 of *Theories of Surplus Value* illustrates how definitions of rent are contingent upon the economic conditions of each epoch and how definitions and apologetics are intimately related. But Marx is primarily interested in the manifestations of rent in a competitive market economy and it is this topic that he pursues most thoroughly. He lists three basic kinds of rent which typically arise under the capitalist mode of production:

(*i*) *Monopoly rent* arises because it is possible to charge a monopoly price "determined by the purchaser's eagerness to buy and ability to pay, independent of the price determined by the general price of production as well as by the value of the product." (*Capital* volume 3, 775). The opportunity to charge a monopoly price creates the opportunity for the landowner to reap a monopoly rent. This form of rent is not thought to be very important in agriculture (Marx mentions vineyards with special characteristics as a case where monopoly rent can arise). But in a number of passages (*Theories of Surplus Value* Part 2, 30, 38, for example) he indicates his belief that monopoly rents are crucial in the case of urban land and property and that there may be conditions, particularly in densely populated areas, in which house and land rents are "only explicable" as monopoly rents. It is an interesting question whether monopolistic competition of the sort analysed by Chamberlin (1933) and Lösch (1954) yields monopoly rents in Marx's sense of the term. It would appear to me that rents achieved in spatial competition are a classic case of *absolute rent* (defined below) and that monopoly rents in Marx's sense arise only through substantial imperfections in spatial competition.

(*ii*) *Differential rent* is usually associated with the name of Ricardo (1817), but Marx shows that Ricardo's doctrine is a special case which arises out of differentials in fertility with diminishing returns to successive inputs of labour and capital. Marx disputes the generality of Ricardo's assumptions and objects to the restrictive way in which the implications of the doctrine are worked out. He chides Ricardo for analysing rent as if landed property did not exist and as if land possessed "original and indestructible powers" when it is clearly a condition of and not a force in production. Marx accepts the existence of differential rents. They arise simply out of the difference between "the individual production price of a particular capital and the general production price of the total capital invested in the sphere of production concerned" (*Capital* volume 3, 646). Differential rent obviously cannot enter into the cost of production or the price of products for it merely arises out of excess profits to certain producers by virtue of their advantageous situation. These excess profits can be pocketed by landowners in the form of rent. Advantageous situations exist for a variety of reasons and Marx discusses these in a far more general fashion than Ricardo differentiating between intensive and extensive applications of capital and labour under different conditions. Differences in fertility are important, but Marx indicates that differential rent can arise irrespective of whether cultivation is extended from rich to poor soils or *vice versa* (*Capital* volume 3, 659). Also there is no necessity to assume diminishing returns and differential rent can arise simply out of differential application of capital and labour. Relative locational advantage is explicitly built into the picture (and it is instructive to note that Marx draws much of his inspiration in this regard from William Petty, who in 1662 recognized the significance of location to the determination of rent—von Thünen is not mentioned). Marx then combines all of these elements and shows how various combinations of soils in different locations with different characteristics exploited in different sequences with different quantities of capital can give rise to various patterns of differential rent (*Capital* volume 3, 650, 668–73; *Theories of Surplus Value* Part 2, 310–12). He also points out that "in the case of ground rent on houses, situation constitutes just as decisive a factor for the differential rent as fertility (and situation) in the case of agricultural rent" (*Theories of Surplus Value* Part 2, 365). Most contemporary location theorists would agree with this assertion.

Differential rent takes on its meaning in a relative space which is structured by differentials in productive capacity at different locations and which is integrated spatially through transport cost relationships. Differential rent, it seems, cannot be conceptualized without projecting a relative space. But differential rent is created, in Marx's view, through the operation of the capitalist mode of production in the context of the institution of private property.

(*iii*) *Absolute Rent* is distinguished from monopoly rent in that it gives rise to monopoly price, whereas an independently determined monopoly price allows monopoly rent to be gained. Ricardo denied the existence of absolute rent—a position he was forced into, in Marx's judgement, by his confusion of value and price. Marx avoids this confusion by arguing that the value of agricultural products can be higher than their price if more money is advanced for wages in proportion to constant capital, compared to the ratio of wages to constant capital necessary in other spheres of production. Under these conditions, a greater quantity of surplus value (which is derived from surplus labour power) can be extracted from agriculture than is possible elsewhere. This condition is necessary for the existence of absolute rent in a particular sphere of production, but it can be realized only if there is some barrier to the overall equalization in the rate of profit among the different spheres of production. Various barriers can exist, including lack of geographical and social mobility, lack of mobility in capital, and so on (*Capital* volume 3, 196–7). Excess profits can therefore "fleetingly" emerge in all areas of production (and here Marx appears to be proposing something akin to Marshall's quasi-rents). But in agriculture excess profits are institutionalized into absolute rent through the monopoly power of private property:

"If capital meets an alien force which it can but partially, or not at all, overcome, and which limits its investment in certain spheres, admitting it only under conditions which wholly or partly exclude that general equalization of surplus value to average profit, then it is evident that the excess of the value of commodities in such spheres of production over their price of production would give rise to surplus profit, which would be converted into rent and as such made independent with respect to profit. Such an alien force and barrier are presented by landed property when confronting capital in its endeavour to invest in land; such a force is the landlord vis-à-vis the capitalist. Landed property is here the barrier which does not permit any new investment of capital. . . without levying a tax, or in other words, without demanding a rent." (*Capital* volume 3, 761–2.)

Capitalist production cannot afford, in Marx's view, to destroy the institution of private property (in the way it had destroyed many other feudal institutions) because its own existence is predicated on the private ownership of the means of production. Capitalism is therefore prepared to pay a tax on production (rent) as the price for perpetuating the legal basis for its own existence. Such a tax obviously must enter into the costs of production and in this regard absolute rent (and monopoly rent) are to be distinguished from differential rent. There has been considerable criticism of Marx's concept of absolute rent (for example, Emmanuel, 1972, 216–26). The difficulty arises because Marx does not provide an adequate reply to the question posed in *Theories of Surplus Value* (Part 2): "if landed property gives the power to sell the product *above* its cost-price at its *value*, why does it not equally well give the power to sell the product *above* its value, at an arbitrary monopoly price?" The distinction between monopoly and absolute rent can perhaps be rescued by regarding the former as operating at the individual level (a particular owner has something which someone particularly wants or needs) and the latter as something which arises out of the general conditions of production in some sector (it is a class monopoly phenomenon which affects the condition of all agricultural landowners, all owners of low-income housing, etc.).

Once rent is institutionalized it can appear under various guises. The investor in land, for example, equates rent with interest on capital and treats it as the latter when it is really still the former. This creates the illusion that land is itself a productive factor which must be paid for and whose cost must enter into production costs. This cost is in fact the tax (rent) extracted by private property as absolute or monopoly rent. There is, however, some confusion surrounding ground rent on the one hand and interest as a return on capital improvements on the other. Marx accepts that there is a legitimate distinction to be made here, but he argues that capital improvements which are relatively permanent and which are incorporated into the attributes of the land (and he includes permanent structures in this) should be analysed from the point of view of rent rather than interest. Marx's views in this respect roughly correspond to those of Gaffney among contemporary analysts.

Marx concedes the significance of "the friction of distance" in the failure to achieve the equalization of profit throughout all spheres of production that permits the extraction of absolute and monopoly rents. But he underestimates the way in which distance in itself may be an "alien force" which can create the conditions for the owners of land and property to gain absolute and monopoly rents. The distinction between rent as it arises through competitive bidding for the use of the land, and rent as the reward for monopoly has been pervasive in the literature on urban land use (see, for example, Chamberlin, 1939, appendix D; Alonso, 1964, 43; Lösch, 1954). But the monopoly aspect has not been well understood for it can arise either in the absolute or monopoly forms as Marx categorizes them. In both cases monopoly pricing is involved, but in the case of absolute rent it is rent which determines monopoly price rather than the other way round. This distinction is relevant to our understanding of spatial competition. Monopoly prices are created under perfect spatial competition—this, of course, was Lösch's fundamental contribution. On a perfectly homogeneous plain with perfect competition among producers of an undifferentiated product, we will still observe a rental surface; monopoly power exists within the vicinity of a producer because alternative producers in other locations incur higher transport costs. This kind of rent can be identified as absolute rent because it arises out of the technical and social conditions affecting a particular sector as a whole. It merges into monopoly rent (in the Marxist sense) as producers within that sector establish cartel arrangements among themselves, as a single producer operates over many production points, and as the various competitive practices among firms with distinctive territories are restricted or modified to prevent strong competition (Seidel, 1969, provides some interesting observations on this last point). Absolute rent is still a return to landed property, but the technical conditions under which it may arise are more numerous than Marx imagined or accounted for.

The power of Marx's analysis of rent lies in the way that he dissects a seemingly homogeneous thing into its component parts and relates those parts to all other aspects of the social structure. Rent is a simple payment to the owners of private property, but it can arise out of a multiplicity of conditions. It is intriguing to compare this analysis of the rental concept with views on the nature of space, for the two sets of ideas exist in a peculiar relationship to each other. The monopoly privileges of private property arise out of the absolute qualities of space which are institutionalized in a certain way. In the sphere of social activity absolute space emerges as the basis for monopoly rent. But absolute space is in general overcome by the interaction between different spheres of activity in different locations and the relative attributes of space emerge as the guiding principle for the establishment of both differential and absolute rent, although absolute space extracts its tax in all cases through the monopoly privilege of private property. Further, there is a sense in which relational space prevails in the general determination of rental value at different locations —this will be made more explicit shortly. The relational style of analysis used by Marx in fact bears remarkable similarities to the relational analysis of space espoused by Leibniz (1934 edition; see also Whiteman 1967). In the same way that rent cannot be understood without relating the payment that takes place to the social circumstances, so we have to recognize that urban space is not absolute, or relative, or relational, but all three simultaneously depending upon the circumstances of the time. We ought, therefore, to take care in matching our social analyses with our conceptualization of space (and time).

The Marxist categories of monopoly, differential and absolute rent embrace all of the thinking in classical political economy and in fact have not been improved on since. This is not to say that writers prior to Marx (such as Ricardo and Smith) or that writers subsequent to Marx (such as Marshall, Wicksell, and Pigou) accept the Marxist interpretation of these categories. For example, absolute rent, as it arises in Marx's analysis, rests on his distinctive and unique theory of value and cannot be distinguished from it. Subsequent writers have ignored or completely misunderstood this theory (Ollman, 1971 and Hunt and Schwartz, 1972, provide good discussions). Few western economists would deny the significance of absolute rent, but most prefer to attribute it to the fixed aggregate supply of land which, once it is all in use in some way or other, is bound to command some rent. The levels of absolute rent can then be attributed to the relative scarcity of land compared to other factors of production and from this we can arrive at the neo-classical position. Monopoly rents can then be interpreted in the neo-classical tradition as arising through the artificial manipulation of scarcity through producers' manipulation of the supply of land.

Scarcity is, however, socially determined (see chapter 4). Marx restricts the meaning of rent to scarcity achieved through the institution of private property and differentiates it from scarcities induced and realized under other conditions. The neo-classical generalization is useful in certain respects, but it eliminates a distinction which Marx and some subsequent analysts (such as Henry George) are unwilling to forget for obvious ethical reasons. The neo-classical analysis proceeds as if it does not matter how scarcity arises. In Marx's view rent is something "filched" by the landlord—it is an undeserved return. The landlord contributes nothing compared with the capitalist who at least promotes production and the landlord succeeds because he has the power to withdraw substantial resources bound up in land and improvements if it is to his advantage so to do (deliberately holding large office blocks vacant became advantageous to property developers in London from 1966 onwards, for example). Marx spells the rule out explicitly when he states that legal ownership of the land give the landholder "the power to withdraw his land from economic exploitation until economic conditions permit him to utilize it in such a manner as to yield him a surplus" (*Capital* volume 3, 757). Marx sees the rentier therefore as a passive figure who reaps the general benefit of economic growth achieved through the application of social labour (*Capital* volume 3, 637). This view of rent provokes certain further analyses of the way in which scarcity is created to give rise to increments or decrements in rental value.

The ability of land to capture benefits and to be afflicted with costs depends upon its fixity of location relative to all manner of external costs and benefits being generated by social activity in the urban system. Gaffney (1967, 142) thus points out that land rent depends in part on "what the public does free for the owner" as well as on "complementary private activity on other land significantly linked to a given parcel" adding that "positive spillover benefits, cumulating and reinforcing, are emphasized by urban economists as what cities are all about." The classical political economists recognized the connection between economic growth and rising rental values, but this aspect to the problem has subsequently been neglected. The ability of land to capture benefits, to trap consumers' surpluses, and so on, is exceedingly important and it has to do with scarcity in the sense that both public and private activity create scarcity of sites with favourable access to man-made resources (see chapter 2). In this fashion property owners receive benefits or are allocated costs independent of their wills except insofar as they can influence public and private activity (the legislature, at state or local level, Gaffney notes, is one of the most pervasive of all cartel arrangements for the management of land resources).

But rents are also created in a relationally structured space and time. Adam Smith and Marx argued that all land rents are determined by the price of *the* basic commodity which sustains life (grain). It is better to regard rental values as being simultaneously influenced by alternative and neighbouring uses (and here general equilibrium thinking is relevant). This means that rent is determined relationally over all spheres of production in all locations, with future expectations also incorporated into the calculation. Land and improvements are, according to real estate practice, frequently valued at their highest and best use rather than with respect to their actual use. From this arises the "important sense" in which the value of any one parcel of land "contains" the values of all other parcels at the present time as well as the expectations held of future values. The implications of this for the determination of land value as well as for the calculation of investment opportunity in land are well explored in the land economics literature (see, for example, Ratcliffe, 1949). The consequences for urban land-use decisions are numerous and encompass a whole host of problems varying from that of rampant speculation through those of "ripening costs" and associated blight in zones of land-use transition, to effects which spread throughout the whole urban system, as urban growth and economic growth (of a sort) go on hand in hand. Gaffney (1969, 148) provides one example:

"Today, too many allocation decisions are made under the shadow of impending increments [in land value]. Visualize the hierarchy of land uses as a series of concentric circles. Demand for higher uses is not fully satisfied in their proper circles, because of land holdouts there. Unmet demand probes outward, casting a diffused "floating value" over outer zones. This floating value raises land prices enough so the outer land is too high priced to renew in its present use, although still unripe for the higher use. . . . The socially optimal course is to renew the site in its present lower use. But the floating value factor discourages that. [The landowner] is more likely to let old buildings get old for a while, reserving the land for the higher use. Builders needing land for the lower use are forced out another ring, casting their floating value over the next lower use, and so on in a series of shock waves—result: more sprawl at every margin of land use."

These shock waves (which Engels and Hawley observed) reflect back into the centre however, for as the city spreads outwards, so the value of the land tends to increase at the centre (and here von Thünen's observations are very relevant). But it is not only land value which increases; congestion costs also increase as do all manner of other external costs (Lave, 1970). These costs impinge upon the user of land who is bound to be sensitive to them. In case the message is not clear, the property tax, assessed by convention against the highest and best use, soon lets the user know that his or her use is not consistent with potential exchange value. And filtering (stimulated by new sprawl) and blow-out pressures lead to falling house prices in the inner city. Hence arises the paradox of the American city; house prices are falling most rapidly in what are, from the relational point of view, the most valuable locations.

The high rental value of land in central cities should not necessarily be interpreted as a reflection of differences in marginal productivity of land (as Mills suggests). Absolute and monopoly rents at these locations enter into the costs of production. Differential rents do not. If absolute and monopoly rents are dominant in the determination of land value at central locations then it is land value which determines use. If differential rents dominate then it is use which determines land value. In practice, of course, rent arises out of all three circumstances and it is often difficult to determine what portion of the overall rental value arises out of which circumstance. It is probable that the structure of the transport system and the nature of production in the new industrial and commercial cities of the nineteenth century, meant that differential rent was a major source of rent during that period (the concept is particularly appealing in late nineteenth century Chicago for example). But it is very likely that in the contemporary metropolitan centres (as well as in older commercial and administrative centres such as London in the eighteenth and nineteenth centuries), the reverse process in which absolute and monopoly rents enter into the costs of production and thereby determine use, is of much greater significance. The problem under these conditions is to discover (or generate) firms with production functions which can readily adjust to absorb these costs. It is not surprising to find, therefore, that the highest rent areas in the city are colonized by commercial activities whose productivity cannot be measured—government offices, banks, insurance companies, stockbrokers, travel agents and various forms of entertainment, are good examples. Hence arises the paradox that some of the most unproductive activity in society is found on land which is supposedly of the greatest marginal productivity by virtue of its location. The solution to this paradox is simple. Land and property rent in central locations does not arise out of the land's marginal productivity but out of the processes which permit absolute and, even more importantly, monopoly rents to be charged.

This provides us with the key for understanding the relative success of models of the von Thünen type. Such models rely exclusively upon the concept of differential rent and generally set their analytics in a relative space. They also abstract, as Ricardo did, from the power of private property although individual monopoly control over individual land parcels is always presumed. These models must therefore be viewed as special cases, which describe conditions when absolute and monopoly rents are insignificant, when absolute and relational concepts of time and space are irrelevant, and when the institution of private property is notably quiescent in the land and property markets. It is helpful, of course, to have the analytics spelled out for these restricted conditions, but it is dangerous to regard these models as the foundation for a general theory of land use. Among geographers, planners and sociologists, many of whom are not sympathetic towards or cognizant of the abstractions of the neo-classical economist, the models gain their currency and appeal because they appear empirically relevant devices for understanding the general structure of the urban system—a view which is fed further by the moderately successful testing of their models by Mills (1969) and Muth (1969).

This apparent relevance arises out of an assumption—that "distance from the city centre incurs a 'penalty' in the form of transportation or communication costs" (Mills, 1969, 234). Differential rents are, as it were, "draped" around distance from the centre (usually because a central source of all employment is assumed). The peaking of land values in the city centre is, however, the result of forces which have nothing necessarily to do with differential rent or marginal productivity of the land. It is natural, for example, for relationally established land values in the city, like demographic and retail potential, to tend to peak at or close to the centre. Monopoly rents also tend to be most easily established at or near the centre (if only because there is only one centre and a whole continuum of periphery). Absolute rent (if we appeal to the system of Lösch for example) will be greatest at the centre of the largest metropolitan region. It is therefore the assumption of centricity which gives the appearance of empirical relevance to the models of Alonso, Mills and Muth. By association, the mechanism assumed in the functioning of these models—competitive bidding for the use of the land—receives far greater attention than it warrants. Competitive bidding is undoubtedly significant, but it assumes that land use determines value when in practice the reverse determination is more prevalent in most contemporary capitalist cities. In this regard the analysis here departs in an important respect from that provided in chapter 4.

The von Thünen type models of urban land use are therefore to be regarded as special cases which apply only under very restricted conditions. They gain their currency and credibility, however, from a seeming empirical relevance which is in fact based upon the assumption of centricity.

USE VALUE, EXCHANGE VALUE, THE CONCEPT OF RENT
AND THEORIES OF URBAN LAND USE—A CONCLUSION

Rent is a portion of exchange value which is set aside for the land and property owner. Exchange values relate (through the circulation of commodities) to socially determined use values. If we argue that rent can dictate use, then this implies that exchange values can determine use values by creating new conditions to which individuals must adapt if they are to survive in society. These conditions are relevant not only at the catalytic moments when decisions are reached about land and property in their commodity form, but they also create persistent pressures by the continuous capturing of external costs and benefits by land parcels, through relationally established changes in land value, and so on. The capitalist market exchange economy so penetrates every aspect of social and private life that it exerts an almost tyrannical control over the life support system in which use values are embedded. A dominant mode of production, Marx observed, inevitably creates the conditions of consumption. Therefore, the evolution of urban land-use patterns can be understood only in terms of the general processes whereby society is pushed down some path (it knows not how) towards a pattern of social needs and human relationships (which are neither comprehended nor desired) by the blind forces of an evolving market system. The evolution of urban form is an integral part of this general process and rent, as a measure of the interpenetration of use values and exchange values, contributes notably to the unfolding of this process.

In capitalist economies rent arises in monopoly, differential and absolute forms. Once it has arisen, rent serves to allocate land to uses. When use determines value a case can be made for the social rationality of rent as an allocative device that leads to efficient capitalist production patterns (although the aggregate quantity of rent paid out seems an extraordinarily high price for society to pay for such an allocative mechanism). But when value determines use, the allocation takes place under the auspices of rampant speculation, artificially induced scarcities, and the like, and it loses any pretence of having anything at all to do with the efficient organization of production and distribution. Social policy, it is frequently argued, should be directed towards encouraging the former kind of allocation and discouraging the latter. Unfortunately, the monopolistic power of private property can be realized in its economic form by innumerable strategems. If rent cannot be extracted by one means then it will be by another. Social policy, no matter how well-intentioned, is helpless in the face of these innumerable strategems—the rentier will get that pound of flesh no matter what. It is this fact, however, that lends a certain homogeneity to capitalist city forms in spite of quite marked differences from country to country (and even from city to city) in political, legal and administrative institutions, as well as in production, distribution and the social matrix of life in the community.

Yet there are discernible changes in the way rent is achieved over time. Monopoly rent (in the Marxist sense) and absolute rent (if it is regarded as a class monopoly phenomenon) are far more significant than ever before, partly because cities are larger and geographically more differentiated. Individual and class monopoly rents are now extensively, but differentially achieved, depending upon the location, the particular form of activity, the particular income group of consumers, and the power of the rentier class to manipulate public decisions to their own advantage. Rent has also become confused in the contemporary capitalist economy with interest on capital and increments in rental value have, as a consequence, become as significant to the evolution of capitalism as have increments in output. The confusion between rent and rate of return on capital also arises in urban land-use theory. The point is that rent can, if necessary, be represented as a problem in defining a social rate of return on capital. The problem of rent is then resolved into one of a transfer payment out of this social rate of return on capital. Unfortunately, all the issues raised in this chapter are raised again in the controversies over capital theory (see Harcourt, 1972). If we take the position that there is no such thing as a homogeneous unit of capital and that the exchange value of fixed capital cannot be measured independent of distribution and prices, then to talk of an aggregate or even industry-wide production function is meaningless and all of the work in urban economics, such as that by Mills (1972) and Muth (1969) is equally meaningless. Since all real analysis of urban phenomena has to commence with the fact that a large proportion of fixed capital has no value independent of future use, prices, and the distribution of benefits in society, there is no way in which the problems arising out of rent theory can be saved by a conversion into the realms of capital theory. In other words, if Joan Robinson, Sraffa and the other "neo-Keynesians" (see Hunt and Schwartz, 1972; Harcourt, 1972 and Harcourt and Laing, 1971) are anywhere near correct then Alonso, Mills and Muth are completely wrong.

Urban growth provides a certain way to realize increments in rental value or in the value of fixed capital while it simultaneously provides a field for the disposal of surplus product (see below, pp. 270–73). Not only at the periphery and at the centre, but right throughout the urban system, the expectation is that land and property values will rise and that the productive capacity of fixed capital assets will be made use of; the safest way to achieve this is to stimulate urban growth. Growth can be tempered, but controlling physical growth without controlling anything else merely exacerbates scarcity. The planner in southeast England and the zoning boards in the New York metropolitan region have alike helped to create further opportunities for extracting monopoly rents. The emergence of individual and class monopoly rents as a dominant source of general rent must therefore be seen as one aspect of a process of evolution in the capitalist market exchange economy and its attached political and legal institutions—an evolution which is closely tied to the emergence of a distinctive form of urbanism (see chapter 6). Monopoly capitalism, it seems, goes hand in hand with monopoly rents.

The conclusion to be drawn from this (if it is not already apparent from Marx's analyses) is that rent exists only in a contingent sense—it is dependent upon a mode of production and certain institutions concerning property ownership. If this is the case, and if the relationship between use value and exchange value is likewise a function of the general processes operating in society, then it follows that there can be no such thing as a "general" urban land-use theory. All land-use theories must be regarded as contingent. There are only specific theories which can play specific roles in helping to elucidate existing conditions or in establishing alternative choices under a particular set of assumptions about the dominant mode of production, about the nature of social relationships and under the prevalent institutions of society. The contingent nature of all urban land-use theory, is most clearly exemplified by the way in which particular conceptions of rent produce particular kinds of theory. Mills (1969), for example, appeals directly to the concept of differential rent whereas Gaffney (1961) regards differential rent as "incidental" and argues that rent arises "because land is scarce relative to demand". As a consequence they produce quite different analyses of urban structure. The introduction of absolute space and rent as consumers' or producers' surplus gained in a sequentially occupied land market (outlined earlier in this essay) produces yet another perspective on the dynamics of the urban housing market. How concepts of rent and space are conjoined clearly determines the kind of land-use theory that emerges. The problem then arises of evaluating contrasting theories. This task can only be accomplished if there is a clear understanding of the uses to which the theory is to be put.

If we are seeking for enlightenment concerning our current urban problems, for example, then it must be concluded that the von Thünen type models of urban land use are a disconcerting mixture of *status quo* apologetics and counter-revolutionary obfuscation. The sense in which these models are special cases has already been considered, but this sense is not explained in the literature nor does it appear to be understood. The reliance on various neo-classical devices and the blurring of important distinctions concerning the nature of rent, the nature of space, and the relationships between use value and exchange value, together with a certain spurious testing, allow such models to achieve much greater currency and credibility than they in fact deserve. Geographers, sociologists and planners, on the other hand, provide us with a welter of data and material (sometimes cast in model form) which is so piecemeal that it is difficult to conclude anything of note save the obvious superficial generalities concerning such things as the significance of class and status, transport cost, political power, and so on, to the functioning of the urban system. Such observations as these accounts contain may be perceptive and, on occasion, enlightening as to the troubled nature of the human condition, but there is little real understanding of "how it all hangs together" or "how it all comes about". The closest we come to real enlightenment is in the work of those few land economists, of whom Gaffney is surely the most eminent, who combine a firm grasp of real processes with a flair for evaluating and generalizing about them

193

against the background of social processes in general. The most obvious task, therefore, is to construct "special case" urban land-use theories which are general enough in scope to embrace different concepts of rent and space in the same context. It is here that a preoccupation with the niceties of mathematical analytics can be more of a barrier than a help. Much of what transpires in the urban land and property market is not susceptible to modelling by conventional techniques—it does not deserve to be ignored for this reason. Perhaps the most urgent task in contemporary circumstances is to understand how individual and class monopoly rents arise and to gain some insight into the processes whereby the creation of artificial scarcity, the growth of urban areas, and the ability to realize such rents are intimately related. Urban land-use theory has little to say on this important topic at the present time.

If, on the other hand, we are searching for some normative theory of land use, then the von Thünen type models (and their brethren in the body of location theory) are of considerable interest. Differentials in the productivity of land do exist, the friction of distance does play a role, land uses are interlinked in complex ways, and absolute scarcity in land availability can be significant. These conditions are likely to persist no matter what the mode of production. Out of these conditions emerges a concept of rent as a shadow price which represents social choices foregone and in such a form rent (which does not actually have to be charged of course) can help fashion social attitudes to the use of land and space as well as help determine socially beneficial land-use decisions consistent with the aims of society. It is paradoxical, perhaps, that the neo-classical models, specified in their blurry fashion as outcomes of perfect and pure competition in a capitalist market exchange economy, can provide the basis for revolutionary advances with respect to the creation of socially efficient and humane urban structures. That this is the case testifies, however, to the fact that particular theories or models are not in themselves *status quo, revolutionary* or *counter-revolutionary* (see chapter 4). Theories and models only assume one or other of these statuses as they enter into social practice, either through shaping the consciousness of people with respect to the processes which operate around them, or through providing an analytical framework as a springboard for action.

Chapter 6

Urbanism and the City—An Interpretive Essay

Robert Park once wrote:
"Cities, and particularly the great metropolitan cities of modern times . . . are, with all their complexities and artificialities, man's most imposing creation, the most prodigious of human artifacts. We must conceive of our cities therefore . . . as the workshops of civilization, and, at the same time, as the natural habitat of civilized man." (1936, 133.)

Since urbanism, and its tangible expression, the city, have for so long been regarded as the locus of civilization itself, it is not surprising to find that the phenomenon of urbanism has been scrutinized from many points of view in a variety of cultural and historical contexts. In spite of (or perhaps because of) this intensive scrutiny, we still look in vain, as did Park's colleague Louis Wirth (1938), for "a general theory systematizing the available knowledge concerning the city as a social entity." Since Wirth wrote, things have changed in one important respect—we now possess a voluminous literature on urban theory. This contains a plethora of theoretical formulations some of which are so particularistic that it seems just impossible to incorporate them into any general urban theory, while others are clearly mutually incompatible. The conclusion implied by a survey of this literature is that a general theory of urbanism is probably impossible to construct. Urbanism is far too complicated a phenomenon to be subsumed easily under some comprehensive theory. Theories, like definitions, have their roots in metaphysical speculation and in ideology, and depend, too, upon the objectives of the investigator and the characteristics of the phenomena being investigated. There are, it seems, far too many ideological positions to be defended, too many intriguing speculations to be followed up, too many investigators, and too many contexts in which urban pheno-mena may be encountered, for a general theory of urbanism to emerge easily. At present such a theory would probably prove more stultifying than helpful: it might lead to a premature closure of our ideas about a set of phenomena that is so rich in complexity and ambiguity that we have scarcely begun to understand it in all its possible manifestations.

This lack of general theory ought not to deter us, however, from pursuing general enquiries into those essential qualities of urbanism which lead cities to be "the workshops of civilization". The quantity of information available makes such a general enquiry difficult, yet it does not seem impossible to extract from the literature some fairly simple concepts through which we can gain some insight into the essence of urbanism itself. It is this task which I shall explore in preliminary fashion in this essay.

MODES OF PRODUCTION AND MODES OF ECONOMIC INTEGRATION

Urbanism may be regarded as a particular form or patterning of the social process. This process unfolds in a spatially struc-tured environment created by man. The city can therefore be regarded as a tangible, built environment—an environment which is a social product. A society may be defined as "a group of human beings sharing a self-sufficient system of action which is capable of existing longer than the life span of the individual, the group being recruited at least in part by the sexual repro-duction of its members" (Fried, 1967, 8).

The conditions of self-sufficiency and survival dictate that the group possess a mode of production and mode of social organization which are successful in obtaining, producing and distributing sufficient quantities of material goods and services. Individual actions must therefore be so coordinated and inte-grated with each other that enough individuals survive to guarantee the survival of the group. The exact way in which societies meet this challenge is subject to enormous variation in its details. But it is, perhaps, possible to generalize concerning modes of production and their concomitant forms of urbanism (wherever these happen to be present).

MODES OF PRODUCTION

The concept of a mode of production is not easy to grasp. It is complicated and seemingly somewhat ambiguous, and it plays a vital role in Marxist thought, but it is nowhere very fully spelled out. We must therefore piece together its meaning. In the preface to *A Contribution to the Critique of Political Economy*, Marx presents what he calls the "guiding principle" of all his studies. In order to guarantee the survival of society, men are forced, "independent of their will", to enter into social relationships with each other. The form of these relationships must be "appropriate to" the particular stage in the development of productive capacity. Marx then continues:

"The totality of these relationships of production constitutes the economic structure of society, the real foundation, on which arises a legal and political superstructure and to which correspond definite forms of social consciousness. The mode of production of material life conditions the general process of social, political and intellectual life. It is not the consciousness of men that determines existence, but their social existence that determines their consciousness. . . . Changes in the economic foundation sooner or later lead to the transformation of the whole immense superstructure. In studying such transformations it is always necessary to distinguish between the material transformation of the economic conditions of production, which can be determined with the precision of natural science, and the legal, political, religious, artistic or philosophic—in short, ideological forms in which men become conscious of conflict [in the economic basis] and fight it out."

Various sections in *Capital* and in other works by Marx and Engels can be used to gain further insight into the meaning of this passage. Towards the end of his life, Engels was much concerned to refute what he regarded as gross misrepresentations of Marx's position, and in a series of letters written in 1890 he sought to explain what Marx really meant. In a letter to Bloch, for example, he wrote

". . . the *ultimately* determining element in history is the production and reproduction of real life. More than this neither Marx nor I have ever asserted. Hence if anyone twists this into saying that the economic element is the *only* determining one, he transforms the proposition into a meaningless, abstract, senseless phrase. The economic situation is the basis, but the various elements of the superstructure—political forms of the class struggle and its results, to wit: constitutions established by the victorious class after a successful battle, etc., juridical forms, and even the reflexes of all these struggles in the brains of the participants, political, juristic, philosophical theories, religious views and their further development into systems of dogmas— also exercise their influence upon the course of historical struggles and in many cases preponderate in determining their *form*. . . . Marx and I are ourselves partly to blame for the fact that the younger people sometimes lay more stress on the economic side than is due to it. We had to emphasize the main principle vis-à-vis our adversaries, who denied it, and we had not always the time, the place or the opportunity to give their due to other elements in the interaction." (*Marx–Engels Correspondence*, 417–18.)

In a previous letter to Conrad Schmidt, he had also written:

"while the material mode of existence is the *primum agens* this does not preclude the ideological spheres reacting upon it in their turn, though with a secondary effect. . . . All history must be studied afresh, the conditions of existence of the different formations of society must be examined individually before the attempt is made to deduce from them the political, civil-law, aesthetic, philosophic, religious, etc., views corresponding to them. Up to now but little has been done here because only a few people have got down to it seriously. In this field we can utilize heaps of help, it is immensely big, and anyone who will work seriously can achieve much and distinguish himself." (*Marx–Engels Correspondence*, 415–16.)

Part of the seeming ambiguity of the concept of a mode of production stems from the fact that the interpretation put upon the concept varies from society to society. This has been taken by some to indicate that Marx's use of terms was inconsistent. This conclusion is itself inconsistent, however, for it is generally held on the one hand that fixed categories and definitions prejudice our interpretation of past, present and future, while on the other hand "floating" relational definitions of the sort used by Marx (see Ollman, 1971) are held to be inadmissible and confusing. Marx tried to relate his definitions and categories to the society under consideration. Therefore, while it is difficult to determine the meaning of the term "mode of production" in abstract, we ought to be able to say something about its constituent features. The mode of production refers to those elements, activities and social relationships which are necessary to produce and reproduce real (material) life. There are three basic elements, and they remain constant from society to society. They are

1   the object of labour (the raw materials existing in nature),
2   the means of labour (the tools, equipment, fixed capital, etc., built up by past labour)
3   labour power.

These three elements must be brought together into an activity pattern that fashions the products and services necessary to produce and reproduce real life in society. The activity patterns can vary immensely, depending upon the technological arrangements for production, the division of labour, the products needed as means for future production, the consumer needs of societies in different environments, and so on. The social basis for coordinating individual activity in production consists of social relationships: these can vary both with the co-ordinating mechanism (which may be different in different societies) and according to the mode of production. The social relationships form a social structure which is maintained through political, legal, and other forces. In some societies, for example, kinship provides a social structure through which activity can be coordinated. In another society, a status system based on some form of property ownership may perform the same function, in this case serving to assign production roles to participants. In contemporary western society, the price system serves to coordinate a large number of individual activities through market behaviour and the requisite social structure is here a stratified class society. Socialist societies seek to replace the market mechanism by something else, such as a centralized or decentralized planning system. These various coordinating mechanisms—modes of economic integration— are an integral part of the economic basis of society, for it is through them that the various elements in production are brought together, and the diverse socially productive activities of society are welded into something coherent. Each society will exhibit a particular blend of elements, a particular mix of activities and a particular patterning of social relationships. All of these, when taken together and insofar as they contribute to the production and reproduction of real life, constitute the mode of production. It is for this reason that Engels's advice to study every society afresh has to be taken seriously. If this point is recognized, the concept of a mode of production loses much of its seeming ambiguity.

Marx and Engels concentrate their analysis, for the most part, on the condition of capitalist society and it is dangerous to generalize from this analysis to all modes of production. This is particularly true when it comes to examining the relationships between the economic basis and the ideological superstructure. Engels, in his letter to Bloch, concedes a certain autonomy of ideological forms (political, juridical, religious, etc.) in the superstructure and rejects the idea of some simple economic determinism. Certain passages in *Capital* (for example, volume 3, 797) and such works as the *Grundrisse* indicate that this was also Marx's view. The essence of the matter is that the totality of interacting political, legal, institutional, and other forms, as well as the state of consciousness, are necessarily both supportive and reflective of conditions in the economic basis of society. The particularities of historical processes and of the relationship between economic basis and superstructure are intricate in their design. Engels, in his letter to Bloch, cited "the endless host of accidents", the "traditions that haunt human minds" and the "conflicts between many individual wills" as being contained in a historical process that contained "innumerable intersecting forces, an infinite series of parallelograms of forces, which give rise to one resultant—the historical event." Ultimately, it is in the sequence of historical events that "the economic movement finally asserts itself as necessary" (Marx–Engels, *Selected Correspondence*, 417–18).

The survival of a society means the perpetuation of a given mode of production. Hence, Marx argues (*Pre-Capitalist Economic Formations; Capital*, volume 3, 879) that a mode of production must create the conditions for its own perpetuation—the reproduction of these conditions becomes as important as production itself. This means the perpetuation of political, juridical, and other ideological forms (including states of social consciousness) which are consistent with the economic basis, as well as the perpetuation of the various relationships (for example, division of labour) within the economic basis itself. The survival of an economic system requires, for example, the survival of the property relations upon which it is based. Marx therefore draws attention to the way in which a mode of production "produces" the conditions for its own existence. Under these conditions a given mode of production becomes "its own prerequisite, and proceeds from itself, creating the presupposition of its maintenance and growth" (Marx, *Grundrisse* 107).

The transformation from one mode of production to another has to be explained. Marx argued that:

"No social order is ever destroyed before all the productive forces for which it is sufficient have been developed, and new superior relations of production never replace older ones before the material conditions for their existence have matured within the framework of the old society. Mankind thus inevitably sets itself only such tasks as it is able to solve, since closer examination will always show that the problem itself arises only when the material conditions for its solution are already present or at least in the course of formation." (*A Contribution to the Critique of Political Economy*, Preface.)

There are two important ideas in this passage. The first suggests that any mode of production will tend to exhaust its own potentialities with respect to either the natural or societal conditions within which it subsists. By exhausting the social possibilities or depleting the natural resource base, a given mode of production will be forced to adapt and change in some way. These adaptations may lead to the stabilization of society through the emergence of superstructural forms (such as states of consciousness, political mechanisms, etc.) which limit population growth, coerce certain sections of the population, and otherwise prevent society from incurring that crisis out of which new economic and social forms can emerge. Or adaptations may open up new potentialities within the existing mode of production. Changes of this sort may bring the forces in the superstructure into conflict with those in the economic basis. For example, technological changes designed to increase command over natural resources may entail new social and legal forms for their implementation (new divisions of labour, new concepts of property rights, and so on). These conflicts may, however, be resolved within a given mode of production. Marx considered capitalism, for example, as being

"permanently revolutionary, tearing down all obstacles that impede it. . . . Capitalist production moves in contradictions which are constantly re-established. The universality towards which it is perpetually driving finds limitations in its own nature, which at a certain stage of its development will make it appear as itself the greatest barrier to this tendency, leading thus to its own self-destruction." (*Grundrisse*, 94–5.)

A particular conjunction of circumstances may make it possible to forge a new combination of social and economic forms to define a new mode of production. This requires that certain social and economic forms, in both the economic basis and the superstructure, carry over from one mode of production to another: indeed, without a certain persistency of these forms, the transition from one mode of production to another would be impossible. Thus different *forms* of production can be found in the same *mode* and similar *forms* can likewise be identified within the different *modes*. Certain forms characteristic of capitalism (for example, commerce, credit, money, interest) can be identified in earlier epochs: these forms played an important role in the transformation from feudalism to capitalism, for it was through quantitative changes in their importance to society that the qualitative change from feudalism to capitalism was achieved. This is the second important idea in Marx's argument. It implies that one historical epoch is not the exclusive domain of one mode of production, even though a particular mode may be clearly dominant. Society always contains within itself potentially conflicting modes of production. Lukacs puts it this way:

"A particular mode of production does not develop and play an historic role only when the mode superseded by it has already everywhere completed the social transformations appropriate to it. The modes of production and the corresponding social forms and class stratifications which succeed and supersede one another tend in fact to appear in history much more as *intersecting and opposing* forces." (1970, 45.)

Part of the ambiguity that has surrounded the concept of the mode of production has resulted from attempts to identify various modes with various historical epochs. This has led some to conclude mistakenly that the mode of production is an "ideal type" concept in Weber's sense—in other words, one that has conceptual utility but no empirical validity. On the contrary, it is clear that a particular historical epoch derives much of its character from the conflict between different modes of production. Or, put another way, society itself is marked by conflict over the proper definition of the mode of production appropriate to its circumstances. Even in stable societies, opposing modes of production are present; but here they are closely held in check by various ideological, social, political and legal devices. It is in this respect that the superstructural elements in society play a vital role in checking the transformation of both the economic basis of society and the social relationships contained in that economic basis. And it is for this reason that it is in the ideological superstructure that "men become conscious of conflict and fight it out". When a particular historical period is described as "feudal" or "capitalistic", therefore, this should always be taken to mean that this historical period was *dominated by* a mode of production which we characterize as "feudal" or "capitalist".

At this juncture I think it is useful to make some preliminary observations on the relationship between urbanism as a *social form*, the city as a *built form*, and the *dominant mode of production*. The city is in part a storehouse of fixed assets accumulated out of previous production. It is constructed with a given technology and is built in the context of a given mode of production (which is not to say that all aspects of the built form of a city are functional with respect to the mode of production). Urbanism is a social form, a way of life predicated on, among other things, a certain division of labour and a certain hierarchical ordering of activity which is broadly consistent with the dominant mode of production. The city and urbanism can therefore function to stabilize a particular mode of production (they both help create the conditions for the self-perpetuation of that mode). But the city may also be the locus of the accumulated contradictions and therefore the likely birthplace of a new mode of production. Historically, the city appears to have variously functioned as a pivot around which a given mode of production is organized, as a centre of revolution against the established order, and as a centre of power and privilege (to be revolted against). Historically, the antithesis between town and country has been a pivot of movement and conflict around which the whole economic history of society has unfolded. In *The German Ideology* (p. 69), Marx and Engels wrote:

"The antagonism between town and country begins with the transition from barbarism to civilization, from tribe to State, from locality to nation, and runs through the whole history of civilization to the present day. . . . The existence of the town implies, at the same time, the necessity of administration, police, taxes, etc.; in short, of the municipality, and thus of politics in general. Here first becomes manifest the division of the population into two great classes, which is directly based on the division of labour and on the instruments of production."

The study of urbanism may therefore contribute significantly to our understanding of the social relationships in the economic basis of society, as well as to our understanding of political and other ideological elements in the superstructure. But like any social form, urbanism can exhibit a considerable variety of forms within a dominant mode of production, while similar forms can be found in different modes of production. For example, certain cities of the medieval period (particularly those dominated by religious institutions) may resemble certain cities in the capitalist period while there may be a tremendous contrast between cities within the capitalist mode of production itself. Yet it seems reasonable to suppose that a dominant mode of production will be characterized by a dominant form of urbanism and, perhaps, by a certain homogeneity in the built form of the city. In an interesting passage in *Pre-Capitalist Economic Formations* (pp. 77–8) Marx attempts a preliminary classification (obviously founded on very sketchy information):

"Ancient classical history is the history of cities, but cities based on landownership and agriculture; Asian history is a kind of undifferentiated unity of town and country (the large city, properly speaking, must be regarded merely as a princely camp superimposed on the real economic structure); the Middle Ages (Germanic [Feudal] period) starts with the countryside as the locus of history, whose further development then proceeds through the opposition of town and country; modern history is the urbanization of the countryside, not, as among the ancients, the ruralization of the city."

The general proposition that some sort of relationship exists between the form and functioning of urbanism (and in particular the various forms of the town–country relationship) and the dominant mode of production appears entirely reasonable. The main problem, therefore, is to elucidate its nature. Marxist and non-Marxist scholars alike have sought to improve upon Marx's classification of the various modes of production and to identify various societies at various points in their evolution in terms of some generally accepted typology. The difficulty with this approach is that the variety of forms in both the economic basis and the superstructure of a strongly dominant mode of production does not permit a unique characterization of that mode. Since much of the tangible evidence we rely on to characterize a society relates to forms (for example, the layout of cities, etc.), one encounters both contention and ambiguity in attempts to define the essential qualities of a particular mode of production. There is, for instance, general agreement on the existence of a mode of production called "feudal" (Marx called it "Germanic"), but disagreement as to what exactly characterizes it and as to the societies to which it may validly be applied. In part, this contention arises because the specific attributes of feudalism were originally established by European historians working in a European context; these attributes have been much modified as scholars have extended their analyses to other contexts such as Japan (Hall, 1962) and early China (Wheatley, 1971).

The argument over the essence of feudalism is polite and refined compared with the argument over capitalism. A great variety of social forms can exist under capitalism. Institutional variations are substantial from country to country and there have been significant changes through time as well. Some consider that capitalism is now qualitatively different from the mode of production which dominated the nineteenth century. Baran and Sweezy (1966), for example, argue that the monopoly form of capitalism is qualitatively different from the typical, nineteenth-century, individualistic capitalism. Others argue that the welfare state in Scandinavian countries and Britain has so essentially changed capitalism that it is no longer reasonable to describe such societies as "capitalist". These arguments are not merely academic, of course, for they represent different analytic positions from which to criticize contemporary society and different prescriptive bases for action. There is, in fact, no mode of production which can be characterized in a fashion that meets with the accord of all observers. It is therefore useful to extend Wheatley's conclusion with respect to feudalism to all modes of production. He suggests

"that a feudal society cannot be categorized under a single inclusive concept, and that feudalism as an ideal type need not be exemplified in its totality by any particular society which is alleged to be feudal. A feudal society is to be viewed as *a mode of social, political, and economic integration* which subsumes a range of essential variables. In defining such a system it is particularly necessary to pay attention to the limits of variability of these elements." (1971, 121.)

The concept of a mode of production when used in the relational manner typical of Marx, is not an "ideal type" construct. But it is, perhaps, too broad and all-embracing to provide the requisite tools for dissecting in any fine fashion the relationship between society and urbanism. Some other conceptual device is thus required, and the one that springs most readily to mind is indicated in Wheatley's phrase "mode of social, political, and economic integration".

MODES OF ECONOMIC INTEGRATION

Karl Polanyi (1968, 148–9) distinguishes between three distinctive modes of economic integration or coordinating mechanisms—*reciprocity, redistribution* and *market exchange*. These may in general be associated with three distinctive modes of social organization called, by Morton Fried (1967), egalitarian, rank and stratified, respectively. The associations between modes of economic integration and social organization are not exact and the schemas put forward by Polanyi and Fried differ in certain respects. In general it appears that reciprocity is exclusively associated with egalitarian social structures, that market exchange (in the restricted sense given to this term by Polanyi) is exclusively associated with stratification, but that redistribution may exist in either rank or stratified social structures. It is also apparent that all three modes of economic integration may be found simultaneously within a given mode of production although one or other is usually dominant. They are not therefore mutually exclusive with respect to each other. But at a particular period in history, one particular mode of economic integration may dominate and be fundamental to the functioning of society. It is thus possible to characterize societies according to the degree of market penetration into human activity, the respects in which reciprocity is relied upon, the extent to which redistributive activity can be observed, and the way in which the three modes function together to bring about that overall coordination of activity upon which the survival of society as a whole relies. We can also characterize the social structure of society by examining the institutional supports and correlative social features of the different modes of economic integration. Polanyi puts it this way:

"Reciprocity, then, assumes for a background symmetrically arranged groupings; redistribution is dependent upon the presence of some measure of centricity in the group; exchange in order to produce integration requires a system of price-making markets. It is apparent that the different patterns of integration assume definite institutional supports." (1968, 149.) The concepts of reciprocity, redistribution and market exchange appear to offer simple and effective tools for dissecting the relationship between societies and the urban forms manifest within them. It will therefore be useful to sharpen these concepts preparatory for use.

1 Reciprocity

Reciprocity involves the transfer of goods, favours and services among individuals in a given group according to certain well-defined social customs. Various kinds of reciprocity are described by Fried (1967). "Balanced" reciprocity indicates a mutual exchange among individuals or production units (such as families) with the amounts exchanged being approximately equal (in the long run) among participants. Many groups exhibit an "unbalanced" reciprocity which ensures that there is a constant movement from those who have to those without. Examples of "negative" reciprocity, which we would call stealing, can also be found. Reciprocity characteristically accords with the existence of symmetrical groupings in the social structure (Polanyi, 1968, chapter 1). Fried calls these societies *egalitarian*, and defines this as meaning that they have "as many positions of prestige in any given age-sex grade as there are persons capable of filling them. . . . As many persons as can wield power—whether through personal strength, influence, authority, or whatever means—can do so and there is no necessity to draw them together to establish an order of dominance and paramountcy." (1967, 33.)

An egalitarian society does not possess the requisite mechanisms for systematic social coercion (which does not preclude the occurrence of individual acts of coercion) and its social coherence is therefore maintained through voluntary cooperation loosely sustained by social custom. Primitive groups are often egalitarian and dominated by reciprocity in exchange. This form of social organization broadly corresponds to what Marx considered to be primitive communism. A number of points need to be made about societies dominated by such a mode of social organization. The first is that they tend to stabilize at their social and resource limits and they are not characterized by social change. In the Marxist sense they have no history, they merely exist in timeless fashion. They simply reproduce their own existence. Also such societies exhibit both a very poorly developed sense of individuality and a consciousness of the relationship between the individual and nature dominated by conditions in the immediate sensuous environment. This consciousness of nature Lévi-Strauss (1966) calls "the science of the concrete", which is a mode of scientific enquiry adapted to perception and imagination but which excludes the abstract conceptualizations of contemporary scientific thought. The science of the concrete is never capable of penetrating beyond naive realism or phenomenal absolutism (Segall *et al.*, 1966) and is permeated by what Gutkind (1956, 11) calls an "I–Thou" relationship between man and the natural world rather than an "I–It" relationship in which man views himself as both separate and different from nature in certain important respects. Egalitarian societies, with their dominant form of economic integration, thus exhibit certain features in their ideological superstructure which reflect both the ability and the need to exploit "the sensible world in sensible terms". Lévi-Strauss thus suggests that the science of the concrete was sufficiently sophisticated to provide the basis for the neolithic revolution in agriculture. Yet it was not sufficiently elaborate to embrace the rise of science which Childe (1942) saw as a

necessary concomitant of the urban revolution in Meso-
potamia.

In general it is accepted by most scholars that egalitarian
societies are incapable of supporting urbanism. The typical
symmetrical groupings do not permit the concentration of
social product necessary for urbanism. Reciprocity can be
found as a residual form in urban society in such diverse places
as the collusive practices of large corporations and in the acts
of friendly exchange and mutual support among good neigh-
bours in a community. But an economy dominated by reciprocity cannot sustain urbanism.

2 Redistributive integration

A *rank society* is defined by Fried as
"one in which positions of valued status are somehow limited
so that not all of those of sufficient talent to occupy such
statuses actually achieve them. Such a society may or may not
be stratified. That is, a society may sharply limit its positions
of prestige without affecting the access of its entire membership
to the basic resources upon which life depends. . . . Accumulation of signs of prestige does not convey any privileged claim to
the strategic resources on which the society is based." (1967, 109.)
Rank societies are characterized by a *redistributive* mode of
economic integration. Redistribution involves a flow of goods
(or in some cases the establishment of rights over production)
to support the activities of an elite. Characteristically there is
a flow of goods into and out of some centre. Fried (1967, 117)
suggests that this centre is typically "the pinnacle of the rank
hierarchy or, as complexity mounts, the pinnacle of a smaller
component network within a larger structure". Urbanism is
thus possible in a rank society. Wheatley (1971, 341) indicates
that urban genesis in northern China involved, among other
things, "the transmutation of reciprocity into redistribution".
In complicated rank societies the social structure may be physically represented by a hierarchy of urban centres of the sort
derived in the locational theories of Christaller and Lösch.
Johnson (1970) provides considerable evidence on this point.
Certainly it would seem that there can be no urbanism and no
hierarchy of urban centres unless there is some significant
hierarchical ordering in the social structure.

A redistributive economy with its correlative social form, the rank society, can, in theory at least, be maintained through voluntary cooperation. Most rank societies in the past have been founded on a religious ideology and in some cases this may have proved sufficient to guarantee the perpetuation of the redistributive economy. A priesthood and a central bureaucracy may be supported willingly by a peasant population. It seems more likely, however, that redistribution will be sustained through the establishment of rights over output or over the means of production (which implies stratification)—rights held by a small elite and guaranteed by force if necessary. The evidence for this lies in the emergence of political institutions and other forms (such as property ownership of some sort) in the superstructure. Fried (1967), after an extensive search, can find no examples of a purely redistributive society which did not contemporaneously possess political and legal institutions. In some cases redistributive societies (such as the feudal societies of medieval Europe) are also stratified, while in some theocratic societies it appears that the rights which guaranteed the perpetuation of the redistributive economy were moral rights over output rather than property rights to the means of production themselves.

3 Market exchange

It is important to distinguish market exchange as a mode of economic integration from the acts of barter and exchange which can occur under reciprocity and redistribution. Polanyi distinguishes between

1   a mere locational movement of a product among people
2   exchange of a product at a price set by some social mechanism
3   exchange which occurs through the operation of price-fixing markets.

He continues:

"In order for exchange to be integrative the behaviour of the partners must be oriented on producing a price that is as favourable to each partner as he can make it. Such a behaviour contrasts sharply with that of exchange at a set price. . . . Exchange at set prices involves no more than the gain to either

party implied in the decision of exchanging; exchange at
fluctuating prices aims at a gain that can be attained only by
an attitude involving a distinctive antagonistic relationship
between the partners." (1968, 154–5.)
Market exchange occurs under a variety of circumstances, but
it functions as a mode of economic integration only when price-
fixing markets operate to coordinate activities. It is in this
latter sense that the term "market exchange" is used throughout this essay.

Regularized exchange through price-fixing markets is a finely
tuned mechanism for coordinating and integrating the activity
of large numbers of individuals acting independently. But to
be effective this system requires that individuals respond appro-
priately to price signals—otherwise there will be no economic
integration. Responses have to be focused on prices and potential profits. It is therefore *exchange value* rather than *use value* (see
chapter 5) that is the focus of exchange. Instead of commodities being sold for money to buy commodities, money is used
to purchase commodities which are then resold (often in a
transformed state) to procure more money. This latter process
of circulation is the hallmark of business behaviour, and it is
this pattern of circulation which provides the focus for Marx's
analyses in *Capital*. Integration through price-fixing markets
is characteristic of the capitalist mode of production: it encourages the division of labour and the geographic specialization of production, and, through competition, it stimulates the
drive towards the adoption of new technologies and the
organization of a reasonably efficient space economy. Consequently, it increases enormously the prospect for the creation
of material wealth in society as a whole. It tends always to
bring about enlarged reproduction. But market exchange rests
on scarcity, for without it price-fixing markets could not
function. So scarcity leads to wealth via the market exchange
system while the preservation of market exchange requires that
scarcity be maintained. Many social institutions in the superstructure are therefore designed to reproduce the conditions of
scarcity upon which price-fixing markets rely. This is particularly true with respect to those institutions which regulate the
ownership of the means of production. As a result, *stratification*
as a social form and market exchange as a mode of economic
integration are related in a very specific way, for differential

access to what Fried (1967, 186) calls "the basic resources that sustain life" permits the social organization of scarcity in the economic basis itself. In a stratified society natural and social features can be characterized as "resources" in a self-conscious manner. Both "scarcity" and "resource" are, however, relative concepts which must be used with circumspection (see above, pp. 80–86; 139). But once a social definition is given to these terms then practical economy, which deals with the allocation of scarce resources, becomes possible.

The market exchange relationship affects the consciousness of the individual participants in a number of ways. The individual replaces states of *personal* dependence (characteristic of egalitarian and rank societies) by states of *material* dependence (Marx, *Grundrisse*, 70–73). The individual becomes "free" yet is controlled by the hidden hand of the market system. The ideology of societies penetrated by market exchange reflects this. Max Weber (1904) and other writers (for example, Tawney, 1937) have recognized an essential connection between changes in religious ideology and the rise of European capitalism. The struggle to achieve a new religious ideology reflected a struggle to replace the social relationships of the feudal order by social relationships appropriate to the capitalist order. An important, perhaps central, aspect to this ideological struggle concerned the meaning of the word "value". To the ancient Greeks, living in a rank society in a condition of hierarchical personal dependence, value referred to the moral worth or "goodness" of a person. As a consequence, the value of an exchange could not be separated from the value of the persons involved in the exchange (Polanyi, 1968, chapter 5). This underlying concept of value, characteristic of all rank societies (such as the Catholic Church of the medieval period), is different from that operating in egalitarian societies: here value lies in the immediate use of a good or favour insofar as it meets the needs (physical or psychological) of the individual. In price-fixing markets, in contrast, value becomes a function of command over resources obtained through acts of exchange. Exchange value, expressed in prices, is an abstract quantity determined through the functioning of a market system based on money as a measure of value. Martin Luther's admonitions on questions of "goodness" and "profit" can therefore be seen as an attempt to conjoin the concept of value in market exchange with the concept of value as moral worth in an uneasy alliance. Hobbes (1651) makes the same attempt in *Leviathan*. On the one hand he asserts unequivocally that "The Value or Worth of a man is as of all other things his Price; that is to say, so much as would be given for the use of his Power. . . . And as in other things, so in men, not the seller but the buyer determines the Price." On the other hand, Hobbes also asserts that "The publique worth of a man, which is the Value set on him by the Common-wealth, is that which men commonly call DIGNITY, and this Value . . . is understood, by offices of Command, Judicature, publique Employment, or by Names and Titles, introduced for distinction of such Value" (p. 151). The clash between these concepts has been an important ideological force ever since the Reformation: the conflict between the old aristocratic order and the newly emergent industrial and commercial class in the early years of the industrial revolution in England can be viewed in these terms for example.

The consciousness of the relationship between man and nature also assumes a new form under conditions of market exchange. Early European rank redistributive societies gave rise, in general, to abstract forms of art and science which were very different from those expressed in "the science of the con-concrete". Called into service to articulate the cosmological symbolism of what was almost invariably a theocratic society, the science of the rank society was abstract and deductive (hence the rise of mathematics in Greece) and its task was to discern the structure of the cosmos in which the image of man, nature and society was fashioned. Applied science frequently aimed to imitate the cosmic order and landscapes were fashioned accordingly—the built form of the city in redistributive economies can, as Wheatley (1969; 1971) brilliantly demonstrates, be interpreted as a projection of cosmological symbolism into the material world. The penetration of the market exchange economy, however, appears to have brought with it a new emphasis in science upon natural philosophy—an emphasis which stemmed from the fact that man now viewed himself as holding a new and different position in relationship to nature. The period since the Renaissance has forged a new consciousness which rests upon "the dichotomy of all reality into inner experience and outer world, subject and object, private reality and public truth" (Langer, 1942, 22). This consciousness, in what Whiteman (1967, 370) calls "The Age of Scientific Dualism", made it possible to differentiate between the public truths of exchange value and price response, and the private truths of use value and actual consumption. Marx portrays one of the consequences as follows:

"Nature becomes for the first time simply an object for mankind, purely a matter of utility; it ceases to be recognized as a power in its own right; and the theoretical knowledge of its independent laws appears only as a strategem designed to subdue it to human requirements, whether as the object of consumption or as the means of production." (*Grundrisse*, 94.)

This conceptualization of the natural world, in which nature is viewed as a "resource" for the use of man, underlies the materialist conception of nature in modern scientific thought (see Whiteman, 1969). The rise of modern natural science should not be viewed, therefore, as a change in ideology which bore no relationship to the penetration of the market exchange economy. It is significant that Leonardo da Vinci worked at the time when Florentine commercial endeavour was at its height, and that Isaac Newton should have been Master of the King's Mint in a period of fundamental revolution in English commercial and banking techniques (Wilson, 1965, 227): applied mathematics, political arithmetic and natural philosophy apparently progressed hand in hand in late seventeenth-century Britain. Scientists do not live in isolation from social circumstances and we should therefore expect science to reflect the social values, attitudes and tensions of the time. Yi-Fu Tuan's delightful study on *The Hydrological Cycle and the Wisdom of God* (1966) documents, for example, how the typical cosmic symbolism of the old order clashed with the natural scientific style of the new in the seventeenth- and eighteenth-century discussion of hydrological phenomena.

Market exchange requires specific legal and political institutions if it is to operate successfully as a mode of economic integration. In Europe the legal and political adjustments necessary to facilitate the new mode of economic integration were legion. These adjustments were not made over night and there has been a continuous evolution in legal and political institutions since the seventeenth century (the emergence of limited liability law, joint stock companies, conglomerate law, and so on). In bringing these new legal forms and institutions into being, free use is always made of a symbolism culled from an older order: the state and other political forms take on, for example, an aura of moral certitude characteristic of the moral rights asserted in theocratic societies. In their practical aspect these institutions serve to sustain and then to perpetuate the new mode of economic integration by legitimizing and in some cases sanctifying it. Ultimately, however, all these institutions depend for their perpetuation on the power to coerce, for, as Fried puts it, "stratified societies create pressures unknown in egalitarian societies and rank societies, and these pressures cannot be contained by internalized social controls or ideology alone" (1968, 186). The market mode of economic integration therefore depends upon the exercise of coercive power, for it is only through such power that the delicate institutions which sustain price-fixing markets can be perpetuated. Because stratified societies operating through market exchange are dynamic and expansionary, we must anticipate contradictions to emerge which call for internal adjustments or new forms of expansion. Since coercion is an essential feature to the market mode of economic integration, it is unlikely that these contradictions can be resolved without the use of violence.

To summarize: reciprocity, redistribution and market exchange are three distinctive modes of economic integration. They are indicative of certain correlative features in the ideological superstructure of society: status, class, the projection of both into patterns of political power, definite supportive institutions and states of social consciousness are perhaps the most significant of these features. Like most simple but crude categorizations, such a schema as this must ultimately be replaced by a finer mesh of concepts in order to catch the more subtle nuances of economic and social organization. But reciprocity, redistribution and market exchange equip us with the conceptual means to characterize a social and economic formation, and provide us with consistent threads to trace the transformation from one dominant mode of production to another.

CITIES AND SURPLUS

Cities are formed through the geographic concentration of a social surplus product, which the mode of economic integration must therefore be capable of producing and concentrating. Herein lies the crucial relationship between urbanism and the mode of economic integration. The concept of a social surplus product is, however, a somewhat slippery one. If it is to be used, as I am proposing here, as a concept through which urbanism and the various modes of economic integration may be related, then its meaning has to be carefully clarified.

THE SURPLUS CONCEPT AND URBAN ORIGINS

The surplus concept as it relates to urbanism has been subjected to the greatest scrutiny in the literature on urban origins. There is general agreement that an agricultural surplus product was necessary for the emergence of city forms. Much controversy, however, surrounds the manner in which we should conceive of the surplus and the way in which surpluses arise, are acquired and are put to use. It may help to examine this controversy. There are two interconnected aspects to it. The first concerns whether the surplus can be defined in an absolute or a relative sense. The second stems from an argument over whether the ability to produce a surplus automatically guarantees that it will be produced to the maximum extent possible and used to foster new social development of which urbanism is a central feature. Embedded in this controversy is a deep cleavage between those who hold to a materialist interpretation of the historical evidence and those who look for some alternative interpretation of the *primum agens* of historical evolution. Our ability to comprehend the main lines of cleavage between the protagonists in the argument is obscured, however, by the tendency for antagonists of the materialist interpretation to pick upon the crude versions of the materialist argument—versions which some "Marxists" have all too frequently propounded but which Marx and Engels clearly disavowed.

A social surplus is usually taken to represent "that quantity of material resources over and above subsistence requirements of the society in question" (Polanyi *et al.*, 1957, 321). It is not, however, easy to define these "subsistence requirements". They may be equated to minimal biological requirements, but this is unsatisfactory for, as Orans points out, "subsistence level is inextricably cultural and is not based on uniform biological species requirements" (1966, 25). By confining our attention to biological requirements alone, we can roughly define what Orans calls the "subminimal surplus", which is the difference between total output and the "subminimal requirements" necessary to support purely biological activity (metabolism, activity for production, and reproduction). Cultural and social needs make it certain that no society could survive with output at this level (while separating biological from cultural functions is itself a very suspicious strategem). At best, then, subminimal requirements can indicate what would be left over if the individual were living a "pure animal existence". But we cannot establish the existence of an absolute surplus by this means.

The definition of an absolute surplus requires that we identify which social and cultural functions are "necessary" for the survival of society and which are "excess" and supported by the production of surplus. This is clearly an impossible if not unreasonable task for "need" (see chapter 3) can be defined only in terms of a particular technical, social, cultural and institutional setting. Even such an elemental thing as hunger cannot be measured independently of some social situation. Marx, for example, suggests that

"Hunger is hunger. But the hunger which is satisfied with cooked meat and fork is another hunger than that which swallows raw meat with the aid of hands, nails and teeth. *The mode of production produces, both objectively and subjectively, not only the object consumed but also the manner of consumption.*" (Quoted in Schmidt, 1970, 84; italics mine.)

The consciousness of need is a social product; it is but a part of the ideological superstructure which rests upon a functioning economic base. The level of need varies from society to society and from time to time; it is contingent on the mode of production itself. In *A Contribution to the Critique of Political Economy* Marx examines the intricate relationships between production, consumption, distribution, need, exchange and circulation and he arrives at the following important principle:

"Production produces consumption: (1) by providing the material of consumption; (2) by determining the mode of consumption; (3) by creating in the consumer a need for the objects which it first presents as products." (p. 197.)

Most workers have accepted that the surplus is something relative, but few non-Marxist scholars recognize how the *nature* of the surplus is in turn produced by the conditions internal to society. Pearson, for example, merely accepts without further elaboration that:

"Relative surpluses are simply material means and human services that are in some sense set aside or mobilized apart from the existing functional demands which a given social unit—a family—a firm—a society—makes upon its economy." (Polanyi *et al.*, 334.)

Rosa Luxemburg agrees that surpluses appear out of a particular kind of social and economic situation. She holds that "every society performs surplus labour" because non-workers (particularly children and sometimes the sick and the old) are maintained by workers and because it is frequently necessary to maintain a "fund of social insurance against the elementary disaster which may threaten the annual produce" (1913, 77). This may lead, even in egalitarian societies, to the creation of a central communal storehouse and social mechanisms for the distribution of stored produce. An operating surplus of some sort is necessary for the long-term survival of society for no society is prescient enough to be able to calculate exactly what its future needs and circumstances are likely to be. Most societies therefore set aside something over and above what is necessary to meet immediate needs. As society changes, so may the quantity of material product set aside as well as the purposes for doing so. Definition of what is or is not surplus is therefore contingent upon the social conditions of production in society.

It is consequently possible to increase the quantity of surplus by instituting social changes which alter the social definition of surplus (or, what amounts to the same thing, changing the concept of need) without actually increasing the total quantity of material product. Religious functions which make material demands may, for example, be regarded by some as "necessary" to the survival of society. But should all elements in society decide that organized religious activity is not necessary then the material product allocated to these functions would be designated as surplus. This would also happen if it were decided, in like manner, that the material resources currently allocated to military ventures and defence were not necessary for survival. Each mode of production and each mode of social organization has implicit within it a particular definition of surplus. Since society invariably contains different modes of production in conflict with each other there is bound to be a corresponding conflict over the social definition of the surplus. For this reason the concept of surplus has ideological content and political meaning. Those who appropriate surplus product for their own benefit go to elaborate lengths to persuade those who contribute it that the activities and functions of the appropriators are invaluable, necessary and beneficial for the survival of society—the ideological blandishments of the ancient priesthood and of the military industrial complex have certain things in common. This implies that a surplus should be defined as that quantity of product over and above what is necessary to guarantee the survival of society *as individuals know it*. The surplus has to be defined in a way which is internal to the workings of a particular mode of production. In society at large what is defined as surplus by some will be construed as essential by others.

This view of the surplus condemns us to a formless relativism —a position that, as we shall shortly see, appears quite acceptable to many western scholars. If the surplus concept is to play a critical role we must, however, construct some more general vantage point from which it can be viewed in relationship to diverse modes of production, modes of economic integration and the varieties of urbanism. To do so requires that innumerable parochialist definitions of surplus be superseded by a concept which can bridge cultures, epochs and classes. The Marxist version does this by relating the surplus concept to a view of the universal human requirements of man's existence as a species. This relationship may be seen in Marx's work from a juxtaposition of *The Economic and Philosophic Manuscripts of 1844* and the *Grundrisse* on the one hand and *Capital* on the other. From this we may conclude that the surplus has two forms. It may firstly be an amount of material product (over and above that which is necessary to reproduce society in its existing state) that is set aside to promote improvements in human welfare. Rosa Luxemburg (1913) thus points out that there can be no advances in civilization without the initial creation of a surplus that can be used for purposes of overall social advancement. Secondly, the surplus may be regarded as an estranged or alienated version of the first: it appears as a quantity of material resources that is appropriated for the benefit of one segment of society at the expense of another. In all historically occurring modes of production (save those which exhibit primitive communistic forms of social organization) the surplus has appeared in its estranged or alienated form. In these societies the surplus may be equated with the product of alienated labour.

The Marxist conception of the surplus (with its relationally established meanings) has been misunderstood in the western literature (and among Marxists as well) in part because the Marxist view of universal species requirements has been confounded with arguments in support of the concept of an absolute surplus. But there is also a more serious misunderstanding of the relational role of the surplus concept in the overall structure of Marxist thought. Western scholars, such as Pearson, Adams and Wheatley, have been exceedingly critical of Marx's argument, particularly as represented in the work of Gordon Childe on urban origins. Childe, it must be admitted, was not always unambiguous in his presentation of the Marxist view, but he did not hold to some of the views usually attributed to him. We will take up this matter shortly, but it is instructive to enquire how the alternative view, held by many western scholars, unfolds.

The stance of rather formless relativism with respect to the surplus concept adopted by scholars such as Pearson, Adams and Wheatley, has certain consequences for their conception of urban origins as well as for their fundamental conceptualization of the nature of urbanism itself. Because the surplus is conceived of as individual and special to each and every society, it is difficult or impossible to say anything of any great import about its specific role in either the emergence of urban forms or in the functioning of urbanism in general. A surplus has to be produced, to be sure, but it can be produced by all manner of means. Notice, for example, how Pearson shifts from consideration of the surplus to other aspects of social organization:

"Since we are not searching for absolute consumption levels

after which surpluses automatically appear, research interest is directed towards the positive factor of the institutional means by which the course of the ongoing economic process is altered to support the material requirements of new or expanded societal roles." (Pearson *et al.*, 1957, 334.)

Once it is established that institutional forms are the "positive factor" then the problems attached to the production of a surplus, although real enough, become of secondary significance. Social change is thus attributed to a moving force in the minds of men rather than to a necessary evolution of social practice determined by the transition from one dominant mode of production to another as the conditions supportive of an initial mode of production are slowly exhausted through its own internal development and expansion. The surplus is always, it is argued, there for the taking. Pearson writes:

"there are always and everywhere potential surpluses available. What counts is the institutional means for bringing them to life. And the means for calling forth the special effort, setting aside the extra amount, devising the surplus, are as wide and varied as the organization of the economic process itself." (Polanyi *et al.*, 1957, 339.)

Wheatley echoes Pearson's view closely:

"A 'social' surplus, then, is designated as such by the society in question, and its realization depends on the existence of a locus of power capable of extracting products or services from the hands of its members. No primitive peoples have ever spent all their waking hours in eating, breeding and cultivating: even the most debilitated, by squandering some of their resources in non-utilitarian ways, have demonstrated the existence of a surplus. Those administrators charged with the mobilization of resources in redistributive economies long ago discovered that the human frame was almost infinitely extensible and that, consequently, it was almost always possible to wring from the most wretched of cultivators yet another exaction for the support of the central bureaucracy." (1971, 268.)

Adams likewise concludes that "the transformation at the core of the Urban Revolution lay in the realm of social organization" (1966, 12). Which aspect of social organization played the decisive role in the emergence of urbanism is the subject of controversy. Pearson accepts a wide range of possibilities, while Wheatley strongly favours a transformation from shrine to ceremonial centre and hence focuses on religious institutions. In fact a whole gamut of social and organizational features, many of which Marx would characterize as superstructural, are paraded as possible candidates for the role of *the* positive factor or factors which led to the genesis of urbanism. There is considerable diversity of opinion among western scholars, but their views differ markedly from those of Marx who held, quite simply, that any and every society contains inherent contradictions which permit and ultimately necessitate an internal transformation of society if it is to survive. In the course of these internally generated transformations a new mode of production may come into being. And each particular mode of production gives definition and tangible form to the concept of a surplus in much the same way that it produces the superstructural forms necessary for the perpetuation of its own existence.

The version of the materialist argument rejected by Pearson and subsequent writers is substantially different from that advanced by Marx. Pearson thus describes what he calls the "surplus theorem" as a two-stage argument in which surpluses are first supposed to appear with advancing technology and productivity to be followed by "social and economic developments of prime importance". Such things as "trade and markets, money, cities, differentiation into social classes, indeed civilization itself, are thus said to follow on the emergence of a surplus" (Polanyi *et al.*, 1957, 321). Pearson subsequently rejects this straw-man argument, saying firstly that cities do not arise because surpluses appear at a certain stage of economic development; secondly, that "the interrelationship between the material and societal aspects of existence are such that they cannot be separated into 'first', 'then' sequences", and thirdly that the surplus cannot be regarded as even a necessary-but-not-sufficient cause of the social and economic change which underlies the emergence of urbanism. Adams likewise rejects the idea—which both he and Wheatley (1971, 278) attribute to Gordon Childe—that there is

"an inherent tendency for agriculturists to advance in productivity towards the highest potential level consistent with their technology, that is, to maximize their production above subsistence needs and so to precipitate the growth of new patterns of appropriation and consumption involving elites freed from responsibilities for food production." (1966, 45.)

A curious feature about this argument concerning the relationship between surplus production and urban origins is the way in which arguments put forward to counteract materialist views attributed to Childe (a Marxist of sorts) have led a number of contemporary western scholars to take up positions which, in certain respects at least, resemble those of Marx. There remain, of course, some fundamental disagreements. Marx would not allow the institutional and social forms in the superstructure the autonomy that writers such as Pearson and Wheatley clearly impute to them. Although the surplus is to be thought of as relative in both arguments, Marx had a highly structured view of the manner in which it could be regarded as relative (see Ollman, 1971, 12–42). But neither Marx nor Childe argued that the surplus was absolute or that it was causally efficacious in giving rise to urban forms. Childe, for example, wrote:

"The worst contradictions in the neolithic economy were transcended when farmers were persuaded or compelled to wring from the soil a surplus above their own domestic requirements, and when this surplus was made available to support new economic classes not directly engaged in producing their own food. The possibility of producing the requisite surplus was inherent in the very nature of the neolithic economy. Its realization, however, required additions to the stock of applied science at the disposal of all barbarians, as well as modifications in social and economic relations." (1942, 77.)

The ability to produce a surplus and the ability to realize it in a form consistent with urbanism are clearly recognized here as two different things. The latter depended upon the emergence of a form of social and economic organization capable of persuading or compelling the neolithic farmer to produce more than was necessary for mere subsistence. Childe apparently regards the ability to produce a surplus as a necessary, but not sufficient, condition for the emergence of urbanism. Marx, however, provides a better viewpoint from which to grasp how the surplus was created and instituted—a viewpoint usually misrepresented and deserving explanation.

SURPLUS VALUE AND THE SURPLUS CONCEPT

The Marxist concept of the surplus arises out of Marx's analysis of the alienated form of surplus value as it is brought into existence in capitalist society. Surplus value is that part of the total value of production which is left over after constant capital (which includes the means of production, raw materials and instruments of labour) and variable capital (labour power) have been accounted for. Under capitalist conditions, surplus value is in part realized in the three forms of rent, interest and profit. If production is to be maintained and the capitalist mode of production is to survive, then sufficient value must be allocated to labour to permit it to sustain and reproduce itself through the consumption of the goods which that value can purchase. The quantity of goods consumed must at least be equal to the quantity necessary for biological survival (and here Marx appears to invoke an idea which is similar to the concept of a subminimal requirement level proposed by Orans). But there will obviously be certain social needs depending upon the social conditions and relationships necessary to maintain production. Transformations in society inevitably bring about transformations in actual and perceived needs for, as Marx puts it in *The Poverty of Philosophy* (147; see also p. 40), "all history is nothing but a continuous transformation of human nature". The quantity of surplus value thus depends upon the quantity of product necessary to meet the social and biological needs of labour. Part of the objection which Marx voiced against the capitalist mode of production was that the drive to maximize the capitalist forms of surplus value inevitably leads the capitalists as a class (even against their own individual wills) to drive down the levels of subsistence in the labouring population closer and closer to the subminimal requirement line. In the process labour is dehumanized and reduced to an "animal" existence. The performance of the early industrialists, in particular, does not seem to have been remarkably different from that of those early bureaucrats of the Chou dynasty who, as Wheatley infers, found it possible to "wring from the most wretched of cultivators yet another exaction for the support of the central bureaucracy".

In a capitalist economy, surplus value is a quantity measured in exchange value or money terms. In a redistributive economy value is equated to moral worth. Since, however, value arises out of the application of socially necessary labour, the production of surplus value in both types of society can be equated to the extraction of surplus labour power. A portion of the labourer's day is devoted to producing surplus value and a portion of it is allocated to producing the equivalent of whatever it takes to maintain and reproduce labour power. Surplus labour is therefore that labour power expended by the labourer for the support of someone or something else. From this arises the connection between the Marxist concept of an alienated surplus and alienated labour. In *Capital* Marx writes:

"It is every bit as important, for a correct understanding of surplus value, to conceive of it as a mere congelation of surplus labour time, as nothing but materialized surplus labour, as it is, for a proper comprehension of value, to conceive it as a mere congelation of so many hours of labour, as nothing but materialized labour. The essential difference between the various economic forms of society, between, for instance, a society based on wage-labour, and one based on slave labour, lies only in the mode in which this surplus labour is in each case extracted from the actual producer, the labourer." (Volume 1, 217.)

In a later passage Marx puts it this way:

"Capital has not invented surplus labour. Wherever a part of society possesses the monopoly of the means of production, the labourer, free or not free, must add to the working time necessary for his own maintenance an extra working-time in order to produce the means of subsistence for the owners of the means of production, whether this proprietor be the Athenian Καλὸς Κἀγαθός, Etruscan theocrat, civis Romanus, Norman baron, American slave-owner, Wallachian Boyard, modern landlord or capitalist." (p. 235.)

Surplus value in capitalist society must therefore be viewed as a manifestation of surplus labour under market exchange conditions. In egalitarian societies, as Luxemburg points out, this surplus labour is brought into existence to support the weak and to hedge against environmental uncertainties. In redistributive societies, however, surplus labour takes on an alienated form. A transmutation from egalitarian to redistributive societies thus entails a social redefinition of surplus labour, which is probably not willingly undertaken. Marx thus argues (*Capital* volume 1, 512–15) that there is "no inherent quality of human labour to furnish a surplus product" and that before labour is expended "in surplus labour for strangers, compulsion is required". The capacity to perform surplus labour does not guarantee the alienation of the surplus. Nor is the surplus to be conceived of in anything other than a relative sense depending upon whatever is socially designated as surplus. The surplus concept is relational like all the other concepts in Marx (Ollman, 1971; also see Chapter 7) and it therefore becomes possible to distinguish societies according to the ways in which the surplus is designated and extracted. Marx drew the most significant distinction between alienated and unalienated concepts of the surplus. But he also distinguished within the alienated category between redistributive economies—in which the objective is the acquisition of use value and where there is a natural limitation to the quantity of surplus products that can be absorbed—and market exchange economies, in which the objective is the acquisition of exchange value and in which the only limitation placed upon extracting surplus labour arises from the necessity to sustain and reproduce labour power for purposes of future production. The latter mode of economic integration therefore leads to a far more vigorous pursuit of surplus labour power than does the former. In other words, slave labour by itself tends to be less exploitive than wage labour.

The extraction of surplus labour power does not necessarily give rise to urbanism: urbanism relies upon the concentration of a significant quantity of the social surplus product at one point in space, and it is quite possible for the social surplus to be extracted and yet remain dispersed. Pearson points out that "the practice of mutually obligatory sharing typical of reciprocity is . . . not conducive to the individual building of surpluses since it insures against the very personal uncertainties which induce saving" (Polanyi *et al.*, 1956, 336). The patterns of exchange under reciprocity are not conducive, either to the building of social surpluses in any large quantities or to the concentration of the surplus in the hands of one segment of society. The lack of urbanism under reciprocity can be attributed to the way the surplus is designated, the limited availability of potential surplus, and the inability to concentrate the surplus on a permanent basis. A redistributive mode of economic integration, on the other hand, does imply an ability to concentrate the product of surplus labour, though whether the concentration is on a permanent and large enough basis to give rise to urbanism is another matter. However, it is the market exchange mode that most typically leads to permanent concentrations of surplus value which are then put into circulation once more to reap further surplus value. The three different modes of economic integration are associated with different institutional and organizational arrangements and we may note in passing that contemporary Western scholars tend to emphasize these institutional and organizational arrangements as explanatory of the emergence and expansion of urbanism as a social form.

There is, however, a deeper economic problem to be resolved in the shift from reciprocity to redistribution and the ultimate emergence of market exchange. This is the problem of expanded production which leads in turn to the problem of primitive accumulation. Rosa Luxemburg puts it this way:

"simple reproduction as a mere continuous repetition of the process of production on the same scale as before can be observed over long periods of social history. . . . But simple reproduction is the source and unmistakable sign of general economic and cultural stagnation. No important forward step in production would be possible without expanding reproduction; for the basis and also the social incentive for a decisive advancement of civilization lies solely in the gradual expansion of production beyond immediate requirements." (1913, 41.)

The transformation from reciprocity to redistribution involves a purely economic problem of replacing simple reproduction by expanding reproduction. Marx and Luxemburg both argue that this entails "primitive accumulation", which Marx defined as "nothing else than the historical process of divorcing the producer from the means of production"—a process of expropriation "written in the annals of mankind in letters of blood and fire" (*Capital*, volume 1, 714–15). Primitive accumulation means the exploitation of a certain section of the population—either through the appropriation of accumulated use values existing as fixed assets, or through the appropriation of labour power—in order to gain a surplus product to invest in enlarged reproduction. The key factor in this process, as far as Marx was concerned, is the emergence of new relationships in production (in the economic basis) in which a certain proportion of the population finds itself divorced from control over the means of production. Thus primitive accumulation relies upon the emergence of a stratified society which, although it may initially be dominated by redistribution, contains within itself the seeds for the emergence of market exchange.

Rosa Luxemburg's subsequent analysis of primitive accumulation is more penetrating, although she does not entirely solve the problem that Marx posed in outline. She makes three points of specific interest in the context of urbanism. Firstly, a part of the surplus has to be used to create new means of production. Insofar as this investment assumes a fixed form, it may contribute to the built form of the city. Secondly, primitive accumulation requires the concomitant growth of an effective demand for the surplus product produced. Under the capitalist mode of production this poses a peculiar difficulty in that the capitalist class is directly interested in expanding exchange value and in order to do this an effective demand—through the expansion of old or the creation of new uses—has to be created. In redistributive economies—which are bound to use values—this problem does not arise in the same way. But in both cases we find that the city functions as a locus for disposing of surplus product. Monumental architecture, lavish and conspicuous consumption, and need-creation in contemporary urban society, are all different manifestations of this same phenomenon. The city can thus partly be interpreted as a field for generating effective demand. Thirdly, Luxemburg argues that there is an absolute necessity for an expansionary mode of production, such as capitalism, to seek proportionate amounts of primitive accumulation; the most important mechanisms for this increase in primitive accumulation were, in her view, economic imperialism and an ever-increasing penetration of the market-exchange mode of economic integration into more and more aspects of social life and into new territories. Although there are good grounds for not regarding this as the whole story of primitive accumulation, there can be no doubt that contemporary urbanism, which might be called "global metropolitanism", is embedded in a global form of economic imperialism. All of which points to the question: how is the surplus defined and where does it come from under the conditions of contemporary urbanism?

When Pearson, Wheatley and others focus on institutional and
organizational transformation as underlying the emergence of
urbanism, we can see they are really drawing attention to certain correlative features of that process whereby primitive
accumulation took place. Clearly, the surplus, even in its
socially designated form, did not have causal efficacy—to
suppose so is to indulge in that crude materialist interpretation
of history of which Marx and Engels so heartily disapproved.
The point is that fundamental changes in the economic basis
of society lead to a redesignation of the surplus concept and
to new social relationships in production which match that
designation. The changes are not, and can never be, simply
generated out of the ideological superstructure of society: the
economic conditions have to be right for the emergence of the
new form of economic integration. These economic conditions
contain accumulations of past assets. The material conditions
for the emergence of redistribution have already to be present
or at least in the course of formation (see above, p. 201). In
Capital Marx puts it this way:

"At the dawn of civilization the productiveness acquired by
labour is small, but so too are the wants which develop with
and by the means of satisfying them. Further, at that early
period, the portion of society that lives on the labour of others is
infinitely small compared with the mass of direct producers.
Along with the progress in the productiveness of labour, that
small portion of society increases both absolutely and relatively. Besides, capital with its accompanying relations springs
up from an economic soil that is the product of a process of
development. The productiveness of labour that serves as its
foundation and starting point, is a gift, not of Nature, but of a
history embracing thousands of centuries." (Volume 1, 512.)
It is this argument that Childe is echoing. So the real question
which the surplus concept poses is : what were the relevant
conditions in the economic basis of society which allowed redistribution and ultimately market exchange to emerge as modes
of economic integration?

The basic features in the transformation from reciprocity to
redistribution have to be accounted for. Firstly, the population

(or at least some portion of it) has to be divorced from part of its output or from access to the means of production. Secondly, the aggregate productivity in society has to be sufficient to support the non-productive portion of the population. There is no question but that Marx's and Childe's arguments with respect to these two features are frequently too simplistic. Childe focused on technological changes which increased agricultural productivity. This obviously has significance, as Adams (1966, 45) concedes. But an increase in total population can generate a larger aggregate surplus without any necessary changes in productivity. For example, Orans (1966) makes a good case for an integral relationship between total population, stratification and surplus-creating activities. It can also be argued that density of population is important. Since in redistributive economies, the extraction of surplus labour power involves spatial integration of the economy around an urban centre, this means that a more proximate population combined with ease of communication makes it possible to extract larger quantities of total surplus labour power with less effort. There is a further point. Populations yielding up surplus labour power do not usually do so willingly. Slaves may run away, and a mobile population will simply move out of range of some centre of exploitation. It is important, therefore, for the population yielding surplus labour to be immobile. This partly indicates a mode of production in which fixed assets—such as field clearances—make it difficult to move, and perhaps a high density of population or physical barriers which make it difficult to find living space out of range of the exploitative city centre. Surplus labour power has therefore to be bound (and it is not inconceivable that this should be by ideological preference) either to the urban centre or to the land within range of the urban centre.

Clearly, no one single set of conditions can be identified as being necessary to guarantee the survival of redistributive forms of economic integration. Nevertheless, some combination of the conditions described above appears necessary. Specifying what conditions is a matter for historical scholarship. But it is easier to extract large quantities of product designated as surplus (in the form of alienated labour) under some conditions (such as settled agriculture, high densities of population, easy forms of communication, high natural productivity under

230

a given technology, and the like) than it is under other conditions. Further, these conditions are the result of a history "embracing thousands of centuries". This is all that Childe's version of urban genesis need imply. In the face of this argument, it is difficult to sustain Pearson's and Wheatley's view that there were no necessary conditions for the production of a surplus and that, as a consequence, urbanism could emerge almost anywhere provided the right organizational and institutional arrangements were brought into being.

The conditions that enabled the transformation from reciprocity to redistribution were crucial for the emergence of urbanism; they were instrumental in concentrating surplus product in a few hands and in a few places. The emergence of urbanism and the appropriation of a social surplus product were inextricably related. If surplus value is regarded as a particular manifestation of surplus labour under capitalist (market exchange) conditions, then it follows that urbanism in capitalist societies can be analysed in terms of the creation, appropriation and circulation of surplus value. It is not sufficient, however, merely to assert such an important proposition *a priori*. The truth of it can be attested to only by a study of urbanism under the capitalist mode of production.

In a capitalist economy, accumulated surplus value is in large part put to work to create even greater quantities of surplus value. This process does not occur with similar intensity in all sectors or territories of the capitalist economy. Its intensity depends, among other things, on the degree of market penetration in the sector or territory in question. It is therefore important to examine the spatial and sectoral patterns of circulation of surplus value as profits are invested for the purpose of realizing further profits.

The simplest form of spatial circulation arises when a city extracts surplus product from an agricultural hinterland. Internal differentiation in the economy of the city is associated with the circulation of surplus value within the city, and with the rise of industrialism the city becomes a locus for the production as well as the extraction of surplus value. The establishment of commercial relationships between cities expands the patterns of circulation so that the surplus value can be extracted through commerce and trade. Contemporary global metropolitanism is a combination of all of these elements and the spatial and sectoral patterns of circulation of surplus value are extraordinarily intricate (Frank, 1969, provides a perceptive analysis of this circulation). Global metropolitanism is embedded in the circulation patterns of a global economy, out of which surplus value is being extracted. Different city forms are contained within that economy. Castells (1970), for example, differentiates between the metropolitan forms of North America and Western Europe and the dependent urban forms of much of the rest of the world. Dependent urbanism arises in situations where the urban form exists as a channel for the extraction of quantities of surplus from a rural and resource hinterland for purposes of shipment to the major metropolitan centres. This colonial form of urbanism is currently characteristic, for example, in much of Latin America (Frank, 1969) but in the early nineteenth century it was, as Pred (1966) notes, dominant in the United States. Within countries functioning hierarchies of city types provide channels for the circulation and concentration of surplus value while at the same time providing for the spatial integration of the economy. Swirls in circulation occur too within the large metropoli (between, for example, city and suburb in the contemporary United States): these, however, are minor compared to the massive global circulation of surplus value in which contemporary metropolitanism is embedded.

In all these complex patterns of circulation, local concentrations may arise, but the distinctiveness of the city form, once so apparent as a geographical phenomenon, disappears. Contemporary urbanism may still be regarded, in the fashion propounded by Adams and Wheatley, as a form of social and economic organization which successfully mobilizes, creates, concentrates and (perhaps) manipulates the product of surplus labour in the form of surplus value; but it no longer makes sense to think of the city as a tangible entity which expresses the processes of circulation in fixed and distinguishable form. Nonetheless, simple models of circulation, such as that based on a town–country pattern of circulation, can be helpful in explaining certain basic features of contemporary urbanism: in the sections that follow I will make use of such a simple model for demonstrative purposes.

Capitalism relies upon the circulation of surplus value. The role the city plays in this process depends upon the social, economic, technological and institutional possibilities that govern the disposition of the surplus value concentrated in it. Hoselitz (1960, chapter 8) draws a useful if somewhat simplistic distinction between "generative" and "parasitic" cities. A generative city contributes to the economic growth of the region in which it is situated, whereas a parasitic city does not. A generative city will allocate a considerable amount of the surplus value accumulated within it to forms of investment that enlarge production. The investments may be in the city or in the surrounding rural area (in the latter case they are basically designed, of course, to facilitate an increased rate of extraction of the surplus from the rural area in question). There is therefore a necessary but not sufficient connection between urbanism and economic growth. In this situation the city does return certain benefits to the rural area and hence arises the view, common to Adam Smith (1776, Book 3) and Jane Jacobs (1969), that the city is beneficial to the countryside because the city is the centre of technological innovation and the catalyst for general economic growth and economic advancement. From the city the country receives new products, new means of production, technological innovations, and the like. Adam Smith thus resolves to his own satisfaction what has the appearance of a serious moral dilemma—the fact that "the town may very properly be said to gain its whole wealth and subsistence from the country." The solution, of course, is that "the gains of both are mutual and reciprocal, and the division of labour is in this, as in all other cases, advantageous to all the different occupations." It is noticeable here that Smith ignores the problem of primitive accumulation and circumvents thereby the simple but unassailable fact that towns have historically been founded upon the extraction and concentration of a social surplus product. If the social surplus is used to enlarge reproduction, the total product of society will undoubtedly increase, and thus an increase in the total quantity of social surplus produced has historically been associated with the activity of urbanization—here both Jane Jacobs and Smith are correct. Urban centres have frequently been "generative" but the need to accomplish primitive accumulation militates against the process being naturally and reciprocally beneficial as both Adam Smith and Jane Jacobs envision it, for the processes of primitive accumulation are, in Marx's words, "anything but idyllic".

Parasitic cities, on the other hand, are characterized by a form of social and economic organization which is dedicated to consuming the social surplus, often through enterprises that are conspicuously wasteful from an economic point of view (whatever their religious or military significance). Wolf (1959, 106–9) regards the theocratic centres of early Mexico as parasitic and C. T. Smith (1967, 329) indicates that many towns in eleventh-century Europe also exhibited parasitic qualities. A parasitic city is geared to simple reproduction rather than to that enlarged reproduction upon which advances in civilization and economy are based. Since this simple reproduction involves the movement of a social surplus to a non-working and all-consuming urban elite, the parasitic form of urbanism plainly reflects the parasitic nature of the urbanized elite. Parasitic cities are vulnerable unless the urban elite has strong ideological, economic, or military control over the surplus-producing population. Generative cities are in this respect more robust, if only because they at least promote the illusion of mutually beneficial patterns of circulation of surplus value. Johnson (1970) thus observes that market integration is a much more powerful tool for the preservation of urbanism and spatial integration than ideological and military control. On the other hand, societies engaged in simple reproduction can be very stable and fairly free of internal economic contradictions. Thus parasitic cities tend not to be so much internally vulnerable as vulnerable to outside forces. This distinction between generative and parasitic cities can manifest itself in a number of different guises. Gramsci (*Prison Notebooks*, 90–102) perceptively distinguishes, for example, between the parasitic urbanism of the Italian South in the 1930s in which there was a "literal subjugation of the city to the countryside" (because the city was the home of a rentier class and a bureaucracy which lived off a surplus extracted from agriculture), and the generative urbanism of the Italian North in which there was a continual enlargement of production through industry and commerce, together with a concomitant creation of a large industrial urban proletariat. In both cases, surplus labour was being mobilized for the production of surplus value, but the circumstances, although both "urban", were quite different.

This discussion suggests a possible dilemma when policies towards urbanism are devised in socialist countries. On the

one hand it is conceded that surplus labour is necessary to promote the advancement of society, while on the other primitive
accumulation is regarded as a painful destructive process. This
is really a problem in the theory of socialist development, but
it would seem that there is no way of enlarging reproduction
without primitive accumulation; and so the non-idyllic development experiences of Russia, China and Cuba would appear
inevitable under the circumstances (which is not necessarily
to defend the actual form they took and are taking). This
view has to be modified, however, to the extent that the transition to socialism involves a redefinition of the surplus concept.
This redefinition eliminates the form of rent, interest and profit
and focuses on what is socially necessary labour for the production of socially beneficial use values (instead of exchange
values) for both present and future members of the population.
In other words a socialist surplus arises, in principle at least, out
of unalienated labour. The surplus so redefined loses its class
character: all members of the society who are able to yield up
a certain quantity of their surplus labour for socially defined
purposes. It is from this theoretical perspective that we have
to gauge the emergence of new urban forms.

In socialist societies it is necessary that a surplus of some sort
be produced but there is no *a priori* reason why it should need
to be concentrated. Both Marx and Engels took the view,
for example, that a socialist society required tha the historical
antithesis of town and country disappear. This is much too
simplistic a recommendation in view of the very complex
patterns of surplus circulation in contemporary capitalist and
socialist countries. But we can weave an argument around it.
Part of the surplus brought into being in a socialist society will
presumably be put to new investment to expand production.
Insofar as that investment will be more efficiently deployed in
concentrated form (through economies of scale, economies of
agglomeration, and the like), there is every reason to accept
some form of urban agglomeration. But much of the surplus
product won in socialist societies will presumably be distributed for the use of the population in general and it is here that
geographic concentration should be avoided at all costs. The
conscious attempt in Cuba to disperse medical care from its
previous heavy concentration in Havana to a comprehensive
regional health care system for the whole country is a good

235

example of this kind of policy. The situation is relatively simple in Cuba, of course, but the principle remains the same with respect to the intricate circulations of the surplus in advanced productive societies. Above all, however, urban forms in socialist society presumably have no role comparable to the promotion of effective demand in capitalist society. The degree to which changes in city form have occurred in "socialist" societies (in situations usually dominated initially by a legacy of capitalist urban forms), relative to the theoretical perspectives formulated above, is some measure of their success in achieving their professed aims. The indications to date in the Soviet Union and Eastern Europe are not particularly encouraging, for the dominance of urban centres has not been transformed into a new configuration, nor has urban structure itself been radically altered (Musil, 1968; Castells, 1970). As Lefebvre puts it: "the same problems [of urbanism] may be found under socialism and under capitalism with the same absence of response" (1970, 220). In China the situation appears to be different. The socialist revolution here was rural-based and the historical tension in Chinese life between town and country had to be dealt with directly.

In Maoist thought the tension between town and country is regarded as a primary contradiction in the social organization of the people—a contradiction which encompasses "three great differences: between urban and rural areas, industry and agriculture, and intellectual and manual labour" (Committee of Concerned Asian Scholars, 1972, 104). These contradictions are examined in Chinese revolutionary theory and much recent Chinese history can be interpreted as an attempt to resolve them (Mao Tse-tung, 1966). A central concern of Chinese policy since 1957, for example, has been to change the character of the bureaucratic industrial centres which were initially conceived (on Russian lines) as a central source of social and political power (as well as the focus of socialist surplus circulation) and to integrate the cities into the countryside (in order to achieve a resolution of the town–country antagonism in the fashion advocated by Marx and Engels). The cultural revolution was a part of this process in which the domination of urban intellectuals was challenged and social and political organization made to take on a new form consistent with a fundamental economic aim of releasing the country from the domination of the towns. The policy disagreement between Russia and China is reflective of very different approaches to the three great contradictions of which the urban–rural differentiation is symptomatic. Russian policy appears to be devoted to perpetuating the historical cleavage between town and country; Chinese policy seems aimed to resolve it. This contrast within "socialist" countries takes on an even deeper significance when it is set against the naturally evolving progress of urbanization in the advanced capitalist nations where town–country distinctions are fast being obliterated through a megalopolitan form of spatial organization. In advanced capitalist nations the local conflict between town and country has been overcome only to be replaced on the one hand by a broader and even deeper antagonism between developed and underdeveloped nations, and on the other by a growing antagonism based on the internal differentiation within metropolitan areas. Of all of these paths of development, both socialist and non-socialist, only the Chinese appears directed towards resolving rather than deepening the conflict between town and country. Whether such a resolution is possible or even conceivable given the Chinese level of economic development must be doubted.

URBANISM AND THE SPATIAL CIRCULATION OF SURPLUS VALUE

Urbanism involves the concentration of surplus (however designated) in some version of the city (whether it be a walled enclave or the sprawling metropoli of the present day). Urbanism thus requires the articulation of a sufficiently extensive space economy to facilitate the geographic concentration of the social surplus (however it is designated). Price-fixing markets cannot function, for example, on a parochial basis and require an effective economic integration over space if they are to work. Spatial integration in the economy, the evolution of price-fixing markets and the evolution of urbanism are therefore inextricably interrelated through the necessity to create, mobilize and concentrate the social surplus. A space economy has to be created and maintained if urbanism is to survive as a social form. Expanded reproduction and changing scale in urbanism also require an expanding (geographically) or intensifying space economy. The flows of goods and services throughout this space economy are a tangible expression of that process which circulates surplus value in order to concentrate more of it. This conception of the space economy is more instructive than the conventional one extant in geography and regional science which rests on Adam Smith's notion that everything can be explained by an insatiable consumer demand and mutual gains from trade. It is more realistic therefore, to model an urbanized space economy as a surplus-creating, -extracting and -concentrating device. Liberal policy suggestions of the sort advocated by John Friedmann (1966; 1969) envisage generating economic growth in underdeveloped nations through the creation of an "effective space" within which products and people can be mobilized in a hierarchical form of urbanism: clearly this policy would create a form of spatial organization which would serve merely to increase the rate of exploitation and to create the necessary conditions for the efficient and irresistible extraction of even greater quantities of surplus for the ultimate benefit of the imperial powers (see Frank, 1969).

Policy proposals for the more effective organization of space cannot take it for granted that a mutual benefit to all will result. Under capitalist forms of economic and social organization the reverse will almost certainly be the case.

CONCLUSIONS

The relationships between cities and surplus can be summarized as follows:

Definitions

1   The social surplus is the quantity of labour power used in the creation of product for certain specified social purposes over and above that which is biologically, socially and culturally necessary to guarantee the maintenance and reproduction of labour power in the context of a given mode of production.

2   Surplus value is surplus labour expressed in capitalist market exchange terms.

Propositions

1   Cities are built forms created out of the mobilization, extrac-

tion and geographic concentration of significant quantities of the socially designated surplus product.

2   Urbanism is a patterning of individual activity which, when aggregated, forms a mode of economic and social integration capable of mobilizing, extracting and concentrating significant quantities of the socially designated surplus product.

3   A social surplus product of some sort is produced in all societies and it is always possible to create more of it. The concept of a surplus is itself subject to re-definition as conditions of production, consumption and distribution change. A distinction must be made between an alienated surplus fashioned out of alienated labour and the unalienated form which the surplus can assume in certain societies.

4   It is easier to mobilize, extract and concentrate a certain quantity of a socially designated surplus product under some conditions than it is under others. These conditions are the end-product of a process of historical evolution. Favourable conditions initially stemmed through some combination of the following circumstances:

   a large total population
   b settled and relatively immobile population
   c high density of population
   d high potential productivity under a given set of natural and technical conditions
   e easy communication and access

5   Mobilizing and concentrating the social surplus on a permanent basis implies the creation of a permanent space economy, and the perpetuation of the conditions described in (4).

6   Urbanism *may* originate with the transformation from a mode of economic integration based on reciprocity to one based on redistribution.

7   Urbanism *necessarily* arises with the emergence of a market exchange mode of economic integration with its concomitants—social stratification and differential access to the means of production.

8   Urbanism can assume a variety of forms depending upon the particular function of the urban centre with respect to the total pattern of circulation of the socially designated

surplus product. In contemporary society these patterns are geographically and sectorally complex.

9   There is a necessary but not sufficient connection between urbanism and economic growth. Generative cities promote growth but parasitic cities do not.

10 If there is no geographic concentration of the socially designated surplus product there is no urbanism. Wherever urbanism is manifest, the only legitimate explanation of it lies in an analysis of the processes which create, mobilize, concentrate and manipulate that social surplus product.

MODES OF ECONOMIC INTEGRATION AND THE SPACE ECONOMY OF URBANISM

It remains to examine the relationships between the modes of economic integration, the creation of the social surplus and the various forms of urbanism. To do this successfully requires that we recognize firstly that a particular mode of economic integration can take on a considerable variety of forms (see above p. 199), and secondly the domination of activity by one mode of economic integration does not preclude the continued or incipient presence of other modes (see above p. 202). The latter point leads us to the concept of a "balance of influence" among the different modes of economic integration in a particular historical period. We can thus interpret the historically occurring forms of urbanism by evaluating the balance of influence among the various modes of economic integration at a particular time and by examining the form assumed by each of the modes at that time. This isn't easy. The difficulty is two-fold. Firstly, the terms "reciprocity", "redistribution", and "market exchange" do not have fixed meanings but, like many other concepts we have examined, they are relationally defined; their meanings cannot be established free of some context of which part is the relationship each bears to the other (for example, we may talk of reciprocity in both primitive and capitalist societies, but in the latter case it is a mere shadowy representation of its former self). Secondly, "urbanism", if the interminable squabbles over its definition are anything to go on, likewise has no fixed universal meaning applicable to all societies at all times. We are therefore, trying to relate two sets of relationally defined terms, which would be impossible were it not that urbanism and the mode of economic integration are both aspects of the same social and economic organization. In other words, both help to define each other. We cannot explain urbanism in a causal sense by attributing causal efficacy to a particular mode of economic integration. But we can use the characteristics of the latter to mirror and better understand the qualitative attributes of the former.

Let us first consider how a particular mode of economic integration can exhibit considerable variation within itself. Reciprocity can take on a variety of forms. The pattern of flows in a predominantly redistributive economy can also vary a great deal. The particular structural characteristics of the rank society will be reflected in the built form of the city. Wheatley (1969; 1971) provides some excellent examples of this in his discussion of the symbolic qualities of various city forms. To demonstrate the general point at issue, however, we will examine very briefly the variety of forms assumed by market exchange.

Market exchange, as a phenomenon, has existed since the earliest times and the earliest cities were, among other things, locales where this activity was likely to concentrate. But market exchange as a mode of economic integration resting on price-fixing markets is relatively recent. It is the self-regulatory aspect of price-fixing markets which makes market exchange a distinctive mode of economic integration. Markets, exchange, trade and commerce, money, prices, and so on, can and do exist without the market being self-regulatory. It is only when individuals adjust their allocation of productive resources, their output levels and consumption habits to price movements that the market becomes a mode of economic integration.

Price-fixing markets require participants who are antagonistic to each other and who operate in the medium of exchange value. The participants can be organized in various social configurations and operate under a variety of institutional

241

conditions. Individual producers and consumers may compete one with each other in a highly fragmented atomistically organized market system. Groups may form which compete with other groups. Monopolies in consumption and production may arise. All kinds of combinations can arise with monopolistic production flowing to individual consumers, oligopolistic producers dealing with monopoly consumers and so on. None of this need destroy the self-regulatory character of the market system although certain stresses and tensions are inevitably created. Even in the case of monopoly within a given line of production, the producer is forced to maintain a certain level of profits (otherwise investment will withdraw and move elsewhere). This means that the monopolist will seek to reduce costs and to adjust the quantity produced to the market price or vary the market price to match a certain capacity to produce. Institutional arrangements really provide some rules of the game for antagonistic behaviour, as well as some rules for regulating the organization of the participants (for example, anti-trust regulations). In some instances, too, mediating or facilitating devices for market activity (for example, laws to limit liability) are created by institutional means.

The exact social configuration of the protagonists and the institutional conditions under which they operate give variety to market exchange as a mode of economic integration and also, as we shall later see, distinctive qualitative attributes to urbanism. The different social configurations and institutional forms do not arise accidentally. The end result of fierce competition in some sector of the economy, for example, is the elimination of all competitors and, hence, the emergence of monopoly. This transition from competition to monopoly amounts to a tendency for price-fixing markets to eliminate the conditions necessary for their perpetuation. If market exchange is to be perpetuated, therefore, there have to be continual changes in social configurations and institutions. There is, of course, no unique way in which social configurations and institutional forms have to blend to accomplish this task. But whatever the configuration and whatever the institutional forms, they must jointly act to preserve market exchange or else the self-regulation of the price-fixing market breaks down.

Self-regulating markets did not become general in Europe until the nineteenth century after which they spread rapidly throughout the rest of the world. Before that time activity was fairly closely regulated within the socially accepted mores of the rank society. However, many hints of the self-regulating market economy are evident before 1800 though almost exclusively in trade and commerce within which in some periods self-regulating market activity became a significant integrative force. Trade and commerce therefore appear as the first sectors of activity to be penetrated by market exchange. The extraordinary thing is that market exchange took so long to penetrate other aspects of social life and activity. Even in England, both land and labour remained, by and large, outside of the self-regulating market economy until 1750 or thereabouts: though there were markets for land and labour much earlier, these were not self-regulating. The penetration of land (with the help of the enclosure acts) meant the penetration of agriculture. This generated a pressure to maximize agricultural output for profit. At the same time large numbers of rural dwellers were deprived (by the combination of enclosure and market forces) of control over the means of production and were forced off the land and into the cities. The wage system concomitantly took general command over labour power. Labour became a commodity like anything else. Thus both agricultural and industrial production could become organized on the basis of market exchange as an integrating mechanism. The slow build up of the industrial revolution in Britain thus represented a gradual penetration of market exchange into production (as distinct from trade and commerce) through the penetration of land and labour. As the industrial revolution gained momentum, more and more sectors of activity became integrated through market exchange, and distribution and service activities were also drawn in. The circulation of surplus value in its capitalist form finally broke free from the restraining influence of the rank society and then, through its domination of all the key sectors of society became the medium through which the market mode of economic integration gradually bound society into one cohesive economic system. The rapidly growing cities of early nineteenth-century England stood at the hub of this circulation of surplus value.

Subsequently, market exchange penetrated and integrated new territories into a global capitalist economy throughout which surplus value freely and restlessly roamed in search of expanded reproduction and primitive accumulation. Sub-

243

sequently, too, market exchange penetrated into more and more aspects of life until scarcely anything of importance remained untouched. One condition stands out as being of paramount importance to this progressive penetration. In order for self-regulation to occur, it is necessary for responses of individuals and groups (consumers, competitors, traders, consumers) to price changes to be correct most of the time. Individuals who miscalculate pay an economic penalty, but substantial errors in the price signals themselves inhibit the penetration of market exchange. This error can to a certain extent be reduced by improvements in communication: with adequate transport facilities it is possible to match supplies to demands relatively quickly and information about quantities of supply and demand can be transmitted almost instantaneously. The spatial integration of much of the world into the capitalist system through market exchange was and is contingent upon the existence of adequate means of communication. The more adequate the communication the more probable market integration becomes. Initially, this applies only to private goods which can be exchanged at a price because the individual has a total control over their use. Institutional, legal, and social changes are necessary to transform other spheres of activity so that they can be treated as commodities. The transformation of labour power into the commodity of wage labour requires such changes. It is now possible to trade in commodity futures, public bonds, franchises for the provision of public goods, all manner of rights and obligations, and so on. In general, we can safely assert that there is scarcely a major aspect of urban life that is not now subject to the operations of a self-regulating market of some sort.

There are, of course, some serious questions to be asked about the efficacy of the price mechanism at large. One of the problems that plagues capitalist production is the failure of the price mechanism to transmit the right signals under certain conditions. In this case, the majority of participants in the market exchange process will make the wrong decisions and an economic breakdown inevitably occurs. Marx argued that this condition was endemic to capitalism and that it was bound to become more and more serious as capital accumulation proceeded, while Keynes thought of it as a serious blemish which could be overcome by government intervention (Mattick, 1969). Keynesian policies are designed to cure what is viewed as a structural weakness in the price mechanism. But for Marx the defects in the price mechanism were but a symptom of a deep structural malaise inherent in the circulation of surplus value to create more surplus value. If Marx is correct, then localized breakdowns in the price mechanism (as frequently exhibited, for example, in housing markets) cannot be attributed to mere deficiencies in price information. They are more likely to indicate deep-seated problems in the process of capitalist circulation itself.

To summarize, price-fixing markets can be organized variously depending upon the exact social configuration, the institutional context and the nature of communication. Likewise, different sectors of the economy may at any time be penetrated to a different degree by market exchange. The qualitative attributes of urbanism are sensitive to these variations. Yet throughout the process, there is a certain constancy of behaviour in price-fixing markets which ensures that surplus value continues to circulate and to seek more surplus value in such a fashion that the actions of all participants and groups in the society are drawn into what always remains a self-regulating system of market exchange.

THE CIRCULATION OF THE SURPLUS AND THE BALANCE OF
INFLUENCE BETWEEN THE MODES OF ECONOMIC INTEGRATION
IN THE URBAN SPACE ECONOMY

The contemporary metropolis in capitalist countries is a veritable palimpsest of social forms constructed in the images of reciprocity, redistribution and market exchange. Surplus value, as it is socially defined under the capitalist order, circulates within society, moving freely along some channels while being reduced to a mere trickle along others. Insofar as this circulation is manifest in physical form, through the flow of goods, services and information, the construction of media for movement, etc. and insofar as the social formations depend for their coherence upon spatial proximity, we will also find an intricately expressed but tangible space economy. It is the central thesis of this essay that by bringing together the conceptual frameworks surrounding (1) the surplus concept, (2) the mode of economic integration concept and (3) concepts of spatial organization, we will arrive at an overall framework for interpreting urbanism and its tangible expression, the city.

Every epoch lends to each of these conceptual frameworks a special meaning. If we seek to write a general theory of urbanism in terms of them, it has therefore to be with the proviso that their meanings change and must always be established through a detailed investigation of the circumstances of the time. What, for example, is the meaning of redistribution in ancient China, Theocratic Mexico, feudal Europe, the contemporary United States? And what future meaning can we see for it in social formations that are possible here and now but which have not yet been brought into being? The construction of revolutionary theory of urbanism need not therefore consist in rewriting previous theories, but it can, under certain circumstances, include redefining the terms contained within them. We may, for example, need to give new meanings to words such as "surplus" and "redistribution". For our theory to be effective requires that it be robust enough to apply to a wide variety of situations. It is in this spirit that we can investigate how the concepts propounded in preceding sections of this essay can be put to use to dissect the relationship between urbanism and society in a variety of historical contexts.

1 Patterns in the geographic circulation of the surplus

Urbanism entails the geographic concentration of a socially designated surplus product. This means a geographic circulation of surplus goods and services, a movement of people and, in a money economy, a circulation of investment, money and credit. The space economy so created is subject to all manner of substitutions, interruptions, breakdowns, shifts and growth paths. The reputation and significance of individual cities rest to large degree upon their location with respect to the geographic circulation of the surplus. The qualitative attributes of urbanism will likewise be affected by the rise and fall in the total quantity of surplus as well as the degree to which the surplus is produced in concentratable form.

Disruption in the geographical circulation of the surplus can occur for a variety of reasons, accidents, natural calamities and natural processes. The decline of many a medieval European port, for example, has been attributed, sometimes erroneously, to the silting up of channels (Bruges being the most debated example). The exhaustion of a key resource and the opening up of new resources (through technology or the opening up of new trade routes) can bring about rapid shifts in the circulation of surplus and powerful and important cities into being, and can just as quickly destroy them. Nuremburg, Augsburg and numerous other Bavarian towns were central to the circulation of surplus in medieval Europe because they controlled access to the much valued silver supply. But the importation of large quantities of gold and silver through the Spanish conquest in the sixteenth century relegated the area to a quiet backwater of the European economy. Social conflict, war, the emergence of territorial power-blocs which restrict movement, the imposition of barriers to movement, all interfere with the circulation of surplus. Pirenne (1925) notes how the towns of southern France declined during the Carolingian era as the Muslims came to dominate Mediterranean trade: the towns, deprived of long distance trade, then reverted to local redistributive functions focused on the Catholic Church and the local nobility. The struggle for control over Mediterranean trade between Islam, Byzantium and Western city states had a profound effect upon the circulation of surplus in the early medieval period. Later struggles between Spanish, Dutch, French and British for control over the Atlantic and Baltic trade changed the geography of surplus circulation as did the colonization movements in the nineteenth century. In contemporary times, the shifting allegiance of nations, the interdiction of trade through political action (the partition of Germany, the closure of the Suez canal) have all affected circulation of surplus. Competition between cities, between sets of cities (such as the Hanse) or between countries, for control over the circulation of the surplus will itself alter the geographic pattern of circulation as one side dominates the other through overwhelming economic power (gained from superior organization and economies of scale for instance), through comparative locational advantage, or through the exercise of monopolistic privilege (won by some strategem or conferred from some outside power). The circulation of surplus is constantly changing to new channels. In some cases, geographical shifts succeed in preserving the overall level of urbanization and the overall quantity of circulation of surplus, while individual cities may die off, stagnate or expand:

adaptation and substitution in surplus circulation allow new geographical configurations to emerge in order to replace the old. In other cases, the quantity of surplus in motion increases and urbanization exhibits an overall growth within which individual cities may die, stagnate or expand.

There is an inherent tendency, however, for the circulation of the surplus to be undermined by economic and social failure in the mechanisms that ensure surplus creation. Wolf provides a fascinating example from theocratic Mexico:

"The basic source of power of the priesthood that ruled the holy towns was apparently power over men's minds and power over goods gained in the service of the gods. But there is an inherent limitation to purely ideological power. . . . The theocratic society had brought together holy town and hinterland, priest, trader, artisan and peasant, men who spoke different languages, stranger and citizen. In unifying it had also sown the inevitable seeds of internal dissension and the possibility of revolt. . . . The web of theocratic society contained another fatal flaw: a built-in imbalance between holy town and hinterland, between city and provinces. Ultimately, the towns grew wealthy and splendid, because the countryside laboured and produced. Not that some of the wealth of the centres did not flow back into the rural area. Some benefits must be returned to the ruled in any society. . . . The growing gap between centre and hinterland was not based on an absolute enrichment of the centre while the countryside remained absolutely impoverished. Both grew in their involvement with each other; but the centres grew more quickly, more opulently, and more obviously. . . . In complex societies, this confrontation of hope with the denial of hope pits rulers against ruled, rich against poor, and hinterland and periphery against core and centre. The periphery suffers by comparison while the centre grows bloated with wealth and power. Yet it is also at the periphery that the controls of government and religion tend to be at their weakest; it is here that the forces of dissatisfaction can easily gain both strength and organization. Here the pull of the centre and its ability to compel people to its will are at a minimum. Theocratic society witnessed this rebellion of the periphery against the centre. The fissures opened up. . . ." (1959, 106.)

This sort of structural weakness has been endemic among all

redistributive economies. It was, for example, the crux of the problem for the survival of the Roman Empire and many lesser urbanized societies have ultimately collapsed because of the inability to cope with an inherent structural weakness in their mode of economic integration (*cf.* Johnson, 1970). Weaknesses of this sort are not confined to redistributive economies: in the market exchange mode of economic integration they have shown through in the numerous commercial crises of the nineteenth century, the near-cataclysm of the Great Depression and in the omni-present and potentially threatening balance of payments and monetary crises of the contemporary world. Any mode of economic integration contains within itself the power to undermine the conditions for its own self-perpetuation. This capacity indicates a structural weakness in both redistribution and market exchange potentially able to inflict a severe and perhaps total disruption in the circulation of the surplus upon which urbanism relies.

It appears easiest to check these structural weaknesses in a period of expansion. The redistributive structure of the Roman Empire was partly preserved by rolling back the edges of Empire to overcome disaffection at the periphery. When expansion ceased, collapse quickly followed. Other redistributive societies have sought to perpetuate ideological control within a fairly stable space economy by a mixture of military action and ideological persuasion. Capitalism, however, has shown itself to be an inherently expansionary force; insofar as its existence is predicted on putting surplus value into circulation to increase surplus value, it has to expand in order to survive. Hence arises a process of generating and subsequently overcoming contradictions through expansion (see above, pp. 227-8). Expansion means a progressive penetration of market exchange, greater quantities of accumulated surplus, and a shift in the circulation of surplus value as new opportunities are explored, new technologies achieved and new resources and productive capacities are opened up. Urbanism, as we have seen, plays an important role in this process. The city functions as a generative centre around which an effective space is created out of which growing quantities of surplus product are extracted. Overall economic growth presupposes both a willingness and an ability for those in the urban centre to put surplus value back into circulation in such a way that the city functions as a "growth pole" for the surrounding economy. The resultant growth alters the channels along which the surplus flows and alters the direction and quantities of such flows. In the past, the alterations in the circulation of surplus value contingent upon economic growth have been both substantial in quantity and significant in terms of spatial reorganization. The geographical patterns of circulation of the surplus have been as much altered by economic growth as they have by the disruptions brought about through natural calamities, wars, and so on.

The geographical pattern in the circulation of surplus can therefore be conceived only as a moment in a process. In terms of that moment, particular cities attain positions with respect to the circulation of surplus which, at the next moment in the process, are changed. Urbanism, as a general phenomenon, should not be viewed as the history of particular cities, but as the history of the system of cities within, between and around which the surplus circulates. When Florence declined, Nuremburg and Augsburg took over, when Antwerp fell Amsterdam rose and when Amsterdam fell, London emerged as the main arbiter in the circulation of the surplus. The history of particular cities can therefore be understood only in terms of the circulation of surplus value at a moment of history within a system of cities.

2 The cities of medieval Europe

Marx asserted that "the Middle Ages starts with the country as the locus of history, whose further development then proceeds through the opposition of town and country." (See above, p. 204.) This is a perceptive analysis. The feudal economy dominant in medieval northern Europe consisted basically of a checkerboard of local selfcontained and rurally based economies in which redistribution occurred within either the manorial system or the somewhat larger feudal fiefdoms (Bloch, 1961). A few super-ordinate authorities—the church and the Holy Roman Empire being the most important—loosely presided over this highly fragmented economy. The surplus for the support of the various elements in the rank society was extracted as tithe, work-days and slave labour while privilege was attached to land-ownership (held through laws of heredity) and to position within the church hierarchy. Military power and ideological control were the twin controls which served to maintain society. The urban centres that did exist were, for the most part, fortresses or religious centres; sometimes church and fortress could combine to form a centre of considerable significance. But much of the surplus extracted was not concentrated geographically in an urban form—it remained dispersed throughout the manorial system.

Another quite distinct geographical circulation of the surplus was superimposed upon these local redistributive feudal economies. This was associated with long distance trade and it appears to have remained set apart from local redistributive activity for much of the medieval period. As Polanyi (1944, 58) writes, "markets are not institutions functioning mainly within an economy, but without". Yet long distance commerce is viewed by most commentators as the primary function of the medieval city. The distinction between long distance and local surplus circulation was a tangible reflection of the ambiguous and uncertain relationships between the precepts of the rank society and the activity of trading for profit. In terms of the prevailing sense of value in catholic and feudal society, it was both immoral and dehumanizing to trade for profit and to take advantage of scarcity. The prevailing ethic of the rank society was anti-capitalist in most respects (the laws governing usury being the most conspicuous example). It was not that trade in itself was despised, but that the institutions, the activities and the rather obvious commercial instincts of professional merchants were clearly not consistent with the ideological precepts of the feudal order. Attempts to organize trade on a non-professional basis were insufficient, however, and the rank society was forced to rely on a professional merchant class which appeared, in some respects, to threaten its moral bases.

Feudal society therefore relied to some degree on trade and commerce and the towns provided a locale where that activity could be controlled and monitored. This control provided the opportunity for feudal society to reap valuable new sources of revenue for its own support (taxation, tolls, and so on, were an important source of wealth, and royal finance, in both England and France, became inextricably mixed up with the fate of commerce and, hence, with the fate of the towns, at a relatively early date). The merchants in medieval society were not capitalistic in any fundamental sense, however. For the most part, they did not seek or desire to control production and labour, nor actively to replace a social and economic system which yielded great profit for their ventures and to whose social norms they generally subscribed. The social and economic system of the feudal order was highly decentralized in character and it therefore created numerous parochial economies between which demand and supply differentials could easily co-exist. The failure to create an integrated space economy over and above the local level, which may in part be attributed to difficulties in communication and in part to deficiencies in social organization, provided merchant capital with abundant opportunity for exploitation and profit.

Merchant capital, as opposed to industrial capitalism, relies upon differentials in economic development for its functioning and in fact operates to preserve rather than to eliminate such differentials. Marx suggests that:

"Wherever merchant's capital still predominates, we find backward conditions. This is true within one and the same country, in which, for instance, the specifically merchant towns present far more striking analogies with past conditions than industrial towns. . . . The law that the independent development of merchant's capital is inversely proportional to the degree of development of capitalist production is particularly evident in the history of the carrying trade, as among the Venetians, Genoese, Dutch, etc., where the principal gains were not made by exporting domestic products, but by promoting the exchange of products of commercially and otherwise economically underdeveloped societies. . . . So long as merchant's capital promotes the exchange of products between undeveloped societies, commercial profit not only appears as outbargaining and cheating, but also largely originates from them. Aside from the fact that it exploits the difference between prices of production in various countries . . . merchant's capital appropriates an overwhelming portion of the surplus product partly as a mediator between communities which still substantially produce for use value . . . and partly because under those earlier modes of production, the principal owners of the surplus product with whom the merchant dealt, namely the slave-owner, the feudal lord, and the state . . . represent the consuming wealth and luxury which the merchant seeks to trap." (*Capital* volume 3, 327–33.)

Seen in this light, merchant capital and the urbanism to which it gave rise, must be regarded as a conservative rather than a revolutionary force. The prevention of spatial integration in production, the establishment of monopolies through which the terms of trade could be dictated to producers, the emergence of "urban colonialism" with respect to the surrounding countryside (Dobb, 1947, 95), were all important aspects to the conservatism of merchant capital. Yet it also posed a threat of sorts to the feudal order which was more substantial than a mere ideological diversion. Marx continues:

"The development of commerce and merchant's capital gives rise everywhere to the tendency towards the production of exchange values, increases its volume, multiplies it, makes it cosmopolitan, and develops money into world-money. Commerce, therefore, has a more or less dissolving influence everywhere on the producing organization. . . . To what extent it brings about a dissolution of the old mode of production depends upon its solidity and internal structure. And whither this process of dissolution will lead, in other words, what new mode of production will replace the old, does not depend on commerce, but on the character of the old mode of production itself." (*ibid.*)

The antagonism between town and country, between the urban merchant and the rural feudal order, had a real economic basis. The solution to this antagonism in northern Europe was sought in the isolation and containment of merchant activity to the towns, where it could be regulated and controlled. In addition, merchant activity tended to be confined to long distance trade based on the geographical principle of complementarity or to long distance trade in luxury items (Postan, 1952). The geographical fragmentation evident in northern Europe was therefore in part a response on the part of the feudal order to the possible incursions of merchant activity, as was the strict geographical delimitation of town and country. It consequently appears as if medieval towns were "non-feudal islands in feudal seas" (Postan, 1952, 172; Pirenne, 1925) or, as Polanyi (1944, 62) prefers it, "prisons" within which the potentially disruptive activities of the merchant class were confined. It would be wrong to conclude from this that medieval towns were "entirely alien bodies" in feudal society, however, for it is highly probable that the majority of towns "originated on the initative of some feudal institution, or in some way as an element in feudal society." (Dobb, 1947, 78.)

The relationship between the rank society and urban commerce and trade was frequently ambiguous in its form throughout northern Europe. In some cases the rank society was strongly supportive of commercial activity or allowed trade to operate freely for its own advantage. In other cases the rank society was in conflict with commerce or pretended (and in some cases did) ignore it altogether, so that it had to be conducted surreptitiously outside of the walls of what was almost a purely redistributive city. The feudal patrimony and the market place were conjoined in innumerable ways. Whatever the exact relationship, however, it was clear the commerce of the towns was to be regulated politically by the rank society. This regulation relied initially upon articles of incorporation which gave the city a legal structure and conferred rights and duties on its inhabitants which were markedly different from those which regulated the feudal economy. The city thus assumed the form of a territorial corporation. This corporation was designed to facilitate commerce, but it also sought to promote monopolistic advantages vis-à-vis other cities, as well as to regulate internal conflict. Far from guaranteeing merchants freedom of action, the territorial corporation regulated, controlled and directed merchant activity in ways which were consistent with the perpetuation of the feudal order. In general, the merchants were cognizant of this fact and sought to conform. Postan (1952) and Thrupp (1948) note, for example, the tendency for the active medieval merchant to retire to the status of country gentleman or urban rentier as soon as sufficient wealth was accumulated—indeed Postan in part attributes the financial degeneration of the wealthier northern European cities in the fifteenth century to this aspect of merchant behaviour.

The situation with respect to urbanism in southern Europe was markedly different to that further north in certain important respects. The redistributive society dominated trade and commerce throughout but in Italy in particular it dominated by participation. The corporate state here combined the elements of catholicism, feudalism and merchant capitalism, and evolved a very special and important form of the rank society. In the Italian city-states the rank society (structured mainly through kinship and inherited rights of land-ownership) was supportive of commerce and trade and in fact sought to express its moral and social norms as well as to appropriate the surplus through commercial operations. The catholic church on occasion participated directly and the Vatican became the centre for commercial activity on a number of occasions. Authority and power derived from the institutions of the rank society (and here the catholic church played an even more important supportive role) were used to legitimize trade and commerce as well as various acts of primitive accumulation through piracy and war. This redistributive activity was designed to distribute wealth in a manner commensurate with the social ordering of the prestige-conscious rank society. And it was in this society that certain capitalist forms gained their initial footing, although in a manner which was not destined to give rise to capitalist production. Lopez writes:

"The golden ages of medieval trade (in southern Europe) certainly knew many of the characteristics which we regard as typical of capitalism. When we scan the records from the late eleventh to the early fourteenth century, we cannot fail to notice a steady accumulation of capital in money and in goods; a growing use of credit and a trend towards gradual separation of management from both ownership of capital and manual labour; a constant endeavour to improve the methods of business and to compete with other business men in the same field; a planning of large scale operations with a view to expanding the market; an elevation of trade interests to the importance of state affairs; and above all, a desire for profits as a leading motive for commercial activity." (1952, 320.)

Banking institutions and technical devices, such as double-entry book-keeping, were created to facilitate trade. These capitalist techniques were later to assume great significance as they were transmitted northwards into Europe by Italian merchants (many of whom were primarily tax collectors in the redistributive system which supported the papacy). With the collapse of the city states and the subsequent decline of trade in the Mediterranean in the sixteenth century, these techniques were preserved in countries further to the north.

The argument over whether the Italian states can properly be characterized as capitalist or not is rather unenlightening. Redistribution remained the fundamental mode of economic integration throughout and capitalism did not penetrate production relationships to any substantial degree. Yet on the other hand the surplus was appropriated using capitalist techniques through the circulation of merchants' capital. To assert that redistribution remained dominant implies that self-regulating market activity was either absent or was a minor feature. There was a price system, but in both north and south Europe prices reflected the balance of supply and demand conditions rather than signals to which consumers and producers were reacting. Profits from commerce depended entirely upon the merchant's skill in matching supply to demand, but since production in agriculture and, for the most part, in industry was not organized on commercial lines, the merchant had to make the best out of perpetually changing conditions—indeed, this was what his skill was organized to do. Price signals themselves were also subject to external interference (the variable supply of silver and gold, debasement of the currency, and so on). The tendency for merchant activity to be confined to long distance and geographically complementary trade also made price signals somewhat irrelevant as a guide to behaviour because competition was muted and the uncertainties enormous. In the thirteenth and fourteenth centuries, however, the relative stability of what Lopez calls the "inner" area of long distance trade (mainly around the margins of the Mediterranean) lent a different character to this trade:

"It was a highly competitive market, where success depended mainly on efficiency, quickness and almost meticulous weighing of transport charges, tolls and marketing conditions. Investments were comparatively safe, and profits were usually moderate, even if judged according to modern standards. . . . The reduction in the margin of profit and the tremendous increase in the volume of traffic quickened the development of business techniques and slowly undermined the superiority of the travelling merchant over the sedentary businessman."

Yet this "inner" long distance trade still proceeded independently of local trade and of local production out of which truly price-fixing markets of a modern sort could be expected to emerge. It was only in the declining years of Venice, in the early sixteenth century, that the lineaments of a self-regulating, regionally integrated economy began to appear and this economy was still not integrated with urban industrial production or long distance trade.

The transition to a new mode of production in Europe consequent upon the dissolution of the old mode through the operations of merchant capitalism, depended upon conditions removed from the urban centres themselves. In medieval Europe, Marx (*Capital* volume 3, 334) saw two possible developments. The first, a "really revolutionary path" involved the producer becoming merchant and capitalist. The second, which could not in itself succeed in transforming the mode of production, extended merchant capital's control over production. The advent of industrial capitalism awaited the transformation of producers into capitalists and merchants. Yet it was this transformation that all the economic and institutional forms of feudal society were designed to prevent. Before producers could become merchants and capitalists, therefore, the numerous barriers posed by the feudal order had to be removed. And it was this task that merchant capital accomplished most successfully.

Merchant capitalism was an unstable force. There was a constant temptation and ultimately a necessity for merchant capital to extend its control over production. Merchant capitalism sought for expanded production for it was necessary always to increase the circulation of the surplus if profit levels were to be maintained. This expansion transformed economies from a productive basis designed to yield use values to one designed to yield exchange values and this in part accounts for the "backward integration" of merchants' capital to engage in production. Another, perhaps more telling reason, was the fact that monopoly trading privileges, upon which merchant capital relied if differentials in economic development were to be maintained, became increasingly difficult to sustain and police in the face of growing competition—hence it became very important to gain control over production. The control of production by merchants' capital—evident in medieval Flanders, in Venice and Florence, in many lesser urban centres and in rural areas (for example, the rural woollen industry in England)—did not revolutionize the organization of production along capitalist lines. It promoted new techniques, but the essential task was to control the supply source rather than to capitalize it.

Our ability to interpret medieval urbanism and the later transition to industrial urbanism, depends upon our ability to distinguish the crucial points of transition from feudalism, through merchant capitalism, to industrial capitalism. If our interpretation is correct then we can look for two significant stages in this process:

1   the creation of a regional, national and eventually a supra-national space economy within which resources, people and product could be mobilized through the operation of price-fixing markets;
2   the penetration of market exchange into all facets of production as opposed to its penetration into distribution under merchant capitalism.

The first stage was broadly accomplished under merchant capitalism while the second required a further revolution. The distinction between the redistributive urbanism of feudal society and the urbanism of merchant capitalism lay almost entirely in the fact that the latter achieved a spatial integration above and beyond that typical of the parochialism of the feudal era. Within this effective space surplus value could be accumulated in the merchant centres and all of the financial trappings of capitalist organization (in the way of technical financial expertise, for example) could be built up. By the late fifteenth century, for example, the Dutch had organized a well-integrated regional space economy which provided them with the competitive edge to challenge and defeat the trading monopoly of the Hanseatic League (Postan, 1952, 251-3). The Revolt of the Netherlands in the late sixteenth century symbolized a final and decisive break of merchant capitalism away from the regulation of the older rank society. Amsterdam, with a sudden accession of wealth, population and expertise as merchants fled before the Spanish conquest of the southern Netherlands (which disrupted the trade of Antwerp in particular), became a totally independent centre within which merchant capitalism could rule. The spatial integration of the economy around London followed a similar course. Starting in the early sixteenth century, a well-fashioned agricultural economy operating through price-fixing markets spread to meet the demands of London for food (Fisher, 1935). The growth of this "agricultural intensity island" played an important role for it was in this sphere that price-fixing markets could most easily function. By the early seventeenth century, London was of equal stature to Amsterdam as a centre for merchant capitalism.

Yet there was a fundamental difference between England and Holland—a difference which is significant for understanding the transformation to capitalism. Marx has a succinct explanation which considerable subsequent research (see Wilson, 1941; 1965, for example) has generally borne out:

"It is not commerce which revolutionizes industry, but industry which constantly revolutionizes commerce. Commercial supremacy itself is linked with the prevalence to a greater or lesser degree of conditions for large industry. Compare, for instance, England and Holland. The history of the decline of Holland as the ruling trading nation is the history of the subordination of merchants' capital to industrial capital." (*Capital* volume 3, 333.)

Once the solvent of merchant capitalism had done its work on feudalism the condition was right for the emergence of a new mode of production. Merchant capitalism could not continue on its expansionary path without an increase in production and therefore looked with favour upon anything in the organization of production which served to expand the circulation of surplus value. Merchant capitalism was not, therefore, resistant to industrial capitalism, while the feudal order most certainly was. Yet the urban centres were still, by and large, dominated by the rank society and, as throughout much of the feudal era, manufacturing was regulated and controlled. The history of manufacturing throughout the medieval era is one of strong gild regulation in which activity was ordered according to precepts of prestige, status and moral worth, rather than through a wage system. A wage system did operate, of course, but wages were usually regulated either by urban authority or through state intervention. Industrial activity was frequently forced, as a consequence, to seek out locations in rural areas away from urban influence and regulation. The English woollen industry, for example, underwent several relocations. Only late in the medieval period did industrial production begin to make use of certain capitalist forms of organization (production for profit, investment, speculation, credit financing, futures, and so on). This organization was undoubtedly brought into industry through the operation of merchant capitalism which could, on occasion, even create a substantial proletariat (as in Florence and the Low Countries at the height of their industrial activity). This was not, however, a revolutionary path. The industrialization that ultimately subdued merchant capital was not an urban phenomenon, but one which led to the creation of a new form of urbanism—a process in which Manchester, Leeds and Birmingham were transformed from insignificant villages or minor trading centres, to industrial cities of great productive might. In this process, it must be added, the once dominant trading centres, fashioned as they were by the peculiar ethic of merchant capitalism as well as by an economic function which was basically parasitic, diminished in economic and political significance. Amsterdam bowed to London and Bristol bowed to Birmingham. The penetration of self-regulating market activity into industrial and agricultural production created new urban centres as well as a new form of urbanism: class stratification now became the most significant feature, instead of the rather older kinds of differentiation which were based partly on stratification (under the legal conditions governing property rights and rights to production in general) and partly on the traditional criteria of the rank society.

The built form of the medieval and merchant capitalist city reflected the kind of social order of the times and was quite different from the social order of the new industrial city. In the early medieval period, the triple themes of fortress, religious institution and market place were everywhere evident. In the later period when merchant activity grew to dominate, the larger cities evolved an ecological structure exhibiting considerable residential segregation as well as segregation of activities. These patterns were not so much a result of functional segregation of work forces, as they were territorial and symbolic representations of relative position in the prestige scaling of the medieval order (Sjoberg, 1960). Even the distinctive artisan quarters in the larger cities reflected considerations of prestige as much as they did economic necessities imposed through an increasingly elaborate division of labour. Some activities, particularly those involving the movement of heavy materials, were located with efficient location in mind. Wealth, however, was an indicator of prestige and prestige locations were, for the most part, close to the symbolic centre of the medieval redistributive city. Land values reflected the competition for prestige locations. Yet it was use that determined exchange value in the rank society's urban land market, contrasted with later periods when return on investment came to dictate use entirely. There was a good deal of manipulation in the urban land market, of course, and the occupation of rentier was favoured as well as prestigious (to say nothing of lucrative and stable).

All in all the spatial structure of the medieval city reflects the typical criteria of the rank society. The built form reflects, in this manner, the necessity for those in positions of power and prestige in society to use space and architectural form either as symbolic representations of that power or as symbolic representations of those cosmic images to which the rank society continued to appeal for its moral sustenance. The distinctive features of city structure were constructed to reflect the characteristic values of the time—values which were ideological expressions of the dominant mode of production, its characteristic mode of economic and social integration, and, on occasion, of the solvent that presaged the emergence of a totally new mode of production.

3 The market exchange process and metropolitan urbanism in the contemporary capitalist world

Marx's characterization of modern history as "the urbanization of the countryside" is simple but true. In the *Manifesto of the Communist Party* Marx and Engels also wrote:

"The bourgeoisie has subjected the country to the rule of the towns. It has created enormous cities, has greatly increased the urban population as compared with the rural, and has thus rescued a considerable part of the population from the idiocy of rural life. Just as it has made the country dependent on the towns, so it has made barbarian and semi-barbarian countries dependent on the civilized ones, nations of peasants on nations of bourgeois, the east on the west. The bourgeoisie keeps more and more doing away with the scattered state of the population, of the means of production, and of property. It has agglomerated population, centralized means of production, and has concentrated property in a few hands." (pp. 47–8.)

The penetration of the self-regulating market exchange economy into all facets of social activity, and in particular into production, allowed capitalist forms to escape their urban confines and to integrate the whole economy, at first on a national and later at an international scale. The domination of market activity by the moral criteria of the rank society was finally terminated. The whole of society was now basically regulated and fashioned by the self-regulating market. Technically and economically this allowed the production of goods through innumerable stages, the proliferation of linkages between and among industries, a tremendous increase in the number of transactions necessary to produce a finished product, and an enormous increase in the potential for division of labour. All kinds of new ways were opened up in which the surplus, now universally designated in its exchange value form, could be created and appropriated. As a consequence the total product as well as the quantity of surplus value in circulation increased enormously, as did the urban centres and the populations they contained.

There are some important differences in degree between previous forms of urbanism and its contemporary manifestation in developed capitalist countries. "Contemporary metropolitanism" is embedded in a global economy of great complexity. That economy is hierarchically ordered with local centres dominating local hinterlands, more important metropolitan centres dominating lesser centres, and all centres outside of the communist nations being ultimately subordinate to the central metropolitan areas in North America and Western Europe. This economic structure, elaborated theoretically and empirically most perceptively in the work of Lösch (1954) has to be interpreted in terms of surplus appropriation and extraction. Frank hypothesizes and documents from Latin American history an interpretation of spatial organization similar to that formulated in the analytics of Lösch, but understood in terms of the *modus operandi* of contemporary capitalism. This interpretation rests on an:

"exploitation relation which in chain-like fashion extends the capitalist link between the capitalist world and national metropolises to the regional centres (part of whose surplus they appropriate), and from these to local centres, and so on to large landowners or merchants who expropriate surplus from small peasants or tenants, and sometimes even from these latter to landless labourers exploited by them in turn. At each step along the way, the relatively few capitalists above exercise monopoly power over the many below, expropriating some or all of their

economic surplus and, to the extent that they are not expropriated in turn by the still fewer above them, appropriating it for
their own use. Thus at each point, the international, national,
and local capitalist system generates economic development for
the few and underdevelopment for the many." (1969, 31–2.)

The tendency for rich nations to grow richer and for poor
nations to grow poorer has been the subject of detailed investigation (Myrdal, 1957). Within the general structure of surplus
circulation associated with this tendency, the meaning of the
town–country antagonism changes. Fanon argues, for example,
that the town–country relation within the colonial world is restructured by the particular position of colonial countries in
the chain of exploitation of which Frank speaks:

"The originality of the colonial context is that economic
reality, inequality and the immense difference of ways of life
never come to mask the human realities. When you examine
at close quarters the colonial context, it is evident that what
parcels out the world is to begin with the fact of belonging to or
not belonging to a given race, a given species. In the colonies
the economic substructure is also a superstructure. The cause
is the consequence; you are rich because you are white, you are
white because you are rich. This is why Marxist analysis should
always be slightly stretched every time we have to do with the
colonial problem." (1967, 31–2.)

The urban structure that results is strongly differentiated:

"The settler's town is a strongly built town, all made of
stone and steel. It is a brightly-lit town; the streets are covered
with asphalt, and the garbage-cans swallow all the leavings,
unseen, unknown and hardly thought about. . . . The settler's
town is a well-fed town, an easy-going town; its belly is always
full of good things. The settler's town is a town of white people,
of foreigners. The town belonging to the colonized people . . .
is a place of ill fame, peopled by men of evil repute. They are
born there, it matters little where or how; they die there, it
matters not where, nor how. It is a world without spaciousness;
men live there on top of each other, and their huts are built one
on top of the other. The native town is a hungry town, starved
of bread, of shoes, of meat, of coal, of light. The native town is
a crouching village, a town on its knees, a town wallowing in
the mire. It is a town of niggers and dirty arabs." (*ibid.*)

The economic antagonism between town and country is here

replaced by "the antagonism which exists between the native who is excluded from the advantages of colonialism and his counterpart who manages to turn colonial exploitation to his account" (p. 89). The historical struggle between town and country in China, Algeria and Vietnam has to be interpreted in these terms, and our conception of urbanism has to be modified accordingly.

Although the major appropriative flow in the surplus is from the underdeveloped nations to the advanced capitalist powers, the metropolitan centres of the latter are themselves internally differentiated by the process through which surplus is appropriated in the "transaction maximizing system", the contemporary metropolis. Surplus value may be extracted at every transaction point whether it be in the primary, secondary (manufacturing), tertiary (distribution and services) or what may be designated quaternary (financial and money manipulating activities) sectors of the economy. In the midst of this welter of transactions, it is not easy to distinguish between productive and unproductive activity. But as metropolitan areas have increased in size and significance, so the proportion of surplus value extracted through socially unnecessary and unproductive transactions has increased. The contemporary metropolis therefore appears vulnerable, for if the rate at which surplus value is being appropriated at the centre (if profit levels are to be maintained) exceeds the rate at which social product is being created, then financial and economic collapse is inevitable. Financial speculation is not productive activity (although some would argue that it helps to coordinate productive activity) and money is worth only what it will buy. All activity must ultimately be supported by that simple conversion of naturally occurring materials into objects of utility to man—appropriation has to relate to the production of socially needed goods and services, otherwise the rate of profit is bound to fall.

The vulnerability of the contemporary metropolis in the advanced capitalist nations stems from the fact that the production of socially needed goods and services (the production of use values) takes place in large measure in other parts of the world—only in industrial manufacturing and in the provision of those services which Marx regarded as "unproductive but socially necessary", does the contemporary metropolis contribute enormously to the production of wealth. This vulnerability can be tempered by the effectiveness of the price mechanism in coordinating activity through the self-regulating market in such a way that the "hidden hand" ensures a flow of surplus into the metropolitan centre. Yet perfect competition of the sort envisaged in the analytics of western economic thought is a destructive force. In fact all aspects of society are threatened by the potentially destructive power of the market exchange system. Polanyi (1944) puts it this way:

"To allow the market mechanism to be the sole director of the fate of human beings and their natural environment, indeed, even of the amount and use of purchasing power, would result in the demolition of society. For the alleged commodity "labour power" cannot be shoved about, used indiscriminately, or even left unused, without affecting also the human individual who happens to be the bearer of this peculiar commodity. In disposing of man's labour power the system would, incidentally, dispose of the physical, psychological, and moral entity "man" attached to that tag. Robbed of the protective covering of cultural institutions human beings would perish from the effects of social exposure; they would die as the victims of acute social dislocation through vice, perversion, crime and starvation. Nature would be reduced to its elements, neighbourhoods and landscapes defiled, rivers polluted, military safety jeopardized, the power to produce food and raw materials destroyed. Finally, the market administration of purchasing power would periodically liquidate business enterprise, for shortages and surfeits of money would prove as disastrous to business as floods and droughts in primitive society."

These destructive tendencies of the self-regulating market economy are all too clearly evident in the history of capitalism since the beginning of the nineteenth century and the effects are as marked in the contemporary metropolis as they were in the early industrial city. The survival of capitalist society and the metropolitan centres to which it gives rise thus depends upon some countervailing force to that expressed through the operation of self-regulating markets. In part this countervailing force lies in the reconstitution of reciprocity and redistribution to play the role of container to the destructive powers of market exchange. But in part, also, the market exchange system is so organized as to contain certain checks which in themselves serve to stave off (at least for a time) its most destructive aspects. The two most important features here are the various forms of monopoly control (monopoly, oligopoly, cartel arrangements, informal non-competitive arrangements, etc.) and a rapid rate of technological innovation.

Monopoly forms and technological innovation are related to each other in a very important way. Monopoly must eventually lead to the frustration of the self-regulating market and therefore to the collapse of the capitalist economic system. Innovative activity opens up new lines of activity and new types of production which can be competitively organized, so that the self-regulating market can generate new activity which will eventually supersede the older activities (usually organized monopolistically). Innovation, competitive growth, monopolization and supersession appears to be quite a standard sequence in capitalist history. Technological innovation can also help perpetuate oligopoly since firms can compete through innovation rather than through price competition.

Monopoly forms of economic organization and technological innovation have great significance for the understanding of contemporary metropolitan urbanism, particularly when they are seen in relationship to each other. The metropolis provides a field for the application of technological innovations as well as a locale for the operations of large corporations. At the same time the metropolis is organized to reflect the growing power of monopolistic forms of organization in certain spheres of activity.

The growth of monopoly is itself a problem to be confronted. On the one hand the theoreticians of capitalism view monopoly as a threat to the traditional order and to the ability of price-fixing markets to be perpetuated. Some Marxist theoreticians (such as Baran and Sweezy, 1968) regard it as the reason why capitalist collapse has been staved off so long. The truth of the matter is that competition has ever been ameliorated by monopoly and that monopoly is inevitably the ultimate consequence of competition (Marx, *Poverty of Philosophy*, 161). Monopoly has always been essential to capitalism and property relationships guarantee restricted access to the means of production and, hence, individual monopoly control over at least some portion of the productive resources of society. Competition is never open and free, but takes the form of competition among many localized monopolies which, through time, may consolidate into larger monopolies. Historically, urban centres have been the locus of monopoly power and even under capitalism this urban mercantilism has not disappeared. Veblen (1923) argues that the country towns in nineteenth century America functioned basically as centres of monopoly control over wholesaling, retailing and the shipment of agricultural products. Vance (1970) likewise provides examples of monopoly power and urban roles under capitalist market exchange conditions. The connection between urban centres and monopoly power thus seems quite general. What has really changed in the last fifty years, of course, is the *scale* of monopoly enterprise and there can be no doubt that this change of scale has produced certain qualitative changes in the social form of contemporary metropolitanism. The self-regulating market has always operated under legal and institutional restraints; but it now frequently appears as if market prices are determined and dominated by a few powerful vested interest groups, who use their power in much the same way that the patrician clans in Venice of old expressed their moral and social norms through market exchange activity.

The contemporary form of monopoly is very different however. The control which large corporations exercise in the market place is largely illusory. In a self-regulating market economy surplus value has to be put back into circulation to create more surplus value. The rapidity with which surplus value is now circulated is such that wealth is measured as a rate of flow rather than as an absolute quantity of stored product. Wealth is no longer a tangible thing but constitutes a statement of rate of current flow (capitalized over a future time period) supported by paper rights over future flows or debts and obligations outstanding from past flows. The metropolis as a transaction maximizing system reflects this in many ways, the most evident of which is the growing physical instability of the structures it contains as the economy requires a more rapid circulation of surplus value in order to maintain the rate of profit. The large corporation is caught up in this process whether it likes it or not: its objective must be to protect and enhance the rate at which it is circulating surplus value—it cannot do anything else. This objective is realizable all the time it is possible to expand the circulation of surplus value in a given line of production (the automobile industry has succeeded in so doing for fifty years). But as soon as the prospects for expansion decline, profit levels fall and wealth (measured as a capitalized rate of flow) is eroded away. The large corporation may look big and all powerful but it is so only as long as it manages to meet the criteria imposed by the self-regulating market. The Penn Central Railroad went bankrupt not because it lacked assets but because the rate at which it could circulate surplus value declined below survival level and because the paper value of its fixed capital assets could not be justified against future expectations of earnings. Rolls-Royce had the same problem.

The latest institutional adaptation to this problem of increasing the rate of circulation of surplus value is the financial conglomerate. The smaller conglomerates usually function as "asset strippers", but the large conglomerates are extraordinarily large and flexible financial institutions which switch assets from one line of production to another—they "float" flexibly over a great diversity of operations in many countries, taking over profitable lines of investment and divesting themselves of unprofitable enterprises (Report on Conglomerates, 1971). Conglomerates do not identify with any one line of activity, any one place, or even any one country (they are placeless international institutions). They are an institutional adaptation to the necessity to expand the quantity of surplus value in circulation as well as to increase the rate of circulation—a necessity generated out of the tendency for the rate of profit to fall.

These new institutional and legal forms and the particular form now assumed by the self-regulating market, have had a profound impact upon the structure of the contemporary metropolitan economy. The scale of urbanism has expanded in like fashion to the expansion of corporate enterprise. The complexity of transactions within the urban space economy has increased as the division of labour has multiplied. The geographical concentration of people and productive activity in the large metropolitan centres in the advanced capitalist nations would not be possible without the enormous concentrations of surplus value in superordinate institutions such as large corporations and national government. Nor would this concentration be possible without an elaborate apparatus to protect the hierarchical structure of the global space economy in order to ensure the maintenance of flows from hinterlands to urban centres, from lesser centres to larger centres and from all regional centres into the centres of capitalist activity.

There are also some very specific impacts of the increasing scale of monopoly capitalism upon urban structure that ought to be considered. Chinitz (1958) details some of these. He suggests that an oligopolistically organized metropolitan economy, such as that of Pittsburgh, is less likely to breed entrepreneurial skills and to be less receptive to the in-migration of capitalist entrepreneurs. It follows that such a city is less likely to foster new industries and that it will tend to encourage and apply only those innovations which aid in the relentless drive to cut costs, to improve efficiency and to differentiate product in existing lines of activity. Jane Jacobs (1969) is undoubtedly correct in complaining that large and efficient corporate enterprise (and government activity) create city environments that inhibit a vigorous generative urbanism out of which new work and technological innovation can grow. The most fertile environments are those within which a chaotic assemblage of work, talent and entrepreneurial and financial skills provide a breeding ground for capitalist creativity and invention. This history of Pittsburgh contrasts with New York; the histories of Birmingham (England) and Manchester contrast similarly. Insofar as monopoly control inhibits innovative activity in a particular location, it may be anticipated that supersession will involve geographical shifts in the centres of growth activity and shifts in the geographical patterns of circulation of the surplus.

The large industrial corporation also aims at and normally achieves "financial independence through the internal generation of funds": as a consequence "surplus capital which accumulates inside large multiplant companies is more mobile interregionally within the company than intraregionally outside of the company" (Chinitz, 1958, 285–6). In addition, banks and other financial institutions have increased the scale of their enterprise, so that they find it easier to relate to large industrial corporations than to small time entrepreneurs who usually need small amounts of high risk capital as seed money if new lines of activity are to be opened up. The nature of this concentration is itself significant for the channelling of surplus value among the various enterprises and activities within a metropolitan area. For example, the Wright Patman Report (1968) on *Trust*

Banking in the United States indicated that Trust Banks held one quarter of the $1 trillion assets held by institutional investors. In 221 urban areas surveyed, 210 had 75 per cent or more of these trust assets held by three banks or less. In Baltimore, for example, it was concluded:
"that Baltimore banking, Baltimore finance, and much of Baltimore's commerce and industry are greatly influenced and perhaps even dominated and controlled through the operations of the Mercantile Safe Deposit and Trust Company and corporations closely linked to it." (p. 545.)
A few banks control much of the investment capital available within particular metropolitan areas. The circulation of surplus value from large financial institutions to large industial corporations and back again—often symbolized by interlocking directorships within a fairly closed economic power structure—implies a relatively restricted flow of funds into new forms of production or into sectors of the economy which cannot, for technical reasons, be organized on a large scale. Sectors organized atomistically or on a small scale are usually serviced through some intermediary (a real estate corporation, a mortgage agency, a large landlord operation, a small business loan corporation, etc.). In housing, for example, the policies of large financial institutions and government agencies towards various intermediaries in the housing market have a significant impact upon new construction, rehabilitation, maintenance, home purchasing, and the time horizon in both construction and purchase. The physical structure of the metropolis is in large degree a tangible outcome of such policies.

The influence of monopolistic forms extends far beyond the direct consequences for the organization of investment, production and distribution. Protected from direct antagonistic competition and with large quantities of surplus value at its disposal, the large corporation faces an acute problem of finding a market to absorb expanding output as well as to help expand the rate of circulation of surplus value. The corporation must therefore create, maintain and expand the effective demand for its products. There are various strategems available. Perhaps the most successful is to create a need while eliminating the possibility for that need to be met by a substitution of product. The effective demand for automobiles (as well as oil products, highway construction, suburban construction, etc.) has been created and expanded through the total reorganization of the metropolitan built form so that it is all but impossible to live a "normal" social life without a car (except in areas where congestion is so great as to make automobile access expensive and difficult). A need has been created out of a luxury. And it is essential that this effective demand for automobiles—the linch-pin of the contemporary capitalist economies—be maintained and expanded. Otherwise there will be severe economic and financial disruption throughout the whole economy. On this basis it may be predicted, for example, that public transit systems can be built only insofar as they do not cut into (or effectively expand) the effective demand for transportation equipment. If the United States were suddenly covered by public transit systems, there would be massive unemployment in Detroit and an economic recession far more serious than the collapse of the 1930s. Contemporary metropolitanism apparently functions in part as a field for the necessary disposal of surplus product and as a manipulable source of effective demand. Surplus product has frequently been lavished on the built form of the city in the past (in the form of monumental architecture and the like). But it is now *necessary* for urbanism to generate expanding consumption if the capitalist economy is to be maintained. Much of the expansion of GNP in capitalist societies is in fact bound up in the whole suburbanization process.

Planned obsolescence provides another means for maintaining effective demand and is particularly significant when it comes to expanding the rate of circulation of surplus value. In the redistributive city it was the physical life of buildings which mattered and many buildings were built to last. In the contemporary capitalist city it is the economic life which matters and this economic life-span is contracting as it becomes necessary to increase the rate of circulation of surplus value. Good buildings are torn down to make way for new buildings which will have an even shorter economic life span. It is not a mere cultural passion for newness which leads to the tearing down and building up in metropolitan economies (particularly evident in the United States). It is an economic necessity. Shortening the economic and physical life of products is a typical strategem for accelerating the circulation of surplus value in all sectors of the economy. It operates most intricately in the housing market, where the need to realize profits on speculative investment in suburban land and construction as well as in the land-use transition process, stimulates demand for housing and commercial properties in certain locations while cutting off the flow of funds into other sectors (see chapter 5).

Effective demand depends ultimately upon consumption. If we reject the view that mankind possesses a natural and insatiable appetite for consumer goods (as opposed to a culturally instilled commodity fetishism), then we are forced to consider the origins of effective demand. Within the global economy there is an obvious answer—the unfulfilled and real needs are everywhere apparent. Internally, within the metropolitan economy, there also exists a large potential effective demand in the unfulfilled needs of a poverty population. In the United States this population is substantial—five million or so families were officially defined as living in poverty in 1968 and half of these lived in metropolitan areas (the numbers close to, at or below the poverty line are even more substantial). Such poverty populations have a dual function. They can be viewed as an industrial reserve army (to use Marx's phrase) which can be either used as a threat to organized labour in wage disputes or as a surplus labour force to be drawn upon in times of expansion and relinquished in times of contraction. Marx (*Capital*, volume 1, chapter 25) provides an analysis of the mechanism which links capitalist accumulation and the production of a relative surplus population. The industrial reserve army produced is made up of three components. The first two, which Marx called floating and latent, are those groups which are underemployed or which can be brought into the labour force when necessary (e.g. women). But much of the poverty in advanced metropolitan economies is found in populations who are incapable of joining the work force—the aged, female heads of households, and the like. These elements, which Marx called the stagnant group in the industrial reserve army, typically depend upon welfare for survival and therefore can be viewed as a tool for the manipulation of effective demand through government policies.

Poverty populations therefore function as stabilizing devices within capitalist economies—stabilizing devices which rest on human suffering and degradation. They may be viewed as the result of that institutional creation of scarcity in the commodity labour power, in which some elements are favoured and some denied. It appears inevitable that attempts to eliminate poverty *within* the capitalist system are automatically countered through adjustments in the self-regulating market. The distribution of income in capitalist society is, within certain limits, structurally determined. Since the self-regulating market leads different income groups to occupy different locations we can view the geographical patterns in urban residential structure as a tangible geographical expression of a structural condition in the capitalist economy. Residential segregation in the contemporary metropolis is therefore fundamentally different from the residential segregation exhibited in typical redistributive cities which was largely symbolic.

The growing scale of capitalist enterprise and the increasing quantities of product to which it has given rise, the creation of large-scale as opposed to localized monopolies, the generation of new needs to ensure an effective demand for product, planned obsolescence to facilitate an increasing rate of circulation of surplus value, elaborate mechanisms to ensure the structural maintenance of scarcity—these are but a few of the adaptations which have occurred in capitalism to resolve the difficulties it generates within itself. These adaptations do not however, change its basic character. The self-regulating market operates in a new institutional context. Yet it functions in basically the same manner. The consequences of this functioning mode of economic integration are everywhere apparent in contemporary metropolitanism, whether it be at the periphery in impoverished nations or in the ghetto areas of the capitalist metropolis. These consequences cannot be countered by a return to some idealized system of individualistic capitalism, since such a system never existed: capitalism has always been imbued with monopoly. What is more, a system like this cannot be created, for to do so would be tantamount to releasing an uncontrollable destructive force which, as Polanyi pointed out so succinctly, would undermine the very fabric of urbanized society. To advocate—as Jane Jacobs and Jeffersonian democrats alike appear to be doing—a more open and individualistic capitalism is not only to propose a system that contradicts the historical evidence as to what capitalism is really all about, but also one which, if created, would almost certainly destroy all civilized society.

The internal adaptations which have occurred in social

organization to encompass the problems generated by the self-regulating market economy have been accompanied by a number of other adaptations—in particular the reconstitution of reciprocity and redistribution as countervailing forces to the potential destructive power of antagonistic market exchange.

4 Redistribution and reciprocity as countervailing forces to market exchange in the contemporary metropolis

Whenever and wherever the self-regulating market cast its spell over the organization of the urban space economy, government adapted its functions to support and contain it. Asa Briggs (1963) describes, for example, how city governments during the first wave of industrialization in Britain took on a redistributive function to provide those public goods and services (such as sewers and sanitation facilities) that private entrepreneurs did not find profitable, as well as to alleviate to some degree the worst impacts of the wage system on the poorest groups in society (through the regulation of work conditions, housing conditions, and the like). These government interventions, minor at first, have become more and more significant over time. The public provision of public (and sometimes private) goods, together with private and public planning of the urban community "in the public interest", are now of major significance in shaping the geography of the contemporary city. Public or quasi-public projects, such as urban renewal schemes and new-town construction, have also served to transform the chaotic individualism of the early industrial city and the "privatism"—as Sam Bass Warner (1968) calls it—of the American city into an urban pluralism in which the public sector acts as a countervailing force to potentially destructive market exchange, while supporting the structural conditions necessary for the survival of capitalist forms. The political and bureaucratic system partly functions as a redistributive agent within a self-regulating market economy (see chapter 2).

The indirect effects of this redistributive activity require some elucidation. Government intervention in capitalist countries has two broad aims. The first is to keep market exchange functioning properly. The second is to ameliorate the destructive consequences stemming from the self-regulating market. Policies in the first arena vary from the creation of instruments of coercion to preserve an institutionalized scarcity (military power abroad and police power at home), through direct support of financial institutions, to the construction of a variety of mechanisms to keep the market functioning as a self-regulating system. In the last respect government may intervene either to absorb risks in an economy that relies more and more upon long term and large scale investment if its structure is to be preserved, or to prevent (and in certain circumstances to encourage) the emergence of monopoly in a particular sector of the economy. These policies have a variety of impacts and, indeed, are designed to accomplish different objectives depending upon the circumstances. The growing role of the state in an urbanizing society has to be understood against the background of the growing accumulation of capital, the expanding power of production, the increasing penetration of market exchange and "the urbanization of the countryside" on a global scale. The state, together with supra-national organizations (in which we may include alliances of states), have to intervene wherever crises, most of which are generated out of the internal dynamics of capitalism, arise. State intervention occurs at the international level as artificial barriers are erected to the flows of capital, labour power, resources, goods and services and as technical manipulations within the international monetary system serve to preserve the chains of exploitation which Frank (1969) describes, largely through a forced pattern of unequal exchange (Emmanuel, 1972). The growing power and significance of state intervention in the twentieth century has to be seen as a response to the "permanently revolutionary force" that is capitalism.

Within nations state policies have considerable consequences for the built form of the contemporary metropolis. The Federal Housing Administration (FHA) legislation in the United States, for example, was set up to support mortgage financing of housing in the 1930s, but its main effect was to support financial institutions which were deeply troubled by the reverberations of the depression. The consequence has been, however, to stimulate suburbanization, because FHA loans are mostly geared to financing purchase of new rather than old stock (Douglas Commission, 1968). This policy also led to a more rapid rate of economic obsolescence in the housing sector and thereby increased the potential for circulating surplus

value at an increasing rate. This kind of government intervention appears to be more and more necessary and it now extends
to the creation of jobs and employment, and production and
allocation of economic resources to areas of "national interest"
(which usually means defense but which could and does also
extend to health, pollution control, education, and the like).

In seeking to ameliorate the worst impacts of market exchange, government policy can also generate substantial
changes in urban structure. The end result of competition is a
very lop-sided distribution of income in society which, it has
been recognized, is not beneficial to those in control over the
means of production since it diminishes effective demand while
reducing the quality of labour power. There is therefore a
permanent need for some redistribution of income and wealth.
This redistribution may be facilitated by permitting the organization of labour. Otherwise it is necessary to tax certain portions of the surplus in circulation. Insofar as this surplus is held
by one part of society and directed to the use of another, the
taxation system is progressive or regressive depending upon
which group is taxed and which group is provided for. Taxation
and the public provision of goods, services and financial resources, is exceedingly complex and money flows in both ways.
In general it appears that society is much more progressively
redistributive than in fact it is, for there are numerous hidden
flows as well as taxation schemes (particularly purchase taxes
and sales taxes) which distribute in the other direction. Nevertheless, government policies in these areas have transformed
the meaning of unemployment, underemployment (which is
estimated to run as high as 30 per cent or more of the labour
force in many American cities), and inability to work. The
combination of capitalism with welfare state policies has
wrought a substantial transformation in metropolitan forms.

The changing distribution of disposable income among the
various groups in society is reflected in the appearance of
contemporary urbanism. This impact is most clearly evident in
those countries, such as Britain and in Scandinavia, which have
pursued welfare state policies with some persistency. In these
countries society has achieved a dual structure in which a private
sector is strongly differentiated from a public sector. This
dualism is reflected in physical design. In British towns public
housing is clearly distinguishable from private and goods and

services rendered throughout the public sector are likewise differentiated from private action in fields such as health and education. The urban dualism of Britain and Scandinavia is writ large in the urban landscape giving urbanism there a particular character distinguishing it from the urbanism of the United States where dualism has to large degree been avoided by the ideological commitment to privatism, except when it comes to provision for the wealthiest in society. Socialism for the rich, which appears to be the way government intervention is organized in the United States, creates a very different kind of urban structure from social welfare for the poor.

Yet welfare policies, if pursued too far, pose a threat of sorts to capitalist market exchange. An industrial reserve army has to exist somewhere and primitive accumulation has also to take place somewhere. The case of Sweden, frequently held up as a model welfare state society, is instructive here. Sweden has eliminated the worst aspects of material deprivation yet has maintained its capitalist economic basis. It has succeeded in this because it draws upon the industrial reserve army of southern Europe and accomplishes primitive accumulation indirectly through its links to the global capitalist economy (for instance, trade with the United States and Britain). Sweden is in effect an affluent suburb of the global capitalist economy (it even exhibits many of the social and psychological stresses of a typical suburban economy). The moral of this example, is that a particular territory can succeed in its welfare policies beyond a certain limit only insofar as it can shift some of the major problems associated with capitalist market exchange outside of its borders. There is no limit to the effectiveness of welfare state policies within a territory, but there is an overall limit to progressive redistribution within the global economy of capitalism as a whole.

Commentators such as de Jouvenal (1951) have been much more perceptive in this regard than have those socialists who blindly and religiously believe that socialism can be accomplished by redistributive policies without fundamentally altering capitalist production. The limit to redistribution is reached at the point where it seriously impairs the operation of the self-regulating market and the circulation of surplus value. In a large scale economy such as that of the United States, it is difficult to shift all of the burden elsewhere and redistribution

could not probably proceed to the degree to which it has proceeded in Scandinavia. In an intermediate size economy, such
as Britain, attempts to redistribute are likely to be frustrated by
natural adjustments through the self-regulating market. Titmuss
(1962) and others have shown that this is indeed the case and
that a substantial effort to redistribute income and wealth in
Britain resulted in very little change in the structure of income
distribution in the economy. Government can, and frequently
does, pursue all kinds of policies, but the compensating effects
of a dominant self-regulating market mechanism will always
tend to produce some sort of "natural" balance between market
exchange and redistributive activity. This balance is roughly
what is necessary to perpetuate the economic basis of capitalist
society.

This has implications for comparative urban studies. The
superficial if impressive differences between urbanism in
Sweden, Britain and the United States, for example, largely
disappear in the face of this analysis. Swedish urbanism may be
regarded as something achievable in a small jurisdiction in a
large scale capitalist economic system and it has to be compared
therefore to urbanism in Connecticut (USA) or Sussex
(England). In all of these areas many of the characteristic
problems of capitalist economies have been transported elsewhere. What is remarkable is not that urbanism is so different
but that it is so similar in all the metropolitan centres of the
world in spite of significant differences in social policy, cultural
tradition, administrative and political arrangements, institutions
and laws, and so on. The conditions in the economic basis of
capitalist society together with its associated technology put an
unmistakable stamp upon the qualitative attributes of urbanism
in all economically advanced capitalist nations.

Although redistributive activity is usually equated with
government action, it would be wrong to ignore certain other
respects in which the social characteristics of the rank society
have been reconstituted in the context of contemporary capitalism. Market exchange reduces every human being to the status
of a commodity. Few individuals find this an adequate measure
of their own value or an adequate criterion by which to
establish their own self-identity. Nor do many find it entirely
satisfying to locate their total identity in a commodity fetishism
which proclaims that "I am what I can buy" or "I am what I

278

possess." Other measures of value are therefore very important. Here the criteria of moral worth inherent in the older rank societies provide an apparent relief to counter the impersonal and dehumanizing criteria of the market place. Status, rank, prestige and privilege provide more appealing ways of identifying self than that provided through commodity relationships in the market place. Organizations are thus organized hierarchically, governmental and corporate bureaucracies are internally ordered, professional groups exhibit official or unofficial prestige orderings, each division of labour in society is organized like a mini-rank society, while certain occupations are designated "high status" by different ethnic, racial and religious groupings.

These manifestations of the rank society are significant to the way in which people regard themselves and hence to the way in which they become aware of conflict and fight it out. Issues stemming from the economic basis of society will frequently be translated into political and ideological issues spelled out in the language of the rank society. For example, issues of unemployment may be translated into issues of racial or ethnic discrimination in the job market. Urban politics and government at large are permeated by such translations and insofar as action occurs with respect to the translation of the issue rather than with respect to the underlying economic issue, we can expect conflicts to be resolved in a manner which moves the problem around (sometimes geographically) without touching its underlying structure—it is tempting to hypothesize that this is much of what contemporary politics is about in capitalist nations.

There is a deep and underlying resistance even to interpreting problems in market exchange terms, for to do so is to admit that market exchange is the ultimate determinant of value in society —a notion which the very condition of being human makes us rightly revolt against. Yet it is only when we recognize the conditions under which we exist for what they are that it becomes possible to confront them directly. It is this aspect of analysis that the Marxist theory of alienation is most clearly directed towards (see Mészáros, 1970). Representing issues of market exchange as issues of status and prestige merely serves to blind us to action and thereby helps to preserve the *status quo*. Unfortunately, as T. S. Eliot observed in *Four Quartets*, "mankind cannot bear very much reality." Or, put another way, most of us are victims of false consciousness most of the time.

The prevailing concern with the trappings of the rank society is real enough and produces tangible results in the urban space economy. Dominant organizations and institutions make use of space hierarchically and symbolically. Sacred and profane spaces are created, focal points emphasized, and space is generally manipulated to reflect status and prestige. The contemporary city therefore exhibits many similar features to those found in redistributive cities which Wheatley (1969; 1971) interprets as symbolic constructs reflecting the mores of the rank society. It is usually held, for example, that western cities exhibit a focusing of activity at their centre for it is here that maximum accessibility exists to all market activity. In the contemporary city this is scarcely true any longer (the centres are maximally congested). The centre is still a prestigious location, however, and firms bid with prestige and status in mind. It may seem strange to think that what firms are bidding for in the heartless and cold analytics of the von Thünen–Alonso–Muth models is prestige, status and perhaps even divinity at the *axis mundi* of the capitalist city, but this is probably closer to the truth than the argument that they are bidding for relative locational advantage.

The moulding of the contemporary metropolis to fit the trappings of a superficially constituted rank society is self-conscious and aware enough. Urban renewal in the United States had an overt symbolic as well as an economic function. It was (and still is) designed to create confidence in the dominant institutions of capitalist society and in so doing made self-conscious use of an ancient technique for projecting "images of cosmic order on to the plane of human experience, where they could provide a framework for action" (Wheatley, 1971, 478). Consider the Charles Center urban renewal project in Baltimore, the heart of which is Hopkins Plaza, used solely by lunch-hour strollers and reserved for occasional ritual gatherings (the City Fair, the annual anti-war demonstrations). To the south the plaza is bounded by a monumental slab of a building which houses Federal government offices; to the north, slightly taller and more elegant, is the home of the Mercantile Safe Deposit and Trust Company (the dominant commercial institution in Baltimore). To the west an unsuccessful restaurant (who wants to dine in church really?) and to the east a well-fashioned but small theatre. In the centre an impressive fountain. City Hall is hidden away four blocks to the east. Large commercial buildings and some prestigious apartment blocks cluster eagerly around the centre. Is all of this really so different from Wheatley's description of the ancient Chinese city?

"The supremely sacred central precinct, the *axis mundi*, was usually reserved for ritual purposes. Building in this zone was then restricted to habitations of gods and of those élites who, in societies structured in the image of a hierarchical cosmic order, were either conceived of as occupying positions close to divinity, or were experts in the technics of ceremonial and ritual service."

Although the basic lineaments of residential structure in the contemporary metropolis are determined by competitive bidding power, its many nuances can be interpreted only as the result of individuals turning to the criteria of a rank society to differentiate themselves in the face of an homogenizing market exchange process. The *Urban Mosaic* described by Timms (1971) has to be interpreted as redistribution and rank superimposed upon market exchange and stratification. People attempt by all manner of means, to differentiate what the market place has in fact rendered homogeneous. Hence the urban space economy is replete with all manner of pseudo-hierarchical spatial orderings to reflect prestige and status in residential location. These orderings are very important to the self-respect of people, but are irrelevant to the basic economic structure of society.

In the same way that redistribution and the rank society have been reconstituted in capitalist society, so reciprocity has also emerged in a new form to act as a countervailing force in the face of a dehumanizing market process. Reciprocity comes closest to performing its traditional function in the neighbourhood and in the local community. It became particularly important, for example, in the early years of the industrial revolution when working-class communities typically evolved a neighbourly warm-hearted reciprocity that did much to assuage the worst ravages of an insensate wage system. The sense of community has been significant as a protective device in the industrial city ever since. In the early stages of industrial urbanization reciprocity was typically based on extended kinship relations, ethnic or religious identifications, or on the coming together of particular population groups under some threat (the sense of community is very strong in mining areas for example). Increased mobility and rapid changes in social structure have done much to loosen these bonds. The former has also meant a lessening of attachment to any one particular locale. Spatial propinquity, geographical immobility and reciprocity in the community are undoubtedly related.

The decline of this traditional form of reciprocity in urban communities (much lamented by writers such as Jane Jacobs) has changed the functioning of the urban community. In the American city, ethnic bonds and a close-knit community structure have done much in the past to help resist the penetration of market exchange relationships into the daily life and hence of human relationships within the community. The consequences of reciprocity are generally held to be beneficial within the community: behaviour based upon this mode of economic integration provides far surer mechanisms for the provision of public goods and services than result from a logic of collective action based upon individual self-interest (see Olson, 1965). Reciprocity based on mutual respect and support among individuals in the community can therefore provide a potent source of resistance to human commodity relationships implicit in the market exchange system. Insofar as this mode of economic integration has declined, it has allowed the further penetration of human relationships by market exchange.

Reciprocity has not declined though as much as many observers think. It has evolved new forms. In the community "neighbourly behaviour" has been redefined (Keller, 1969); it has become particularly significant as a mode of behaviour which is resurrected by communities under threat. The political reaction of urban communities to the threat of highway clearance, the threat of noxious facilities in the neighbourhood, the progress of avaricious real-estate speculation, and so on, is explicable as the emergence of reciprocity when it becomes apparent to all that action based on individual self-interest automatically presages defeat.

There are also numerous parochialist institutions in which reciprocity can flourish. Local political clubs, the Chamber of Commerce, trade unions, and so on, all can be marked by reciprocity of behaviour within the organization. This behaviour may be tacit and implied—a philosophy of "you scratch my back and I'll scratch yours" put into daily practice. There need be no conspiracy, no explicit rules of the game, for there can evolve an unwritten code of conduct among people or organizations who regard themselves as equals for ideological and pragmatic reasons. This code applies in politics and business as well as in areas of social action. Most parliaments have a certain "club-like" atmosphere and businessmen can relate sympathetically to each other even though they may be titular competitors. Under these conditions reciprocity becomes a mode of economic integration in the economic basis of society. It operates under limited but very important conditions— whenever it is apparent to competitors that antagonistic competition will lead to the destruction of all concerned. Baran and Sweezy (1968, 50) note how the three large automobile companies in the United States behave with respect to each other on the basis of reciprocity, since each recognizes each of the others has enormous retaliatory power. It is therefore a deliberate calculated policy to avoid antagonistic confrontations and provocations, and a tacit reciprocity of behaviour takes over. A similar relationship exists between the very large corporations, particularly the international conglomerates (such as ITT) and national governments. Wherever competitive behaviour appears too threatening to the survival of the capitalist economic system, reciprocity of behaviour may emerge as an alternate mode of economic integration.

Reciprocity and redistribution are ancient and well-tried modes of economic integration. Far from being abandoned with the penetration of market exchange into all aspects of life, these older modes of economic integration and the social forms with which they are associated, have adapted to take on new and very significant roles. The modes of economic integration cannot be understood in isolation from each other. Each is defined with respect to the role it plays vis-à-vis the others. Urbanism as a way of life comprises all three modes of economic integration as well as the societal forms with which each is associated. Class and rank differentiation and patterns of mutual respect and support, are carefully intertwined in the life of the contemporary metropolis. Similarly the physical structure of the city reflects the peculiar combination of each with each. The symbolic downtown centre with its emphasis on prestige and status, the fashionable neighbourhoods, the areas of public housing, the cosy architecture of the working class or ethnic neighbourhood within which reciprocity can flourish, the areas of residential and commercial blight as exchange value becomes the criterion of use in the hands of speculators and commercial operators—these are all tangible representations of the various modes of economic and social integration present in contemporary society. The nuances are many and the interactions are complex. But even in the contemporary metropolis, with all of its manifest complexity, it appears that these interpretive devices serve us well as we seek to construct a theory of urbanism which realistically encompasses the necessity to concentrate and circulate surplus value as well as the necessity to construct a space economy in which the various modes of economic integration can function effectively.

Part three

Synthesis

Chapter 7

Conclusions and Reflections

The previous six chapters of this volume are characterized by analysis. It remains to take a final step into synthesis—to try to distill some conclusions. This is not too awesome a task if we are prepared to undertake a reconstitution of method, a re-formulation of the sense in which we may validly speak of a "theory" of urbanism, and a re-evaluation of the nature of urbanism in its historical and geographical contexts. These are big "ifs" however. But since the essays here assembled are positioned on an evolutionary path of thought and experience, it seems proper to try to provide some conclusions which we can hold up as a mirror in order to reflect back upon what has been said. These conclusions cannot be arbitrary. They have to be present, albeit in disguised and latent form, in the material already presented. A conclusion should not be permitted to introduce new material, but it should be permitted to re-constitute the old.

ON METHODS AND THEORIES

A persistent theme throughout this book has been the search for appropriate methods and an appropriate conception of theory through which we may effectively investigate a phenomenon of great complexity like urbanism. It seems right, therefore, to begin by sorting out some conclusions concerning method and theory.

I think it is true to say that the most important thing to be learned from the study of Marx's work is his conception of method. And it is out of this conception of method that theory naturally flows. Certain features in Marx's method are to be found in the writings of his precursors. Leibniz and Spinoza provide relational modes of thought and a concept of totality which Marx broadly accepted. Hegel provides a version of the dialectic, Kant provides innumerable dualisms to be resolved, the English political economists provide practical methods for investigating the material activities of production in society. Marx brought together all of these diffuse elements (and more) and constituted a method which, by the fusion of abstract theory and concrete practice, allowed the creation of a theoretical practice through which man could fashion history rather than be fashioned by it. Marx saw what no one else had seen before him, that the innumerable dualisms that beset western thought (between man and nature, between fact and value, between subject and object, between freedom and necessity, between mind and body and between thought and action) could be resolved only through the study of and, where necessary, through the creation of human practice. It is indeed unfortunate that many so-called Marxists have not understood this method for they have thereby lost the most precious tool to be gained from a study of Marx's works. Fortunately, these works stand as living testimony to his method and narrow dogmatism cannot for long conceal its inherent power. Fortunately too, living scholarship leads to the rediscovery of the method by those who might not otherwise regard themselves as "Marxist". Perhaps the most outstanding example in recent times is Piaget. In his summary work on *The Principles of Genetic Epistemology* (1972a) and in his philosophical works on *Structuralism* (1970) and *Insights and Illusions of Philosophy* (1972b), Piaget arrives at a conception of method that is very close indeed to that practiced by Marx—a fact which he insists "is a matter of convergence not of influence" (1972b, 204). And it is exactly this kind of convergence that occurs through the essays assembled in this book. This convergence has to be accounted for.

What constitutes Marx's method and how can it be represented? These are difficult questions to answer in abstraction for the method can be fully understood only through its practice. Yet we can say something about it, erect a few signposts if you will. Ollman (1971; 1972) has attempted to create a guide for us and has, I believe, succeeded most admirably. So I shall take two steps along the pathway he charts and examine Marx's ontology and epistemology pausing at each stage to consider how these aspects of Marx's method come to influence the analyses in this book.

1 Ontology

An ontology is a theory of what exists. To say, therefore, that something has ontological status is to say that it exists. Marx evolves in his work certain fundamental assumptions regarding the way in which reality is structured and organized. Ollman puts it this way: "the twin pillars of Marx's ontology are his conception of reality as a totality of internally related parts, and his conception of these parts as expandable relations such that each one in its fullness can represent the totality" (1972, 8). Let us examine this statement. Many writers have argued that society has to be understood as a totality. But there are different ways in which we can think of "totality". In the first case we may think of it as an aggregate of elements—a mere sum of parts—which enter into combination without being fashioned by some pre-existing structure within the totality. If a structure (such as a class structure) arises in the totality it can be explained as something contingent upon the way in which the elements just happened to combine. In the second case, the totality is viewed as something "emergent" that has an existence independent of its parts, while it also dominates the character of the parts it contains. Explanation in this second case has to focus on the laws governing the behaviour of the totality and can proceed without reference to the parts. There is a further case to be considered:

"Over and beyond schemes of atomistic association on the one hand and emergent totalities on the other, there is a third, that of operational structuralism. It adopts from the start a relational perspective, according to which it is neither the elements nor a whole that comes about in a manner one knows not how, but the relations among elements that count. In other words, the logical procedures or natural processes by which the whole is formed are primary, not the whole, which is consequent on the system's laws of composition, or the elements." (Piaget, 1970, 9.)

Marx might be surprised to find himself described as an "operational structuralist" but the concept of totality to which Marx appealed was exactly of this third sort as Ollman (1971) points out. This concept of totality (which is not too different from that proposed by Leibniz) leads us on to ask how totalities are structured and how these structures change. To deal with the problem of change Piaget introduces the concept of a *structure under transformation* arguing that "were it not for the idea of transformation, structures would lose all explanatory import since they would collapse into static forms" (1970, 12). The relationships between elements within the structure are therefore regarded as expressing certain transformation rules through which the totality itself comes to be transformed. In other words, the totality is in the course of being structured by the elaboration of the relationships within it.

This last sense of totality is quite different from the other two and it is this conception that is common to both Marx and Piaget. Ollman (1972) points out how this view of things affects the ways in which we think of the relationships between the elements and between the elements and the totality. The totality seeks to shape the parts so that each part functions to preserve the existence and general structure of the whole. Capitalism, for example, seeks to shape the elements and relationships within itself in such a way that capitalism is reproduced as an ongoing system. Consequently, we can interpret the relationships within the totality according to the way in which they function to preserve and reproduce it. A further consequence is that each element (rather like Leibniz's monads) reflects within itself all of the characteristics of the totality because it is the locus of a set of relationships within that totality. Concepts such as labour power and surplus have to be treated, for example, as reflections of all social relationships occurring within a given mode of production. But these relationships are not necessarily in harmony with each other. They are frequently in contradiction and out of this contradiction flows conflict. Transformations occur through the resolution of these conflicts and with each transformation the totality is restructured and this restructuring in turn alters the definition, meaning and function of the elements and relationships within the whole. New conflicts and contradictions emerge to replace the old.

It follows from Marx's ontology that research has to be directed to discovering the transformation rules whereby society is constantly being restructured, rather than to finding "causes", in the isolated sense that follows from a presupposition of atomistic association, or to identifying "stages" or "descriptive laws" governing the evolution of totalities independent of their parts. Marx thus directs our attention to the processes of inner transformation in society. He does not speak of causes in the ordinary sense of the word, nor does he propose an historicist evolutionary schema as some seem to think he did. The transition from feudalism to capitalism, for example, is not some step on an arbitrarily determined evolutionary schema which Marx dreamed up, but is seen as a *necessary* transformation within society as the tensions and contradictions of feudal society were overcome. Dialectical materialism is likewise not a doctrine arbitrarily foisted on phenomena to interpret their meaning, but a *method* that seeks to identify the transformation rules through which society is restructured. Marx's dialectic is, as both Althusser (1969) and Godelier (1972) point out, fundamentally different from that of Hegel since the latter did not, among other things, possess an adequate concept of totality to turn the dialectic into a rich rather than an arbitrary and barren tool.

So far, we have treated of totalities and structures as if they were synonymous and we have failed to consider how totalities and structures may be defined. It would be rather too glib to assert that a totality is simply everything there is and a careful study of Marx's works indicates that he never took such a view in practice. He implied, rather, that separate structures exist within a totality and that these structures can be differentiated from each other. Structures are not "things" or "actions" and we cannot therefore establish their existence through observation. To define elements relationally means to interpret them in a way external to direct observation. The meaning of an observable action, such as cutting a log, is established by discovering its relation to the wider structure of which it is a part. Its interpretation will vary depending upon whether we view it in relation to capitalism or socialism, or whether we place it in relationship to some quite different structure (the ecological system, for example). A structure must be defined, therefore, as a system of internal relations which is in the process of being structured through the operation of its own transformation rules. It follows from this that structures have to be defined through an understanding of the transformation rules that shape them. From this we can derive two distinct ways in which structures relate to each other.

A higher order structure may be obtained from a lower by way of a transformation. Under these conditions a hierarchy of structures can emerge through a process of internal differentiation. Lower and higher order structures may thus co-exist. This appears to be an adequate way of dealing with the relationship between, say, Newtonian mechanics and relativity theory or between a system of local government and the system of national administration. But such a hierarchical view does not seem adequate to interpret the relationship between, say, a mode of production and an ecological structure. In this last case we cannot derive one structure from another through a transformation. This suggests a rule. Structures may be regarded as separate and differentiatable entities when no transformation exists whereby one may be derived from another. The inability to identify a transformation does not prove, of course, that one does not exist. Indeed the history of ideas is replete with examples in which a transformation has been discovered through which seemingly independent structures have been unified (mathematics provides numerous cases). But it appears wise, as a general rule, to treat structures as distinct from each other until a transformation can be identified.

One consequence of this rule is that we are obliged to distinguish between contradictions *within* a structure and contradictions *between* structures. Mao Tse-tung (1966), for example, distinguishes between contradictions among the people (between intellectual and manual work, for example) and contradictions between the people and their enemies (different approaches to property, for example). The two different kinds of contradiction present quite different problems and require different measures for their resolution. Godelier has recently amplified this point by a careful examination of contradiction in Marx's works (1972). He suggests that many of the contradictions which Marx exposed were of the internal variety, but that some of the more fundamental ones are to be interpreted as contradictions between structures. For example, the structure of the forces of production comes into conflict with the structure of the relations of production—a conflict that is expressed in the increasingly social character of capitalist production and the enduringly private character of capitalist control and consumption. Likewise, the superstructure of which Marx frequently writes, has to be regarded as being made up of separate structures (political, ideological, juridical, and so on) none of which can be derived either from each other or from the structures in the economic basis of society by way of a transformation. But to say that structures can be distinguished from each other is not to say that they evolve autonomously without interacting with each other. The separate evolutions in the superstructure are thus seen as sources of contradiction, while there frequently exist fundamental conflicts between the economic basis and the structures in the superstructure. In asserting the primacy of the economic basis Marx was proposing two things. First, he is suggesting that the relationships between structures are themselves structured in some way within the totality. In a conflict between the evolution of the economic basis of society and elements in the superstructure, it is the latter that have to give way, adapt, or be eliminated. Some structures are therefore regarded as more basic than others within a totality. Structures can therefore be ranked in order of significance. Marx obviously decided that the conditions concerning the production and reproduction of material life were fundamental—he certainly argued most strenuously for this view. And this led him to his second main point. When we attempt to view society as a totality, then ultimately everything has to be related to the structures in the economic basis of society. In other words, it was the production and reproduction of material existence that formed the starting point and end point for tracing out the relationships between structures within the totality. From this vantage point it was possible to identify transformation rules through which seemingly quite separate structures contributed to the process of structuring and restructuring society as a whole.

It is evident, then, that Marx distinguishes between the totality and the structures which it contains. The choice of the economic basis as the foundation for all analyses is open to dispute of course. Modern environmentalists would argue for the primacy of the ecological system. The demise of capitalism could thus be interpreted in the same manner as Godelier's "frivolous" example of the dinosaur that did not perish through "the spontaneous development of its own contradictions, but through a contradiction between its internal physiological structure and the structure of its external conditions of existence" (1972, 362). In focusing on the economic basis of society, Marx was not discounting arguments of this sort or necessarily assuming that the economic basis was superior to all other structures with which it might come into conflict. Indeed, Marx specifically suggests that the capitalist mode of production will systematically diminish its own resource base and thereby destroy the conditions essential for its own continuance. The evolution of society as a totality must therefore be interpreted as the result of contradictions established both within and between structures. This theme flows throughout Marx's work and flows naturally from his basic ontology.

These questions of ontology are difficult to grapple with when posed in abstraction. But they are quite fundamental to understanding many of the issues raised in this book. Should we regard urbanism as a structure which can be derived from the economic basis of society (or from superstructural elements) by way of a transformation? Or should we regard urbanism as a separate structure in interaction with other structures? I shall leave these questions aside for the moment, for they will be the foundation for the second part of this conclusion. For the moment I shall remain content to show how Marx's conception of totality, structure, inter-relatedness and transformation relates to the materials assembled in this volume.

It is evident, for example, that the controversy between Marxist and non-Marxist interpreters of urban origins, and the argument over the surplus in particular, can be traced to ontological differences. Following Marx, the only valid way to approach the question of urban origins, is to seek out the internal and external contradictions present in pre-urban society and to show how these contradictions were resolved through the transformation to urban forms of social organization. This transformation involved a restructuring and a reconstitution of the elements and relationships prevailing in pre-urban society into some new configuration. Within this new configuration new elements and relationships could form. Thus the nature and concept of the surplus were transformed as were the realities of labour, value, nature, society, and the like. Such a transformation generated new contradictions and tensions (in particular the antagonism between town and country) which eventually would have to be resolved. The focus in Marx's analysis is therefore on contradiction within and between structures and consequent transformation of the totality. This is a very different conception of things to that forged by non-Marxist (and some "Marxist") scholars, who typically operate under a presupposition of atomistic association—hence the constant parade of "factors" that are reputed to have caused urban genesis (including the economic factors promoted by some "Marxists")—or who appeal to ideas about emergent totalities (such as the concepts of mechanical and organic solidarity advanced by Durkheim and made much of by writers such as Wheatley). The argument over urban origins can thus be represented as an argument over method and in particular over ontological presuppositions. Once these fundamental questions of method are resolved much of the argument over the evidence will disappear.

The same contrast exists between the method employed in Part 1 and that employed in Part 2 of this volume. An example can best be used to establish the point. Redistribution of real income in an urban system is the subject of chapter 2. Attention is immediately focused on the definition and meaning of "income". Policies that are designed to accomplish a redistribution of income may be offset by a change in the social definition and meaning of income and this may return the distribution to the original position—this is an example of the totality shaping the relationships within itself to preserve its structure. To deal with this problem we require an expanded definition of income. The definition which emerges in chapter 2 is that of "command over society's scarce resources". It would be possible to expand the definition even further as, for example, Miller and Roby have recently done in their work on *The Future of Inequality* (1971). Yet all of these expansions run into the same difficulty. Both "resource" and "scarcity" are socially defined while "heterogeneity in social and cultural values plays havoc with any simplistic theory of the redistribution of real income" (p. 81). Expanding the definition of income does not resolve the problem—it merely shifts it elsewhere. Besides, there is no apparent limit to the possible expansion of the concept. These expansions and shifts in meaning of the concept are occasionally revealing. It becomes apparent in chapter 2, for example, that the social and cultural conditions that give meaning to the concept of income are not arbitrarily determined—they are themselves the products of certain other conditions and they are certainly structured in some way. Yet the full implications of this fact cannot be understood because the appropriate method to do so has not yet been brought into existence. Society is being viewed in Part 1 as a totality with interacting parts but the parts are seen as interacting with each other in contingent fashion as in an aggregate. Consequently the struggle to escape from a formless relativism and to give some deeper meaning to the income concept never succeeds.

The approach of Part 2 is different for here an appropriate methodology begins to be fashioned to deal with these kinds of questions. Society comes to be viewed as a set of structures in the process of continuous transformation. The concept of a mode of production comprised of structures which are in conflict with each other emerges in chapter 6 as the key to understanding questions of distribution. Within a mode of production states of consciousness are produced, not in some arbitrary or instantaneous fashion, but by transformations and pressures which take deeply rooted ways of thought and reshape them so that they become broadly supportive of the existing structure of production in society. Thus the states of consciousness attached to reciprocity and redistribution as modes of economic integration are transformed to meet the needs of a society now based on market exchange. The definition of income is transformed as consciousness is transformed. The meaning and definition of income can therefore be seen as something which is "produced" under a given mode of production—it expresses the social relationships existing in a particular historical period. In seeking to redefine the concept of income Titmuss and Miller and Roby are simply seeking to keep pace with the way in which social relationships are changing in society. Furthermore, the separateness of production and distribution disappears. I can do no better than let Marx speak directly to this point:

"Production, distribution, exchange and consumption are . . . links of a single whole, different aspects of one unit. Production is the decisive phase. . . . That exchange and consumption cannot be decisive elements is obvious, and the same applies to distribution in the sense of the distribution of products. Distribution of the factors of production on the other hand, is itself a phase of production. A distinct mode of production thus determines the specific mode of consumption, distribution,

295

exchange, and the specific relations of these different phases to one another. Production in its narrow sense, however, is in its turn also determined by the other aspects. For example, if the market, or the sphere of exchange, expands, then the volume of production grows and tends to become more differentiated. Production also changes in consequence of changes in distribution, e.g., concentration of capital, different distribution of the population in town and countryside, and the like. Production is, finally, determined by the demands of consumption. There is an interaction between the various aspects. Such interaction takes place in any organic entity." (*A Contribution to the Critique of Political Economy*, 204–5.)

It is through this sort of formulation that the formless relativism from which chapter 2 never escapes can be averted without appealing to those abstract principles of "eternal morality and justice"—to use Engels's phrase—that permeate much of chapter 2, are the subject of explicit investigation in chapter 3, and are finally rejected together with the fact-value distinction in chapter 4. The processes identified in chapter 2 can consequently be reinterpreted in the light of a different methodological stance which emerges in Part 2.

The conception of society as a totality of internally related parts with inner laws of transformation cannot be assumed *a priori* to be a superior conception of things. Marx appealed to history as proof and affirmation of his ontology and sought to demonstrate its superiority through the practice of the method it defined. This practice made use of a distinctive epistemology and so we must take the second step down the path towards an understanding of Marx's method.

2 Epistemology

Epistemology seeks to uncover the procedures and conditions that make knowledge possible. In Marx's work ontology and epistemology are related. Knowledge is seen as a part of human experience and as growing out of human practice—it is an internal relation within society viewed as a totality. Consciousness and knowledge are products of a social situation. But gaining knowledge is productive activity and is therefore seen as a part of that more general process whereby society is transformed. Marx suggests:

"Since the process of thought itself grows out of a situation, itself is a process of nature, truly conceptual thought is in the same position, and can only differentiate itself gradually, in accordance with the level of development, including that of the organ of thought." (Quoted in Schmidt, 1970, 31.)

In *A Contribution to the Critique of Political Economy* Marx elaborates further on how he sees knowledge arising:

"To consciousness, therefore, the evolution of categories appears as the actual process of production . . . whose result is the world; and this is true in so far as the concrete totality regarded as a conceptual totality, as a mental fact, is indeed a product of thinking, of comprehension. [This conceptual totality] is by no means a product of the idea which evolves spontaneously and whose thinking proceeds outside and above perception and imagination, but is the result of the assimilation and transformation of perceptions and images into concepts." (p. 207.)

The concepts and ideas thus established can then become a material force in production. To do so, however, requires that concepts which exist as mere abstractions be translated into human practice. Many concepts remain barren in this regard. But many do not for "at the end of every labour-process we get a result that already existed in the imagination of the labourer at its commencement" (*Capital*, volume 1, 178).

Underlying Marx's epistemological position is a certain view of the relationship between subject and object. This view is a particular expression of those ontological concepts which we have already examined. Subject and object are to be seen not as entities but as relationships one to the other. This conception is very different indeed from that proposed in traditional empiricism—which assumes that "all cognitive information has its source in objects that the subject is instructed by what is outside of him"—and from that proposed in the many varieties of *a priorism* and innatism which commonly assume that the subject "possesses from the start endogenous structures which it imposes on objects" (Piaget, 1972a, 19). Both of these views are rejected by Marx and Piaget in favour of what the latter calls a "constructivist position" of the following sort:

"Whereas other animals cannot alter themselves except by changing their species, man can transform himself by transforming the world and can structure himself by constructing structures; and these structures are his own, for they are not entirely predestined either from within or without." (1970, 118–19.)

The subject is thus regarded as both structuring and being structured by the object. As Marx puts it in *Capital*, "by acting on the external world and changing it, [man] at the same time changes his own nature" (volume 1, 175).

A number of basic principles can be derived from Marx's basic ontology and epistemology. These principles can aid us in forging a very specific conception as to what theory is all about and how it can be constructed. The "assimilation and transformation of perceptions and images into concepts" of which Marx writes, proceeds through reflective abstraction on the part of the observing subject. The result of this process has to be understood in the light of Marx's ontology. Concepts and categories cannot be viewed as having an independent existence, as being universal abstractions true for all time. The structure of knowledge can be transformed, it is true, by its own internal laws of transformation (including those social pressures internal to science considered in chapter 4). But the results of this process have to be interpreted in terms of the relationships they express within the totality of which they are a part. Concepts are "produced" under certain conditions (including a pre-existing set of concepts) while they also have to be seen as producing agents in a social situation. It is irrelevant to ask whether concepts, categories and relationships are "true" or "false". We have to ask, rather, what it is that produces them and what is it that they serve to produce? Hence arises the distinction, hit upon in chapter 4, between revolutionary theories which are productive of change, *status quo* theories which are derived out of and help to preserve an existing situation, and counter-revolutionary theories which produce only confusion, obfuscation and frustration. Hence also arises the view that these theories in turn cannot be made use of in abstraction from an existing situation, but have to be applied through a study of the ways in which theories become a "material force" in society through their impact upon social action.

Through conscious recognition of the role which concepts and categories play in society, Marx attempts to use them rather than be used by them. He criticizes the categories of the English political economists and recognizes how they were all "prisoners of the categories handed down to them". He seeks to devise new categories—such as that of surplus value—through which we can restructure our understanding of society. And in the process he makes use of a fundamental technique—a technique which as Piaget points out has become standard method in logic and mathematics (1970, 124)—namely, construction by negation. Marx is thus prepared to turn problems into solutions and solutions into problems. This strategy is the foundation for the investigation in chapter 4 of this volume.

Since "truly conceptual thought can only differentiate itself gradually", it is important at each stage to understand the way categories relate to each other inside of the general body of knowledge handed down to us. Thus *Capital* is simultaneously an investigation of capitalist society and the categories used to describe and analyse that society. This conception of things provides us with certain insights when it comes to interpreting both social history and the history of thought. The evolution of theory is seen as a gradual differentiation and restructuring of knowledge out of which can emerge a hierarchy of concepts which relate to each other in a particular way. Piaget points out that

"between two structures of different levels there can be no one-way reduction, but rather there is reciprocal assimilation such that the higher can be derived from the lower by means of transformations, while the higher enriches the lower by integrating it." (1972a, 93.)

It was, of course, this kind of transformation that Marx sought and partially achieved in *Capital* and in *Theories of Surplus Value*. And it is transformations of this type that are littered throughout the history of science and which are so well described by Kuhn (1962).

The restructuring of knowledge through this transformation process mirrors the transformation process as it operates in society as a whole. Knowledge can therefore be viewed as a structured body of information subject to its own internal laws of transformation. Internal contradictions (anomalies) become the foundation for new theories. Insofar as knowledge becomes a material force, the restructuring which occurs on the conceptual plane can expand throughout the totality of society and ultimately be registered in the economic basis. Movements in the economic basis are likewise registered on the conceptual plane. But ultimately the latter has to be related to the former if it is to be understood.

The epistemological position of Marx gradually comes to affect the analyses presented in this book. Concepts and categories are subjected to critical scrutiny in the light of the relationships they express to the reality of which they are a part. In chapter 5, for example, the basic concepts inherent in urban land-use theory are examined in critical fashion. Rent, it is shown, has been accorded a position of great importance in that theory and has come to be treated in the neo-classical models as a universal category with a fixed meaning. Returning to Marx's analyses we can see that rent is not a universal category, but is a concept which takes on specific meaning only in specific social situations. Rent is nothing outside of the particular set of relationships in production and it can arise in a variety of ways depending on how these relationships are structured. From this position it is possible to forge a critique of contemporary urban land-use theory. In the course of examining the rental concept, the controversy over the meaning and measurement of capital is briefly alluded to. This controversy has fundamental implications for location theory as it has for all economic analysis. It arises, of course, out of the fact that capital has no meaning independent of the social structure of which it is a part and within which it performs a specific function. Likewise the concept of space which presents such great philosophical difficulties in chapter 1 (and which degenerates as a consequence into a formless relativism) is rescued in chapter 5 by recognizing that the philosophical problems it presents have solutions only through the study and creation of human practice. Concepts of social justice also have to be considered as being both produced by and producers of social conditions. The abstracted analysis of social justice in chapter 3 is tacitly transformed in chapter 6 into an examination of how the sense of value which underlies the sense of social justice arises under the conditions of egalitarian, rank and stratified societies and how these conceptions can, when transformed into a dominant ideology, contribute to the support and maintenance of the social relationships within a mode of production.

The intervention of a new epistemological position akin to that held by Marx is most evident in chapter 6. The concepts of reciprocity, redistribution and market exchange are here made use of in a relational fashion. As social relationships alter so the meaning of each concept is adjusted. Fundamental to this technique is the view that categories and concepts bear a relationship to each other (or at least can be made to do so) which mirrors conditions in society itself. Again, I can do no better than to quote Marx:

"Since, furthermore, bourgeois society is only a form resulting from the development of antagonistic elements, some relations belonging to earlier forms of society are frequently to be found in it, though in a crippled state or as a travesty of their former self, as for example communal property. While it may be said, therefore, that the categories of bourgeois economy contain what is true of all other forms of society, the statement is to be taken *cum grano salis*. They may contain these in a developed or crippled or caricatured form, but always essentially different." (*Grundrisse*, 39–40.)

Under the domination of market exchange, redistribution (in the form of the state in particular) becomes a developed form of its former self, while reciprocity is reduced to a mere travesty. In this fashion the concepts, properly transformed, can be used to reflect, as in a mirror, the transformations that have occurred in society.

Enough has been said regarding Marx's method and the conception of theory that flows out of it for us to reach some fundamental conclusions. I have already indicated that a radical transformation of method occurs between Part 1 and Part 2 of this book. This transformation in method does not negate the formulations of Part 1. It enriches them by assimilating them to higher order concepts. It also brings about a convergence towards an ontological and epistemological position akin to that held by Marx. This convergence is not induced by the sense of moral outrage that frequently besets Englishmen who move to the United States, nor is it a consequence of a changing political climate that makes it possible (even fashionable in some circles) to dabble in Marxism. These factors are incidental. They merely aid and abet something more fundamental. And the more fundamental explanation lies in the *necessity* of the transformation and consequent convergence if the dilemmas that beset Part 1 are to be resolved. These dilemmas did not arise out of thin air of course. They arose out of a social situation in which the thoughts and intellectual efforts of innumerable people were being devoted to what were perceived as pressing and serious problems. The issues which dominated in the late 1960s were those of urbanization, environment and economic development. These issues plainly could not be regarded as separate from each other and each appeared to demand an "interdisciplinary" approach if it was to be tackled effectively.

Piaget, in his book on *Structuralism*, concludes that "the search for structures cannot but result in interdisciplinary coordinations" (1970, 137). I prefer, as the result of the experience expressed in this book, to invert that conclusion. Any attempt to create an interdisciplinary theory with respect to a phenomenon such as urbanism, has perforce to resort to the operational structuralist method which Marx practices and which Ollman and Piaget describe. In other words, and this conclusion will be unpalatable to many, the only method capable of uniting disciplines in such a fashion that they can grapple with issues such as urbanization, economic development and the environment, is that founded in a properly constituted version of dialectical materialism as it operates within a structured totality in the sense that Marx conceived of it.

ON THE NATURE OF URBANISM

Out of a set of studies designed to say something about urban problems, we have extracted a fundamental conclusion regarding method. The justification for such a conclusion lies in the supposed ability of that method to reveal important insights into urban problems. If the method cannot yield up such insights then clearly the conclusion does not hold good. We must therefore address the question: what insights and revelations do we gain through the use of Marx's method in the investigation of urban phenomena?

A preliminary answer to this question is attempted in chapter 6. I want to stress the word "preliminary" for at this stage I am not prepared to rest the validity of the conclusion concerning method on the substance of that essay. The only other work I can call upon is that of Henri Lefebvre. Unfortunately, the essays in this volume were completed before I had the opportunity to read Lefebvre's *La Pensée Marxiste et La Ville*

(1972) and *La Revolution Urbaine* (1970). In the first of these works Lefebvre examines the treatment of urbanism in Marx's works, while in the second he attempts an investigation of contemporary urbanism making use of Marx's tools. There are parallels between his concerns and mine and there are similarities in content (which is reassuring) and some differences in interpretation and emphasis (which is challenging). Lefebvre's work is more general than my own but it is also incomplete in certain important respects. Nevertheless, I feel more confident in appealing to both Lefebvre's work and the material collected in this volume, in attempting to fashion some general conclusions concerning the nature of urbanism.

What kind of object or entity are we dealing with when we seek to investigate urbanism? We cannot answer that urbanism is a "thing" in the ordinary sense of the word. The city as a built form can, it is true, be regarded as a set of objects arranged according to some pattern in space. But there are few who would argue that cities are just that. Most writers seem to agree that the city has to be regarded as a functioning totality within which everything is related to everything else. Various strategies have been advanced to deal with this totality. They fall, for the most part, in the two categories of atomistic association and emergent evolution that we have explicitly rejected. An example of the former is Wilson's (1970) entropy formulation while the spectacular design-mysticism of Doxiadis (1968) is surely an excellent example of the latter. Systems modelling attempts to trace interaction and feedback within a totality, but by having to define fixed categories and activities it loses the flexibility to deal with the fluid structure of social relationships which exists in reality. It can be used to deal with certain limited problems (the optimal design of some transport system for example), but it cannot be used for broader purposes— "optimizing the city" is a meaningless phrase. When systems modelling attempts to become more general it quickly degenerates, as in the work of Jay Forrester, into "black-box mysticism". Faced with these kinds of difficulties, a certain air of disillusionment frequently attaches to the idea of examining the city as a totality. There is, consequently, a tendency to retreat into partial analyses, usually framed within the safety of some disciplinary womb. Many investigators, after a ritualistic bow to the notion of totality which asserts that cities are not just statistical aggregates of things and activities, quickly reduce their problem (in the name of competency or tractability) to the analysis of things and activities. The insights gained from such investigations are not to be dismissed—in fact they are invaluable raw material out of which we may fashion a conception of urbanism. But their net import is that we learn to deal, as was pointed out in chapter 1, with "problems *in* the city rather than *of* the city".

Urbanism has to be regarded as a set of social relationships which reflects the relationships established throughout society as a whole. Further, these relationships have to express the laws whereby urban phenomena are structured, regulated and constructed. We then have to consider whether urbanism is (1) a separate structure with its own laws of inner transformation and construction, or (2) the expression of a set of relationships embedded in some broader structure (such as the social relations of production). If we assert the former, then we are obliged to identify the transformation laws internal to urbanism and the semi-autonomous processes that structure it as well as the relationship which urbanism bears to other structures in the totality. If we take the second view then we have to establish the process through which urbanism is derived out of other structures.

These questions can be resolved through a study of history as well as from a dissection of urbanism in the contemporary world. The first urban revolution saw the precipitation of an autonomous and separate structure, which we can designate as "urban", out of an homogeneously organized set of social relationships. The transformation from reciprocity to redistribution (examined in chapter 6) involved the creation of hierarchical self-sustaining set of social relationships. Marx regarded this as the crystallization of the first great class struggle in the form of the antagonism between town and country. There can be no doubt that a new structure appeared where there had been no structure before. This structure had limited powers of inner transformation and self-regulation. From this point on the city has to be seen as a separate entity in relationship to other structures. But what kind of entity was it and how did it function? It was born out of the contradiction between the social relations of production and forces of production. Initially it functioned as a political, ideological and military force to sustain a particular pattern in the social relations of production (particularly with respect to property rights). The city had little or nothing to do with production itself. Many of the functions of the city during this period have to be categorized as superstructural. Max Weber's defining characteristics for occidental cities (a fortification; a market; a court of its own and partially autonomous law; a distinct form of association and partial autonomy and autocephaly) indicate this superstructural quality of early urbanism. To say that the function of urbanism was to fashion a superstructure in support of a particular patterning of the social relations of production is not to say that urbanism was a mere product of forces in the economic basis of society. If we regard the superstructure as containing certain separate and partially autonomous structures, in the fashion that Godelier suggests, then I think we arrive at a reasonable conception of urbanism at this stage of its history.

Lefebvre contrasts this first stage of urbanism—the political city—with two later stages—the commercial city and the industrial city. The transformation from the political city to the commercial city can be interpreted as an inner transformation of urbanism itself. The city still functioned as a political, ideological and military force, but partly as the result of the expanding needs of urban populations, the city also had to expand its trading function. Thus the city was transformed to the role of broker between areas of supply and demand within an expanding effective space. This role had always been present, but in the mercantile era it expanded to dominate the other roles. The urban transformation that occurred with the industrial revolution cannot be interpreted as a transformation from within. The new form of urbanism generally arose outside of the older cities and subsequently came to absorb the older more traditional functions of the political and commercial city. Fundamental to this form of urbanism was the reorganization of the forces of production to take advantage of mechanization, technological change and economies of scale in production. Urbanism became as important to the organization of the forces of production as it had previously been with respect to the social relations of production.

It is in the interpretation of contemporary urbanism that Lefebvre seeks to break new ground. He notes that the object of Marx's investigation was industrial society, its modes of organization and the social relationships it expressed. Marx interpreted history in terms of past relationships which were fundamental to the emergence of industrial capitalism. Urbanism, as a focus of concern, diminishes in importance as Marx focuses closer and closer on his object of investigation (compare the early *German Ideology* with the later *Capital*) and where urbanism is considered it is treated in the light of its contribution in preparing the way for industrial capitalism. Lefebvre makes use of the traditional Marxist method of construction by negation and inversion—he seeks to interpret industrial society as a precursor of what he calls the "urban revolution":

"when we use the words 'urban revolution' we designate the total ensemble of transformations which run throughout contemporary society and which serve to being about the change from a period in which questions of economic growth and industrialization predominate to the period in which the urban problematic becomes decisive, when research into the solutions and forms appropriate to urban society takes precedence. . . . The urban problematic imposes itself on a world-wide scale. Can the realities of urbanism be defined as something superstructural, on the surface of the economic basis, whether capitalist or socialist? Or as a simple result of economic growth and the increasing power of the forces of production, as a modest marginal elaboration of the social relations of production? No. The reality of urbanism modifies the relations of production without being sufficient to transform them. Urbanism becomes a force in production, rather like science. Space and the political organization of space express social relationships but also react back upon them." (1970, 13, 25.) Lefebvre then derives his main thesis. Industrial society is seen not as an end in itself but as a preparatory stage for urbanism. Industrialization, he argues, can only find its fulfilment in urbanization, and urbanization is now coming to dominate industrial production and organization. Industrialization, once the producer of urbanism, is now being produced by it. This subordination of industrial society to urban society entails certain further changes which, in turn, contain the seeds of further conflict. Lefebvre argues that as the whole world becomes urbanized so there occurs a counter-movement interior to the urbanization process which leads to greater internal differentiation through the creation of distinctively local habitats. (1970, 1935.) It is at this local level that new and distinctive qualities of urbanism begin to emerge to compensate the homogeneity achieved at the global scale.

Certain of the materials assembled in this volume can be used to support Lefebvre's thesis while others contradict it. There are, of course, certain common points of departure. We both accept the same conception of the totality as inner-relatedness. We also both accept that urbanism has to be understood as a self-sustaining entity which expresses and fashions relationships with other structures in the totality. Neither of us regard urbanism as something simply derived out of other structures. Lefebvre also attempts to incorporate adequate concepts of space into his analysis. He notes the conflict between the dialectics of the social process and the static geometry of the spatial form and he arrives at a conceptualization of the social-process–spatial-form theme which is not too dissimilar from that which underlies the analyses in this volume. Urbanism, insofar as it possesses its own transformation laws, is at least partly moulded out of basic principles of spatial organization. The distinctive role which space plays in both the organization of production and patterning social relationships is consequently expressed in urban structure. But urbanism is not *merely* a structure fashioned out of a spatial logic. It has attached to it distinctive ideologies (urban versus rural images for example) and therefore has a certain autonomous function in fashioning the way of life of a people. And urban structure, once created, affects the future development of social relationships and the organization of production. I therefore like Lefebvre's analogy between urbanism and scientific knowledge. Both possess distinctive structures with their own inner dynamic. Both can alter the structure of the economic basis on occasion in fundamental ways. Yet both are channelled and constrained by the forces and influences emanating from the economic basis and ultimately have to be related to the production and reproduction of material existence if they are to be understood.

The city as a built form and urbanism as a way of life have to be considered separately from each other for they have become separated in reality. What were once synonymous concepts are no longer so. We can see the beginnings of this separation in past epochs, but it is only with industrialization and the penetration of market exchange into all sectors and areas that the

307

antagonism between town and country is finally overcome. City, suburb and rural area are now incorporated within the urban process. The urbanization of the countryside is not complete, of course, and our response to Lefebvre's thesis will depend in part on whether we are thinking of Colombia, China, France, the United States, or wherever. But as the old antagonisms between town and country come to play a much reduced role, so new antagonisms emerge in the heart of the urbanization process itself. At the global level there is the conflict between the metropolitan centres of the world and the under-developed nations (see chapter 6). At the local level we see the import of rural problems into the city—in the United States the migrations of rural Blacks and Appalachian Whites to inner city areas, in much of the Third World the precipitation out of the rural areas of large numbers of people who form an unstable "lumpenproletariat" (as Fanon calls them), usually in shanty towns around the edges of the major cities. Urban poverty is, for the most part, rural poverty refashioned within the city system. It is in this sense that we have to accept Lefebvre's view that the urbanization of the countryside involves a subsidiary ruralization of the city.

New antagonisms also emerge with changing scale and density of city organization. It becomes increasingly difficult to maintain the distinction between public and private particularly through the operation of those externalities discussed in detail in chapter 2. Traditional conceptions of property rights no longer appear adequate and have to be supplemented by the creation of collective property rights through the political organization of space. The antagonism between central city and suburb emerges as a major theme in American politics (again, see chapter 2). The difficulty of distinguishing between public and private (generated out of the urban form of spatial organization) establishes the necessity for greater governmental participation. An ancient mode of economic integration—redistribution—is refashioned to meet a new set of circumstances. Insofar as government is potentially susceptible to democratic control, so the social relations governing production and distribution stand to be fundamentally restructured (as, for example, in welfare state societies). And insofar as these new relationships are in conflict with the organizational requirements of production an ancient antagonism is reinforced. All of these antagonisms (and many more) are partially structured through the urbanization process.

This implies also that urbanism is becoming less homogeneous. Structures grow and proliferate within the urban process. Exchange value has reduced everything to a common denominator (see chapter 5), but other more subtle criteria have emerged to structure urban differentials. As Lefebvre argues, industrial society homogenizes and urban society differentiates (1970, 169). The strong forces working towards cultural heterogeneity and territorial differentiation in the urban system were subject to detailed analysis in chapter 2. The notion of a "one-dimensional man" (Marcuse) living in an "urban non-place realm" (Melvin Webber) was explicitly rejected in that chapter and in this I am in entire agreement with Lefebvre.

One significant element in this general process of differentiation is that *created space* replaces *effective space* as the overriding principle of geographical organization. In preindustrial society natural differentials in resource availability and in natural environments formed the basis for geographical differentiation. Effective space was created out of ecological differentiation by arranging for the flow of goods and services from areas of supply to areas of demand—flows which allowed the accumulation of surpluses in urban areas. Regional and local life-styles could flourish and landscape was fashioned out of subtle symbiotic interrelationships between social activities and organic nature. Industrialization created the power to alter all that. The urbanization of the countryside implies the elimination of regional life-styles through the forces of the world market. The products and objects available for consumption and use become more standardized, more numerous and less tied to the local base. And the once vibrant life-styles of distinctive geographical regions, together with the distinctive landscapes they fashioned, are transformed into something preserved out of the past for tourists to look at. On this dimension we see increasing uniformity. Yet the urban system has also to be viewed, in the manner of chapter 2, as a giant man-made resource system "of great economic, social, psychological and symbolic significance". The growth of this man-made resource system involves the structuring and differentiation of space through the distribution of fixed capital investments. A new spatial structure is created and some of the old lines of regional differentiation are revived to accentuate the structure (a recent example is the revival of ethnic politics in cities in the United States in order to confront issues of urban growth and change). The structuring of space grows more and more important as fixed capital investments become more and more important to the process of living. To put it in Marx's terminology, created space comes to dominate effective space as a consequence of the changing organic composition of capital.

But in whose image is space created? We have already acknowledged that the organization of space can reflect and affect social relationships. But created space has a deeper meaning than just that. In the ancient city the organization of space was a symbolic re-creation of a supposed cosmic order. It had an ideological purpose. Created space in the modern city has an equivalent ideological purpose. In part it reflects the prevailing ideology of the ruling groups and institutions in society. In part it is fashioned by the dynamics of market forces which can easily produce results which nobody in particular wants (see chapter 5). Created space is an "ethnic domain" in only a very limited sense (see chapter 1). Yet created space is an integral part of an intricate sign-process that gives direction and meaning to daily life within the urban culture. The signs, symbols and signals that surround us in the urban environment are powerful influences (particularly among the young). We fashion our sensibilities, extract our sense of wants and needs, and locate our aspirations with respect to a geographical environment that is in large part created. It is probable that our culture, conceived of as an ethnic domain, emanates from created space more than it succeeds in creating space. A frequently expressed alienation from urban culture and an antipathy to the image of the city in part arises out of a deeper estrangement. Neither the activity of space creation nor the final product of created space appear to be within our individual or collective control but fashioned by forces alien to us. We scarcely know how to grapple, either in reality or in the mind, with the implications of created space. For example, we still tend to analyse urban phenomena as if effective space (largely understood as efficiency of movement) were the only appropriate concept.

Almost everything that has been stated so far is reasonably

consistent with Lefebvre's thesis. So wherein lie the differences? Lefebvre asserts that urbanism now dominates industrial society. He arrives at this position through construction by negation. The use of such a dialectical device provides a hypothesis. It does not constitute a proof. And I do not believe the hypothesis can at this point in history be substantiated.

Urbanism possesses a separate structure—it can be conceived as a separate entity—with a dynamic of its own. But this dynamic is moderated through interaction and contradiction with other structures. To say that urbanism now dominates industrial society is to say that contradictions between urbanism as a structure in the process of transformation and the internal dynamic of the older industrial society are usually resolved in favour of the former. I do not believe this claim is realistic. In certain important and crucial respects industrial society and the structures which comprise it continue to dominate urbanism. There are three respects in which this is the case.

(i) The changing organic composition of capital and the growing volume of fixed capital investment which it entails is a product of the internal dynamics of industrial capitalism and it cannot be interpreted as a response to the urbanization process. Created space is fashioned through the deployment of fixed capital investments. It is industrial capitalism that is creating space for us—hence the frequently expressed sense of alienation with respect to created space. The process of urbanization, it is true, exerts certain pressures on industrial capitalism—one set of investments requires another set to complement it. But the dynamics of the process are controlled and constrained by the processes governing industrial capitalism and not by those governing the evolution of urbanism as a separate structure.

(ii) Need creation and the maintenance of an effective demand are produced through the processes governing the evolution of industrial capitalism. Urbanization provides the opportunity for industrial capital to dispose of the products it creates. In this sense the urbanization process is still being propelled by the requirements of industrial capitalism. Urbanization creates new wants and needs, new sensibilities and aspirations, and insofar as these achieve an autonomous development, urbanism puts pressure on industrial capitalism. But the limits of response and the rate of evolution are governed

311

by conditions relating to industrial capitalism rather than to urbanism.

(iii) The production, appropriation and circulation of surplus value have not become subordinated to the internal dynamic of urbanism but continue to be regulated by conditions derived from industrial society. In chapter 6 the relationship between urbanism and the circulation of surplus value is explored. Urbanism is there viewed as a product of the circulation of surplus value. This is a critical and important issue and one which is probably the most important source of disagreement between Lefebvre and myself. I regard the channels through which surplus value circulates as the arteries through which course all of the relationships and interactions which define the totality of society. To understand the circulation of surplus value is in fact to understand the way in which society works. Unfortunately we do not possess the kind of insight into the structure of this circulation to make definitive statements about it. It is in this regard that chapter 6 is most defective and most preliminary in its formulations. It would require a work of at least the magnitude and insight of Marx's *Capital* to unravel all of the complexities. Lefebvre makes a simplistic but quite useful distinction between two circuits in the circulation of surplus value. The first circuit arises out of industrial activity and involves that simple conversion of naturally occurring materials and forces into objects and powers of utility to man. The second circuit involves the creation and extraction of surplus value out of speculation in property rights (of all sorts) and out of returns gained from the disbursement of fixed capital investments. Lefebvre argues "Whereas the proportion of global surplus value formed and realized in industry declines, the proportion realized in speculation and in construction and real estate development grows. The secondary circuit comes to supplant the principal circuit" (1970, 212). This contention requires some consideration. The secondary circuit has some complicated characteristics. The growing quantities of fixed capital investment (resulting from the changing organic composition of capital) are, as Marx puts it, "dead labour". To bring this fixed capital to life requires that living labour set it in motion and that a use value be found (now or in the future) for the products or services it yields up. It is difficult to ensure that the latter requirement be met. Consequently, there is a growing and difficult capital valuation problem besetting industrial society. Speculative activity arises out of this capital valuation problem and feeds off it. Speculative activity has grown in proportion as fixed capital investment has grown and since urbanism is in part the product of the latter it is hardly surprising that urbanism and the circuit of speculative capital are intimately related to each other. The relevance of this idea is demonstrated in chapters 2 and 5 in this volume. But it is premature to argue that the second circuit has replaced the first. The two circuits are fundamental to each other, but that based on industrial capitalism still dominates. Pressures generated out of the second circuit threaten the stability of the first for it now appears that the second circuit is far more crisis prone than the first, while contradiction between the two circuits is a constant source of tension.

The circulation of surplus value in society is a complex topic which requires a good deal more understanding if it is to help us in dealing with the dynamics of urbanization. It is no less a topic for investigation in socialist societies for, as was indicated in chapter 6, the concept of the surplus does not disappear—it merely changes its form.

So where does this leave us with respect to Lefebvre's thesis? To say that the thesis is not true at this juncture in history is not to say that it is not in the process of becoming true or that it cannot become true in the future. The evidence suggests that the forces of urbanization are emerging strongly and moving to dominate the centre stage of world history. Urbanization has become global in scope. Urbanization of the countryside is proceeding apace. Created space is replacing effective space. Internal differentiation within the urbanization process is strongly evident as is the changing political organization of space that parallels this differentiation. In all of these respects Lefebvre is describing some dominant trends. Lefebvre can also be interpreted as presenting a hypothesis concerning the possibilities immanent in the present. Many hopeful and utopian things have been written about the city throughout its history. We now have the opportunity to live many of these things provided we can seize upon the present possibilities. We have the opportunity to create space, to harness creatively the forces making for urban differentiation. But in order to seize these opportunities we have to confront the forces that create cities as alien environments, that push urbanization in directions alien to our individual or collective purpose.

To confront these forces we have first to understand them. The old structure of industrial capitalism, once such a force for revolutionary change in society, now appears as a stumbling block. The growing concentration of fixed capital investment, the creation of new needs and effective demands, and a pattern of circulation of surplus value that rests upon appropriation and exploitation, all emanate from the internal dynamic of industrial capitalism. Patterns in the circulation of surplus value are changing but they have not altered the fact that cities—those "workshops of civilization"—are founded upon the exploitation of the many by the few. An urbanism founded upon exploitation is a legacy of history. A genuinely humanizing urbanism has yet to be brought into being. It remains for revolutionary theory to chart the path from an urbanism based in exploitation to an urbanism appropriate for the human species. And it remains for revolutionary practice to accomplish such a transformation.

Bibliography

ADAMS, R.MCC. 1966: *The Evolution of Urban Society* (Chicago).

ALKER, H. 1969: A typology of ecological fallacies. In Dogan, M. and Rokan, S., editors, *Quantitative Ecological Analysis in the Social Sciences* (Cambridge, Massachusetts).

ALONSO, W. 1964: *Location and Land Use* (Cambridge, Massachusetts).

ALONSO, W. 1967: A reformulation of classical location theory and its relation to rent theory. *Papers of the Regional Science Association* **19**, 23–44.

ALTHUSSER, L. 1969: *For Marx* (London).

ALTHUSSER, L. and BALIBAR, E. 1970: *Reading Capital* (London).

ARISTOTLE: *Ethics* (Harmondsworth, Middlesex: Penguin edition, 1955, translated by J. A. K. Thompson).

ARROW, K. 1963: *Social Choice and Individual Values* (New York).

BACHRACH, P. 1969: A power analysis: the shaping of antipoverty policy in Baltimore. *Public Policy* **18**, 155–86.

BARAN, P. and SWEEZY, P. 1968: *Monopoly Capital* (New York).

BARBOUR, V. 1950: Studies in the development of capitalism in Amsterdam in the seventeenth century. *Johns Hopkins Studies in Historical and Political Science* **67**.

BECKMANN, M. J. 1969: On the distribution of urban rent and residential density. *Journal of Economic Theory* **1**, 60–67.

BERGMANN, G. 1964: *Logic and Reality* (Madison, Wisconsin).

BERNAL, J. D.: *Science in History* (four volumes, Cambridge, Massachusetts, 1971 edition).

BERRY, B. J. L. 1967: *The Geography of Market Centres and Retail Distribution* (Englewood Cliffs, New Jersey).

BERRY, B. J. L. and HORTON, F. 1970: *Geographic Perspectives on Urban Systems* (Englewood Cliffs, New Jersey).

BLOCH, M. 1961: *Feudal Society* (translated by L. Manyon, London).

BORTS, G. H. and STEIN, J. L. 1964: *Economic Growth in a Free Market* (New York).

BOUDEVILLE, J. R. 1966: *Problems of Regional Economic Planning* (Edinburgh).

BRIGGS, A. 1963: *Victorian Cities* (London).

BUCHANAN, J. M. 1968a: *The Demand and Supply of Public Goods* (New York).

BUCHANAN, J. M. 1968b: What kind of redistribution do we want? *Economica* **35**, 185–90.

BUCHANAN, J. M. and TULLOCK, G. 1965: *The Calculus of Consent* (Ann Arbor, Michigan).

315

Bibliography

BURGESS, E. W. 1926: *The Urban Community* (Chicago).

BUTTIMER, A. 1969: Social space in interdisciplinary perspective. *Geographical Review* **59**, 417–26.

BYE, C. R. 1940: *Developments and Issues in the Theory of Rent* (New York).

CARNAP, R. 1958: *An Introduction to Symbolic Logic* (New York).

CASSIRER, E. 1944: *An Essay on Man* (New Haven, Connecticut).

CASSIRER, E. 1955–7: *The Philosophy of Symbolic Forms* (three volumes, New Haven, Connecticut).

CASTELLS, M. 1970: Structures sociales et processus d'urbanization. *Annales, Economies, Societés, Civilization* **25**, 1155–99.

CHAMBERLIN, E. H. 1933: *The Theory of Monopolistic Competition* (Cambridge, Massachusetts).

CHILDE, V. G. 1942: *What Happened in History* (Harmondsworth, Middlesex).

CHINITZ, B. 1958: Contrasts in agglomeration; New York and Pittsburgh. *American Economic Review* **51**, 279–89.

CLAWSON, M. 1969: Open (uncovered) space as a new urban resource. In Perloff, H., editor, *The Quality of Urban Environment* (Baltimore).

CLIFF, A. and ORD, K. 1969: The problem of autocorrelation. In Scott, A., editor, *Studies in Regional Science* (London).

Committee of Concerned Asian Scholars, 1972, *China! Inside the People's Republic* (New York).

COOMBS, C. H. 1946: *A Theory of Data* (New York).

DACEY, M. F. 1965: Some observations on a two-dimensional language. *Technical Report No. 7, ONR Task No. 389-142* (Department of Geography, North-western University, Evanston, Illinois).

DART, F. E. and PRADHAN, L. 1967: Cross-cultural teaching of science. *Science* **155**, 649–56.

DARWENT, D. 1969: Growth poles and growth centres in regional planning—a review. *Environment and Planning* **1**, 5–32.

DAVIES, B. 1968: *Social Needs and Resources in Local Services* (London).

DAVIS, O. A. and WHINSTON, A. 1962: Externalities, welfare, and the theory of games. *Journal of Political Economy* **70**, 241–62.

DAVIS, O. A. and WHINSTON, A. 1964: The economics of complex systems: the case of municipal zoning. *Kyklos* **27**, 419–46.

DENIKE, K. G. and PARR, J. B. 1970: Production in space, spatial competition, and restricted entry. *Journal of Regional Science* **10**, 49–64.

DOBB, M. 1963: *Studies in the Development of Capitalism* (New York).

DOXIADIS, K. 1968: *Ekistics* (New York).

DOWNS, A. 1970: *Urban problems and Prospects* (Chicago).

DUHL, L. J. 1963: The human measure: man and family in megalopolis. In Wingo, L., editor, *Cities and Space: the Future Use of Urban Land* (Baltimore).

EMMANUEL, A. 1972: *Unequal Exchange* (New York).

ENGELS, F.: *The Condition of the Working Class in England in 1844* (London, 1962 edition).

ENGELS, F.: *The Housing Question* (New York, 1935 edition).

FANON, F. 1967: *The Wretched of the Earth* (Harmondsworth, Middlesex).

FISHBURN, P. C. 1964: *Decision and Value Theory* (New York).

FISHER, F. J. 1935: The development of the London food market. *Economic History Review* 5, 46–64.

FRANK, A. G. 1969: *Capitalism and Underdevelopment in Latin America* (New York).

FRIED, M. 1967: *The Evolution of Political Society* (New York).

FRIEDMANN, J. 1966: *Regional Development Policy: a Case Study of Venezuela* (Cambridge, Massachusetts).

FRIEDMANN, J. 1969a: *A general theory of polarized development.* School of Architecture and Urban Planning, University College of Los Angeles. (Mimeo.)

FRIEDMANN, J. 1969b: The role of cities in national development. *American Behavioral Scientist* 22, (5), 13–21.

GAFFNEY, M. 1961: Land and rent in welfare economics. In Ackerman, J., Clawson, M. and Harris, M., editors, *Symposium on Land Economics Research* (Washington D.C.).

GAFFNEY, M. 1969: Land rent, taxation and public policy. *Papers of the Regional Science, Association* 23, 141–53.

GAFFNEY, M. forthcoming: Releasing land to serve demand via fiscal desegregation. In Clawson, M., editor, *Modernizing Urban Land Policy* (Washington D.C.).

GANS, H. J. 1969: Planning for people not buildings. *Environment and Planning* 1, 33–46.

GANS, H. J. 1970: *People and Plans* (New York).

GODELIER, M. 1972: Structure and contradictions in *Capital*. In Blackburn, R., editor, *Idealogy in Social Science* (London).

GRAMSCI, A. 1971: *Selections from the Prison Notebooks* (London).

GRANGER, C. W. 1969: Spatial data and time-series analysis. In Scott, A., editor, *Studies in Regional Science* (London).

GRIGSBY, W. C., ROSENBERG, L., STEGMAN, M. and TAYLOR, J. 1971: *Housing and Poverty*. Philadelphia: Institute for Environmental Studies, University of Pennsylvania.

GUTKIND, E. A. 1956: Our world from the air: conflict and adaptation. In Thomas, W. L., editor, *Man's Role in Changing the Face of the Earth* (Chicago).

HALL, E. T. 1966: *The Hidden Dimension* (Garden City, New York).

HALL, J. W. 1962: Feudalism in Japan: *Comparative Studies in Society and History* 5 (1) 1–30.

HALLOWELL, A. I. 1955: *Culture and Experience* (Philadelphia).

HARCOURT, G. C. 1972: *Some Cambridge Controversies in the Theory of Capital* (Cambridge).

HARCOURT, G. C. and LAING, N. F. 1971: *Capital and Growth* (Harmondsworth, Middlesex).

HARRIS, B. 1968: Quantitative models of urban development: their role in metropolitan policy making. In Perloff, H. and Wingo, L., editors, *Issues in Urban Economics* (Baltimore).

HARVEY, D. 1969: *Explanation in Geography* (London).

HAWLEY, A. 1950: *Human Ecology* (New York).

HEGEL, G. W. 1967 edition: *The Phenomenology of Mind* (New York).

HERBERT, J. and STEVENS, B. 1960: A model for the distribution of residential activities in urban areas. *Journal of Regional Science* **2** 21–36.

HICKS, J. R. 1940: The rehabilitation of consumers' surplus. *Review of Economic Studies* **8**, 108–16.

HICKS, J. R. 1944: The four consumers' surpluses. *Review of Economic Studies* **11**, 31–41.

HOBBES, T. 1651: *Leviathan* (Harmondsworth, Middlesex, Penguin Edition, 1968).

HOCH, I. 1969: The three-dimensional city: contained urban space. In Perloff, H., editor, *The Quality of Urban Environment* (Baltimore).

HOOVER, E. M. 1968: The evolving form and organization of the metropolis. In Perloff, H. and Wingo, L., editors, *Issues in Urban Economics* (Baltimore).

HOSELITZ, B. F. 1960: *Sociological Aspects of Economic Growth* (New York).

HUBERMAN, L. and SWEEZY, P. 1969: *Socialism in Cuba* (New York).

HUNT, E. K. and SCHWARTZ, J. G. editors, 1972: *A Critique of Economic Theory* (Harmondsworth, Middlesex).

HURD, R. M. 1903: *Principles of City Land Values* (The Record and Guide; New York).

ISARD, W. 1956: *Location and Space Economy* (New York).

ISARD, W., SMITH, T. E. *et al.* 1969: *General Theory: Social, Political Economic and Regional* (Cambridge, Massachusetts).

JACOBS, J. 1961: *The Death and Life of Great American Cities* (New York).

JACOBS, J. 1969: *The Economy of Cities* (New York).

JEVONS, W. S. 1871: *The Theory of Political Economy* (Penguin edition, Harmondsworth, Middlesex, 1970).

JOHNSON, E. A. J. 1970: *The Organization of Space in Developing Countries* (Cambridge, Massachusetts).

JOHNSON, H. G. 1971: The Keynesian revolution and monetarist counterrevolution. *American Economic Review* **16** (2), 1–14.

DE JOUVENAL, B. 1951: *The Ethics of Redistribution* (Cambridge).

KAIN, J. F. 1968: The distribution and movement of jobs and industry. In Wilson, J. Q., editor, *The Metropolitan Enigma* (Cambridge, Massachusetts).

KEENE, J. C. and STRONG, A. L. 1970: The Brandywine plan. *Journal of the American Institute of Planners* **36**, 50–64.

KEIPER, J. S. and KURNOW, E., CLARK, C. D. and SEGAL, H. H. 1961: *Theory and Measurement of Rent* (Philadelphia).

KELLER, S. 1969: *The Urban Neighborhood: a Sociological Perspective* (New York).

Kerner Commission, 1968: *Report of the National Advisory Commission on Civil Disorders* (Washington: Government Printing Office).

KEYES, L. C. 1969: *The Rehabilitation Planning Game* (Cambridge, Massachusetts).

KIRWAN, R. M. and MARTIN, D. B. 1971: Some notes on housing market models for urban planning. *Environment and Planning* **3**, 243–52.

KLUCKHOHN, C. 1954: Culture and behavior. In Lindzey, G. editor, *Handbook of Social Psychology* volume 2 (New York).

KOTLER, M. 1969: *Neighborhood Government: the Local Foundations of Political Life* (Indianapolis).

KUHN, T. S. 1962: *The Structure of Scientific Revolutions* (Chicago).

LANGER, S. 1942: *Philosophy in a New Key* (Cambridge, Massachusetts).

LANGER, S. 1953: *Feeling and Form: a Theory of Art* (New York).

LAVE, L. 1970: Congestion and urban location. *Papers of the Regional Science Association* **25**, 133–52.

LEE, T. R. 1968: Urban neighbourhood as a socio-spatial schema. *Human Relations* **21**, 241–67.

LEFEBVRE, H. 1970: *La Revolution Urbaine* (Paris).

LEFEBVRE, H. 1972: *La Pensée Marxiste et la Ville* (Paris).

LEIBNIZ, G. W. 1934 edition: *Philosophical Writings* (Dent: London).

LEVEN, C. 1968: Towards a theory of the city. In G. Hemmens, editor, *Urban Development Models* (National Academy of Sciences, Highway Research Board, *Special Report* **97**, Washington D.C.).

LÉVI-STRAUSS, C. 1963: *Structural Anthropology* (New York).

LÉVI-STRAUSS, C. 1966: *The Savage Mind* (Chicago).

LIEBENSTEIN, H. 1966: Allocative efficiency versus x-efficiency. *American Economic Review*, **61**, 392–415.

LOPEZ, R. S. 1952: The trade of medieval Europe: the South. In Postan, M. and Rich, E. E., editors, *The Cambridge Economic History of Europe* Vol. 2 (Cambridge).

LORENZ, K. 1966: *On Aggression* (New York).

LÖSCH, A. 1954: *The Economics of Location* (New Haven, Connecticut).

LOWENTHAL, D. and PRINCE, H. 1964: The English landscape. *Geographical Review*, **54**, 304–46.

LOWRY, I. 1960: Filtering and housing standards. *Land Economics* **36**, 362–70.

LOWRY, I. 1965: A short course in model design. *Journal of the American Institute of Planners*, **31**, 158–166.

LUCE, R. D. and RAIFFA, H. 1957: *Games and Decisions* (New York).

LUKACS, G. 1971: *Lenin* (London)

LUXEMBURG, R. 1951: *The Accumulation of Capital* (London).

LYNCH, K. 1960: *The Image of the City* (Cambridge, Massachusetts).

MCFARLANE SMITH, I. D. 1964: *Spatial Ability* (New York).

MAKIELSKI, S. J. 1966: *The Politics of Zoning* (New York).

MAO TSE-TUNG 1966: *Four Essays on Philosophy* (Peking).

MARCUSE, H. 1964: *One-Dimensional Man* (London).

MARGOLIS, J. 1965: *The Public Economy of Urban Communities* (Washington).

MARGOLIS, J. 1968: The demand for urban public services. In Perloff, H. and Wingo, L., editors, *Issues in Urban Economics* (Baltimore).

MARX, K.: *The Poverty of Philosophy* (New York: International Publishers Edition, 1963).

MARX, K.: *The Economic and Philosophic Manuscripts of 1844* (New York: International Publishers Edition, 1964).

MARX, K.: *A Contribution to the Critique of Political Economy* (New York: International Publishers Edition, 1970).

MARX, K.: *Critique of the Gotha Programme* (New York: International Publishers Edition, 1938).

MARX, K.: *Pre-Capitalist Economic Formations* (New York: International Publishers Edition, 1964).

MARX, K.: *Capital* (Three Volumes. New York: International Publishers Edition, 1967).

MARX, K.: *Theories of Surplus Value* (Moscow: Progress Publishers Edition, Part 1, 1967; Part 2, 1968; Part 3, 1972).

MARX, K.: *The Grundrisse* (London Macmillan Press, 1971, translated and edited by D. McLellan).

MARX, K. and ENGELS, F.: *Manifesto of the Communist Party* (Moscow: Progress Publishers Edition, 1952).

MARX, K. and ENGELS, F.: *The German Ideology* (New York: International Publishers Edition, 1970).

MARX, K. and ENGELS, F.: *Selected Correspondence* (Moscow: Progress Publishers Edition, 1955).

MATTICK, P. 1969: *Marx and Keynes* (London).

MÉSJÁROS, I. 1970: *Marx's Theory of Alienation* (London).

MEYER, J. R. 1968: Urban transportation. In Wilson, J. Q., editor, *The Metropolitan Enigma* (Cambridge, Massachusetts).

MILLER, S. M. and ROBY, P. 1970: *The Future of Inequality* (New York).

MILLS, C. WRIGHT 1959: *The Sociological Imagination* (New York).

MILLS, E. S. 1967: An aggregative model of resource allocation in a metropolitan area. *American Economic Review* **57**, 197–210.

MILLS, E. S. 1969: The value of urban land. In Perloff, H., editor, *The Quality of Urban Environment* (Washington).

MILLS, E. S. 1972: *Studies in the Structure of the Urban Economy* (Baltimore).

MILNER–HOLLAND Report, 1965: *Report of the Committee on Housing in Greater London* (London: HMSO, Cmnd, 2605).

MINAS, J. S. and ACKOFF, R. L. 1964: Individual and collective value judgments. In Shelly, M. W. and Bryan, G. L., editors, *Human Judgments and Optimality* (New York).

MISHAN, E. J. 1967: *The Costs of Economic Growth* (New York).

MISHAN, E. J. 1968: What is producers' surplus? *American Economic Review* **58**, 1268–82.

MISHAN, E. J. 1969: *Welfare Economics: Ten Introductory Essays* (New York).

MISHAN, E. J. 1971: *Cost-Benefit Analysis* (London).

MUSIL, J. 1968: The development of Prague's ecological structure. In Pahl, R. E., editor, *Readings in Urban Sociology* (London).

MUTH, R. 1969: *Cities and Housing* (Chicago).

MYRDAL, G. 1957: *Economic Theory and Under-Developed Regions* (London).

NAGEL, E. 1961: *The Structure of Science* (New York).

NETZER, D. 1968: Federal, state and local finance in a metropolitan context. In Perloff, H. and Wingo, L., editors, *Issues in Urban Economics* (Baltimore).

NUNNALLY, J. C. 1967: *Psychometric Theory* (New York).

OLLMAN, B. 1971: *Alienation: Marx's Conception of Man in Capitalist Society* (Cambridge).

OLLMAN, B. 1972: *Marxism and political science: prologomenon to a debate on Marx's method* (Unpublished Ms., Department of Political Science, New York University, New York).

OLSON, M. 1965: *The Logic of Collective Action* (Cambridge, Massachusetts).

ORANS, M. 1966: Surplus. *Human Organization* **25**, 24–32.

PAHL, R. 1965: *Urbs in Rure* (London: London School of Economics, Geographical Paper **2**).

PARK, R. E., BURGESS, E. W. and MCKENZIE, R. D. 1925: *The City* (Chicago).

PEARSON, H. 1957: The economy has no surplus: a critique of a theory of development. In Polanyi, K., Arensberg, C. M. and Pearson, H. W., editors, *Trade and Market in Early Empires* (New York).

PIAGET, J. 1970: *Structuralism* (New York).

PIAGET, J. 1972a: *The Principles of Genetic Epistemology* (London).

PIAGET, J. 1972b: *Insights and Illusions of Philosophy* (London).

Bibliography

PIAGET, J. and INHELDER, B. 1956: *The Child's Conception of Space* (London).

PIRENNE, H. 1925: *Medieval Cities* (Princeton, New Jersey).

POLANYI, K. 1944: *The Great Transformation* (Boston)

POLANYI, K. 1968: *Primitive, Archaic and Modern Economies: Essays of Karl Polanyi* (edited by G. Dalton) (Boston).

POSTAN, M. 1952: The trade of medieval Europe: the North. In Postan, M. and Rich, E. E., editors, *The Cambridge Economic History of Europe* Vol. 2 (Cambridge).

PRED, A. 1966, *The Spatial Dynamics of US Urban-Industrial Growth* (Cambridge, Massachusetts).

PROSHANSKY, H. M., ITTLESON, W. H. and RIVLIN, L. G. 1970: *Environmental Psychology* (New York).

QUIRK, J. and SAPOSNIK, R. 1968, *Introduction to General Equilibrium Theory and Welfare Economics* (New York).

RATCLIFFE, R. U. 1949: *Urban Land Economics* (New York).

RAWLS, J. 1969: Distributive justice. In Laslett, P. and Runciman, W. G., editors, *Philosophy, Politics and Society* (Third Series) (Oxford).

RAWLS, J. 1971: *A Theory of Justice* (Cambridge, Massachusetts).

REICHENBACH, H. 1958: *The Philosophy of Space and Time* (New York).

Report on Conglomerates 1971: *House Judiciary Committee (Staff Report)* (Washington: Government Printing Office).

RESCHER, N. 1966: *Distributive Justice* (Indianapolis).

RICARDO, D. 1817: *Principles of Political Economy and Taxation* (Harmondsworth, Middlesex: Penguin Edition, 1971).

RIDKER, R. G. 1967: *Economic Costs of Air Pollution—Studies in Measurement* (New York).

RIESSMAN, F., COHEN, J. and PEARL, A. editors 1964: *The Mental Health of the Poor* (New York).

ROSE, H. and ROSE, S. 1969: *Science and Society* (Harmondsworth, Middlesex).

ROTHENBERG, J. 1967: *Economic Evaluation of Urban Renewal* (Washington).

RUNCIMAN, W. G. 1966: *Relative Deprivation and Social Justice* (London).

SCHMIDT, A. 1971: *The Concept of Nature in Marx* (London).

SCHNEIDER, J. B. 1967: Measuring the locational efficiency of the urban hospital. *Health Service Research* 2, 154–69.

SCHNEIDER, J. B. 1968: Measuring, evaluating, and redesigning hospital-physician-patient spatial relationships in metropolitan areas. *Inquiry* 5, 24–43.

SCHULTZ, G. P. 1969: Facility patterns for a regional health care system. *Regional Science Research Institute, Discussion Paper* 34, Philadelphia.

SEGALL, M. H., CAMPBELL, D. T. and HERSKOVITS, M. J. 1966: *The Influence of Culture on Visual Perception* (Indianapolis).

SEIDEL, M. R. 1969: The margins of spatial monopoly. *Journal of Regional Science* 9, 353–68.

SHEPARD, R. N. 1966: Metric structures in ordinal data. *Journal of Mathematical Psychology* 3, 287–315.

SHERRARD, I. D. editor 1968: *Social Welfare and Urban Problems* (New York).

SJOBERG, G. 1960: *The Preindustrial City* (New York).

SMITH, ADAM, 1776: *An Inquiry into the Nature and Causes of the Wealth of Nations* (New York: Modern Library Edition, 1937).

SMITH, C. T. 1967: *An Historical Geography of Western Europe before 1800* (London).

SMITH, M. B., BRUNER, J. S. and WHITE, R. W. 1965: *Opinions and Personality* (New York).

SMITH, W. F. 1966: The income level of new housing demand. In *Essays in Urban Land Economics* (Los Angeles: Real Estate Research Program, University of California).

SMITH, W. F. 1970: *Housing: the Social and Economic Elements* (Berkeley).

SOMMER, R. 1969: *Personal Space: the Behavioral Basis of Design* (Englewood Cliffs, New Jersey).

SPOEHR, A. 1956: Cultural differences in the interpretation of natural resources. In Thomas, W. L., editor, *Man's Role in Changing the Face of the Earth* (Chicago).

STEINITZ, C. 1968: Meaning and congruence of urban form and activity. *Journal American Institute of Planners* 34, 233–48.

STERNLIEB, G. 1966: *The Tenement Landlord* (New Brunswick, New Jersey).

STEVENS, B. H. and RYDELL, C. P. 1966: Spatial demand theory and monopoly price policy. *Papers of the Regional Science Association* 17, 195–204.

SUTTLES, G. D. 1968: *The Social Order of the Slum* (Chicago).

TAWNEY, R. H. 1931: *Equality* (London).

TAWNEY, R. H. 1937: *Religion and the Rise of Capitalism* (Harmondsworth, Middlesex).

TAYLOR, P. J. 1969: The location variable in taxonomy. *Geographical Analysis*, 1, 181–95.

TEITZ, M. 1968: Toward a theory of urban public facility location. *Papers of the Regional Sciences Association* 21, 25–52.

THOMPSON, W. R. 1965: *A Preface to Urban Economics* (Baltimore).

THRUPP, S. 1948: *The Merchant Class of Medieval London, 1300–1500* (Chicago).

TIEBOUT, C. M. 1956: A pure theory of local expenditures. *Journal of Political Economy* 64, 416–24.

Bibliography

TIEBOUT, C. M. 1961: An economic theory of fiscal decentralization. In Universities National Bureau Committee for Economic Research, *Public Finances; Needs, Sources and Utilization* (Princeton).

TIMMS, D. 1971: *The Urban Mosaic* (Cambridge).

TINBERGEN, N. 1953: *Social Behaviour in Animals* (London).

TITMUSS, R. M. 1962: *Income Distribution and Social Change* (London).

TOBLER, W. 1963, Geographic area and map projection *Geographical Review*, **53**, 59–78.

TUAN, YI-FU 1966: *The Hydrological Cycle and the Wisdom of God* (University of Toronto Press: Department of Geography Research Publications).

VALDÈS, N. P. 1971: Health and revolution in Cuba. *Science and Society* **35**, 311–35.

VANCE, J. E. 1970: *The Merchant's World: the Geography of Wholesaling* (Englewood Cliffs, New Jersey).

VEBLEN, T. 1923: *Absentee Ownership* (Beacon Press edition: Boston, 1967).

WARNER, S. B. 1968: *The Private City* (Philadelphia).

WEBBER, M. 1963: Order in diversity: community without propinquity. In Wingo, L., editor, *Cities and Space: the Future Use of Urban Land* (Baltimore).

WEBBER, M. 1964: Culture, territoriality and the elastic mile. *Papers of the Regional Science Association* **11**, 59–69.

WEBER, M. 1908: *The Protestant Ethic and the Spirit of Capitalism* (New York: Scribner's Edition, 1958).

WEBER, M. 1947: *The Theory of Economic and Social Organization* (New York: Oxford University Press Edition).

WEBER, M. 1958: *The City* (New York: Free Press Edition).

WEISBROD, B. A. 1965: Geographic spillover effects and the allocation of resources to education. In Margolis, J., editor, *The Public Economy of Urban Communities* (Washington).

WHEATLEY, P. 1969: *The City as Symbol* (London: Inaugural Lecture, University College of London).

WHEATLEY, P. 1971: *The Pivot of the Four Quarters* (Chicago).

WHITEMAN, M. 1967: *Philosophy of Space and Time* (London).

WILLIAMS, A. 1966: The optimal provision of public goods in a system of local government. *Journal of Political Economy* **74**, 18–33.

WILSON, A. G. 1970: *Entropy in Urban and Regional Modelling* (London).

WILSON, C. 1941: *Anglo-Dutch Commerce and Finance in the Eighteenth Century* (Cambridge).

WILSON, C. 1965: *England's Apprenticeship* (London).

WILSON, N. L. 1955: Space, time and individuals. *Journal of Philosophy* **52**, 589–98.

WIRTH, L. 1938: Urbanism as a way of life. *American Journal of Sociology* **44**, 1–24.

WOLF, E. 1959: *Sons of the Shaking Earth* (Chicago).

WOOD, R. C. 1963: The contributions of political science to urban form. In Hirsch, W. Z., editor, *Urban Life and Form* (New York).

YOCOM, J. E. and MCCALDIN, R. O. 1968: Effects of air pollution on materials and economy. In Stern, A. C., editor, *Air Pollution* volume 2 (second edition) (New York).

Author Index

327

Subject Index

Accumulation
  of capital 231–3, 244, 249, 255, 269, 272, 275, 309
  of surplus 216–23, 227–8, 231–3, 238–40, 249, 309
  of wealth 53–4, 64–8, 109, 158, 163–4, 254–5
  primitive 227–8, 233–5, 243, 249, 255
Accessibility 56–7, 68–73, 86, 161, 169, 186, 239
Agriculture 204, 236, 243, 258–9
  surplus product from 216–23, 230–31, 262–4
Algeria 264
Alienation 156–7, 279, 311, 314
  in labour 220, 225–6, 230
Allocation of Resources see Investment
Amsterdam 250, 258–60
Anomalies 120–22, 128, 299
Antwerp 250, 258
Architecture 31–2, 228, 261, 280–81, 283
Art 24, 197
Augsburg 247, 250
Automobile 45, 51, 56, 267, 270–71

Baltimore 9, 78, 112, 140, 270, 280–81
Banks see Institutions, financial
Bargaining 72, 74–6
Bavaria 247
Behaviour
  in space 23–5, 27–36, 82–6
  learning 33–6, 83–6
Bid-Rent Function 134–6, 161–2, 176, 189, 280
Birmingham 260, 269
"Blow-out" 173–6, 187
Boston 34
Brazil 84
Bristol 260
Britain 54, 87, 94–5, 110, 112, 130, 276–8
Bureaucracy 110–11, 210, 221, 234, 236, 274, 279
Byzantium 247

Capital 177, 180, 199, 225, 229
  accumulation of see Accumulation
  constant 181, 224
  fixed 51, 158, 191–2, 199, 203, 268, 309–14 (see also Investment, public)

flows see Mobility, of capital; Circulation
  nature of 154, 191–2, 300–301, 313
  organic composition of 310–13
  valuation of 267–8, 313
  variable 224 (see also Wages)
Capitalism 108–16, 126–8, 139–44, 146, 168, 170, 174, 178–91, 199–200, 202, 204–6, 211–15, 224–5, 228, 231, 238, 242–5, 249–52, 255, 261–84, 289–90, 292–3, 299, 306
  as a mode of production 174, 178–91, 202, 205–6, 211–15, 261–84
  origins of 255–62
Categories 12, 120–28, 145–6, 150–51, 198–9, 297–303 (see also Concepts)
Chicago 131–2, 137, 188
China 110, 115, 205, 209, 235–7, 246, 264, 308
Circulation of Surplus (Value) 227, 231, 238–40, 257, 267–73, 276, 312–15
  circuits in 312–14
  geography of 230–40, 243–4, 246–50, 258–9, 262–4, 269, 277
Cities
  built-form of 203–4, 228, 241, 260–61, 271–2, 283–4, 303, 307
  generative 233, 240, 249–50, 269
  nature of 195–6, 203–5, 303–14
  parasitic 233–4, 248, 260
  (see also Urbanism)
City Forms
  ancient 204, 209, 216, 220–23, 227, 293–4, 304–5
  capitalist 213, 232, 245, 261–2, 264–5, 269–73, 276–7, 280–84, 305–14
  colonial 232, 262–5, 308
  feudal 204, 247, 250–61
  industrial 204, 243, 274, 281, 305–14
  merchant 247, 252–61, 267, 305
  redistributive 213, 227, 241, 248, 280–81
  socialist 235–7, 306, 319
  welfare state 276–8
Class 40, 70, 81, 103, 202, 204–6, 209–15, 219, 222, 228, 230, 239, 260, 281–3, 304
  monopoly 170–71, 179, 182, 191, 194
  (see also Stratification)

330

Subject Index

Subject Index

Institutions 26, 97–8, 109–10, 139–42,
146, 168, 191, 207, 221–3, 227,
242, 244, 251, 254–6, 265, 268,
278, 282–3
financial 113, 140, 159, 165–6, 174–
5, 214, 255–8, 268, 275, 280–
81
legal 140, 197, 204, 214–15, 278
political 26, 97–8, 110, 140, 200–
205, 210, 214–15, 254–5 (see also
Political Organization; Political
Power)
religious 32, 204, 222, 234
Interdisciplinary Research 16, 22, 50,
95, 302
Internal Relations see Relational
Modes of Thought
Interest on Capital 182–3, 191–2,
224, 235 (see also Surplus,
value)
Investment 51, 56, 65, 101, 106–8,
110–13, 116–17, 158–9, 164–5,
182–3, 186–9, 235, 242, 256, 259,
268, 270, 310–11
public 68–70, 73–4, 87–91, 93–4,
101, 166
return on 112, 146, 182–3, 261
Italy 234, 254–7

Japan 205
Justice see Social Justice

Kinship 199, 281–2
Knowledge
organization of 127–8, 147–52
production of 121–2, 147–8, 296–
302
(see also Science)

Labour 97, 139, 141–3, 155–6, 177,
180, 199, 224–30, 235–6, 243–5,
252, 262, 293, 297
productive versus unproductive
264–5
Labour Power 155, 199, 224–230,
238–9, 265, 273, 289, 312
Land 14, 55, 243
market 65–8, 158–9, 166–7, 173–6,
261
value see Rent
Land Use 45, 77, 272
theory of 55–6, 63, 65, 131–44,
157–94, 280, 300
change 164–6, 172–6, 186–8
Landlords 138, 140, 164, 170, 174,
185, 270
Language 12, 154
social and spatial 38–41, 46–8
space-time 38–40
substance 38–40
Learning 82–7
Leeds 260

Location
efficiency in 47–9, 88–9, 96–7, 118,
136, 260
games 74–7, 81
of facilities 57–60, 69–73, 87–91,
158, 166
of industry 61–3, 135–6
of retailing 88–9, 158
Location Theory 25, 48–9, 69–70, 80,
87, 96–7, 117, 146, 148, 169, 176–
7, 179–80, 209 (see also Land
Use, theory of)
London 112, 133–4, 188, 250, 258–60
Los Angeles 173

Man–Nature Relationship 208, 213–
14, 287, 293
Manchester 132–3, 260, 269
Manipulation 132–3, 260, 269
Manorial System 225, 250–51, 257
Manufacturing see Industry
Marginalism 127, 134, 146, 153, 155,
161–2
Marginal Productivity of Land 177–
8, 185, 188–9
Market Exchange (as a mode of econo-
mic integration) 139, 206–7,
210–15, 224–5, 227–8, 239–45,
256, 258, 261, 265–84, 301, 307
definition of 210–15
(see also Stratified Societies)
Market Failure 88, 109, 244–5
and externalities 59, 64–8, 70,
88–9
Market Mechanism 59, 64–5, 67–8,
113–16, 133–4, 139–44, 199, 214,
234, 274–5, 310
Materialism 12–13, 121–30, 197–203,
214–16, 229
Megalopolis 237
Merchants 250–62
Merchant Capitalism 252–61
Methodology 9, 37–44, 128–30, 286–
302
Metropolitan Government 87, 94,
111
Metropolitanism 228, 231–2, 237,
245, 261–3, 308
Mexico 234, 246, 248
Military Power 140, 234, 247, 251,
275 (see also Coercion)
Mobility 56, 72, 91, 135, 143, 181,
230, 275, 282–3
of capital 112–13, 174–5, 181–2,
191–2, 249–60, 264–76
Models 55, 96–7
Monopoly 70, 112, 158, 168, 178–9,
181, 194, 205, 242, 257–8, 262,
266–74
and absolute space 14, 158, 167–8
and urbanism 247, 266–74
capitalism 112, 192, 266–74

333